Rehearsals
of Revolution

Rehearsals
of Revolution

THE POLITICAL THEATER
OF BENGAL

RUSTOM BHARUCHA

University of Hawaii Press
Honolulu

Library of Congress Cataloging in Publication Data

Bharucha, Rustom, 1953–
    Rehearsals of revolution.

    Includes bibliographical references and index.
    1.   Theater—India—Bengal—History.   2.   Theater—
Political aspects.   I.   Title.
PN2885.B4B45   1983   792'.0954'14   83–10470
ISBN 0–8248–0845–2

Frontispiece: *The Deaths of Abdul Hannan*, by Probir Guha
of the Living Theater of Khardah.

I want to relive what I'm doing every day. . . .
Theater is true, as real as hunger. It's happening
all the time. My purpose is to make it happen
all over again.

An actor in the Living Theater of Khardah

Contents

Preface

Ever since Sir William Jones published his celebrated translation of Kalidasa's *Shakuntala* in 1789, there has been a tendency in the West to mythologize the Indian theater. From Theophile Gautier's rhapsodic adaptation of *Shakuntala* as a ballet-pantomime (first performed at the Paris Opera House on June 15, 1858), to Lugné-Poe's symbolist experiments on Shudraka's *Mricchakatika* (The Little Clay Cart) and *Shakuntala* in the 1890s, to Tairov's startling production of Kalidasa's masterwork in 1914, a mythology of the Indian theater gradually developed relying on Western stereotypes of the Orient. Shrouded in mystery and endowed with an aura of romance, the Indian theater conjured up images of immanence and grace, subtle evocations of the supernatural, and revelations of cosmic harmony. It seemed to exist in its own time and space, inviolate, sacrosanct, residing serenely in a territory of dreams.

The earliest Western enthusiasts of the Indian theater were dreamers of the East. When Gordon Craig, for instance, discovered the secrets of the Indian theater from the renowned Sanskrit scholar Ananda Coomaraswamy, he tacitly avoided any attempt to demystify his illusions of the Indian theater. He continued to regard it as a "phantom," a "marvel," a source of esoteric insights, and an inspiration of endless dreams.

In his eloquent article "Asia, America, Europe," Craig made it clear to his colleagues that a knowledge of the Indian theater could only lead to "annihilation." In a more pragmatic vein, he argued that the "exquisite fluting of the great and lovely Krishna" could prove to be a dreadful distraction, and therefore, it was better not to be seduced by its sound. As much as Craig was drawn to the Indian theater or, more accurately, his idea of the Indian theater, he feared it tremulously. "I dread for my men lest they go blind suddenly attempting to see God's face," he once wrote to Coomaraswamy. While perceiving the Indian theater as a sacrosanct territory, at once "holy" and "dangerous," Craig insisted that it should be venerated but from a distance.

The idea of distance is integrally related to the shaping of a mythology. The greater the distance between the theaters of East and West, the greater the possibilities of mutual misrepresentation. It is disheartening that the Indian theater continues to be distant for most Western artists and scholars despite developments in international transport, the proliferation of cross-cultural exchanges, and the increased availability of information relating to the Indian theater. The distance of the Indian theater is no longer a geographical issue as it was (in part) for Craig and Tairov and Lugné-Poe. It can be more accurately interpreted today in terms of a certain reticence or inability of Western theater practitioners to confront the reality of the Indian theater and accept it for what it is.

The Indian theater will continue to be distant from the West so long as it is viewed synonymously with the "oriental theater," that nebulous category of varied arts such as Kabuki, Kathakali, Wayang Kulit, Baris, and Legong. Divested of their individuality, these Eastern disciplines become mere presences in an amorphous system. Their differences are less important than their mysterious synchrony. The "oriental theater" (to borrow a construction used by Edward Said in *Orientalism*) is less a body of knowledge about theaters in the East than a luminous sign of the *otherness* that distinguishes the theaters in the East from those in the West.

When I was first compelled to write about the Indian theater, I knew I had to confront this notion of otherness by presenting a concrete, specific, and historical perspective of the Indian theater. Like many of the stereotypes surrounding the Indian theater in the West, the notion of otherness is a fabrication that reflects a Westerner's illusory view of the Orient rather than any historical awareness of the working conditions, the techniques, the disciplines, and the differing modes of dramaturgy that prevail in India.

I am, of course, aware that there are some scholars in the West who are historically informed about arts like Kathakali, Bharat Natyam, and the rituals of the Ramlila. Unfortunately, the dissemination of their knowledge is generally limited to a few students who view the Indian theater from a somewhat academic perspective. This perspective may not be ideal but it is preferable to the impressionistic views on the Indian theater of those performers who may have attended the occasional workshop in Kathakali or Yoga taught by some self-appointed guru of the East. For these performers, the otherness of the Indian theater persists though they may not be aware of it, or perhaps care to admit it. Enhanced by an aura that seems to have its origin in a scattered reference—a gesture, a movement, a rhythm—it is rooted in a fundamental ignorance of the intricacies and philosophical premises of the Indian theater.

It is unfortunate that the only Indian theater that seems to interest Western scholars and Indologists is the traditional theater. Very little is known about the contemporary theater in India or, more accurately, the contemporary theaters in India. Indeed, one of the most common misconceptions about the Indian theater in the West is the tendency to view it as an entity. It needs to be stressed that there is no such thing as *an* Indian theater. It may have existed centuries ago when it was synonymous with Sanskrit classical drama, but today we can speak only of the Bengali theater, or the Marathi theater, or the Tamil theater, and so on. There are as many theaters as there are languages in India. Since many of the sixteen major languages are not understood outside a particular state or region, there is little or no communication among the various theaters. There have not been many translations of regional plays and the few productions of, say, a Marathi play in Bengali or a Hindi play in Gujarati, have not been entirely successful.

Apart from differences in language, there are divergencies of culture. The diversity of India's languages is symptomatic of the bewildering variety of customs, traditions, and folklore that are inextricably linked to particular regions. Consequently, the theaters in India are often specifically related to the cultural inheritance of particular communities. A play set in Bengal, for instance, may not be fully understood by an urban audience in Tamil Nadu while the contemporary resonances of a Marathi play may elude an audience in Rajasthan. It should be remembered that there are difficulties in understanding Indian theaters within India itself.

The mythology of the Indian theater in the West can be confronted only if the specificities of the various theaters in India are acknowledged. I am not aware of any theater scholar who is in a position to analyze all the theaters in India with authority. Each theater has an individual history, a particular performance tradition, an intimate relationship with the lives of the people belonging to a particular region. Each Indian theater has to be studied for what it is. Only after a specific knowledge about the individual theaters in India has been acquired can one hope for some pandit to synthesize this knowledge. Such a synthesis is not possible at the moment despite the many lamentable attempts to provide panoramic surveys of "The Theater in India." Steeped in generalizations, these surveys serve only to enhance the mythology of the Indian theater in the West. They need to be replaced by critical studies of the individual theaters.

I write about the Bengali theater because it is closer to me than any other theater in India. Having lived in Calcutta for twenty-four years, I am aware of the intimate relation between the activity of the theater and the life in the streets. They share a vitality and physical immediacy that never fail to thrill me. When I started going to the Bengali theater on a regular basis between 1972 and 1977, often seeing a particularly provocative production three or four times, I confronted my insularity for the first time. The Bengali theater made me examine the extremities and contradictions of life in Calcutta which I had assimilated without even being aware of them.

The more theater I saw in Calcutta, the more I realized how inadequate it was to think of the Bengali theater without a political perspective. In an impoverished state where millions of people are denied the basic necessities of life—food, water, electricity, accommodation, sanitation, fuel—the theater cannot afford to be mere entertainment. The poverty and destitution of the masses demand a stringently political theater—a theater that confronts the basic problems of the people and exposes the socio-economic injustices that are responsible for these problems. If the theater in Bengal failed to examine the predicament of the people, it would be redundant.

As it happens, there are very few theaters in Bengal that can be described as redundant. Most of the theater groups in Calcutta (the center of cultural activity in Bengal) are politically conscious, and at least some of them are politically engaged. It is a striking fact that one cannot generalize about the political strategies and commitments of the Bengali theater groups. They may share some attitudes, particularly in relation to the censorship and economic survival of the theater, but fundamentally they have their own ways of viewing the political turmoil and the pervasive exploitation of the people in West Bengal. By juxtaposing the theaters of Utpal Dutt and Badal Sircar (which are examined in chapters 2 and 3 respectively), I hope to demonstrate that the political theater in Bengal can be valid and effective in totally different ways.

There could not be two more fundamentally opposed practitioners of the Bengali theater than Dutt and Sircar. Unlike Dutt, who believes that the political theater should be "epic" and reach thousands of workers, Sircar works on a much smaller scale for a predominantly middle-class audience. While Dutt strategically uses the conventions of the commercial theater to preach "the revolutionary struggle of the people," Sircar deliberately works outside the commercial theater framework in order to preserve his integrity as an artist. While Dutt harangues his audience and hypnotizes them with slogans, songs, rhetoric, and spectacular stage devices, Sircar works with the barest minimum of effects and questions his audience quietly, urgently, and with total simplicity.

Perhaps the most crucial difference between the two men inheres in their understanding of politics. Though he may not always adhere to the party line, Dutt interprets his function as an artist according to Marxist-Leninist precepts. As an advocate of "revolutionary theater," he believes that his theater must do more than expose the system that is responsible for the exploitation of the masses: it has to preach revolution in such a way that the overthrow of the system is an imminent possibility. While Dutt sees his theater as a weapon in the struggle of the people, Sircar views his theater in less militant terms. Without adhering to the rigors of the party line or to any specific political ideology, he makes his audience confront its indifference to the suffering of the oppressed people living in Calcutta and the rural areas of Bengal. By playing at once on the guilt and humanity of his spectators, Sircar recommends neither revolution nor the overthrow of the system but rather advocates a heightened awareness of the injustices in this world. All he demands from his audience is a partial responsibility for these injustices. Sircar seems more a humanist than a Marxist, and consequently his understanding of politics is broader and more inclusive of other perspectives concerning the well-being of man than Dutt's more rigorous interpretation of the term.

I must state at this point that I do not believe that the word "politics" can be defined unequivocally. I should also point out that the indeterminacy of the word increases when it is used in specific relation to an activity as variable and dynamic as the theater. There are as many ways to do political theater as there are directors with visions and political beliefs. At the risk of dogmatizing, I insist that there can be no fixed model for the political theater in Bengal or, for that matter, anywhere in the world.

Fortunately, the Bengali theater has no figure like Zhdanov instituting rules and legislating interpretations about the content of political plays. Despite censorship difficulties, particularly during the Emergency Rule of Indira Gandhi, the Bengali theater has been relatively free to comment on the political situation and the repressive policies of the central government in New Delhi. Compared to the rigors and sheer violence of censorship in certain Latin American countries under repressive regimes, the state of censorship in India, bothersome and occasionally asinine as it is, can be reckoned with by wily directors like Utpal Dutt. It is not invulnerable.

Earlier in the growth of the political theater movement in Bengal, the Communist party did exert considerable authority in matters concerning the ideology and subject matter of plays. But this authority lasted only so long as the Party existed as a unified body. Once it splintered into various factions, there were disagreements among the Marxists themselves about the integration of politics with the culture of the people. The emergence of the I.P.T.A. (the Indian People's Theater Association), the first organized political theater movement in India under the aegis of the Communist party, will be discussed toward the end of the first chapter of this book. Earlier in the chapter, I will provide a historical perspective of the central developments in the Bengali theater that eventually led to the formation of the people's theater movement.

If I have concentrated on various aspects of the Bengali theater not related to the contemporary political theater, it is because I do not underestimate the emotional power and entertainment value of the commercial theater in Bengal. As I attempt to demonstrate in my chapter on Utpal Dutt, the techniques of the commercial theater can be most effectively used to enhance the political awareness of the people. I have also sketched the beginnings of the Bengali theater and its colonial inheritance. Since I have assumed that readers in the West may not be familiar with the origins of the Bengali theater, I have also found it necessary to situate (somewhat perfunctorily I must admit) the Bengali theater in the larger, more nebulous context of the Indian theater.

I also examine in the first chapter productions that were considered inflammatory in their time but which may not seem particularly subversive today. At best, they may seem "socially relevant" rather than "political"; nevertheless, the study of political theater is incomplete without a consideration of its historical and social context. It is easy to condescend to what was once radical. An old-fashioned political play in particular is vulnerable to our cynicism. But we should remember that such a play might have had significance in its own time, and we can be aware of this significance only if we study the play in relation to its reception and its impact on the political awareness of the people when it was first produced. Perhaps this awareness is minimal when compared to the increased militancy of the working class in India today, but nevertheless, it deserves to be acknowledged. The first chapter concludes with a discussion of the activities of the I.P.T.A. and the immense contribution of Bijon Bhattacharya to the people's theater movement in Bengal.

Since very few plays by Utpal Dutt and Badal Sircar have been translated into English (or, for that matter, into other Indian languages), I have found it necessary to provide detailed descriptions of some of their plots in chapters 2 and 3. Also, because most of their productions are rarely staged outside Bengal, I have confronted the difficult task of writing about a theater that most of my readers may never see. Consequently, I have attempted to "recreate" some of their productions. Sircar's plays in particular have to be described in minute detail because they are constructed like scenarios. They have no plots that can be summarized, no characters of any consistency. Even the scripts are of a nonverbal nature where words and fragments of sentences are punctuated by gestures, movements, and tableaux. Such a theater should be seen, not written about. But since it is unlikely that it will be performed outside India, I have attempted to visualize it for those who may never see it.

To my surprise as a critic, I discovered that visualizing a production does not necessarily involve mere documentation of details. On the contrary, it involves criticism on an extremely subtle level. The very selection of the images in a play and the juxtaposition of one detail against another reveal a process of thought, even a system of value judgements, that are embedded in the description of the play. I have found the descriptive mode of criticizing the political theater in Bengal at once appropriate and imaginative.

This discussion of the political theater in Bengal ends with a critical survey of the "Varieties of Political Theater in Bengal." The focus is on particular productions that exemplify signficantly different attitudes to fundamental issues of the political theater, notably the responsibility of the artist, the imitation of foreign models, and the use of symbol and allegory in political plays. The validity of an urban political theater is questioned particularly in view of its isolation from the extremities of life in Calcutta.

My discussion of specific productions leads to a statement concerning the involvement of the people in the creation of political plays. In a state where millions of people live in rural areas, there should be a politically active theater that enables the people to participate not only as spectators but also as performers. Without the active participation of the people, the political theater in Bengal cannot fully develop its potential.

If the political theater has a raison d'être, it is surely its allegiance to people who have been denied their fundamental human rights. As I implied earlier, this allegiance can be manifest in a number of ways with or without the support of a specific political ideology. Sometimes a very conspicuous "revolutionary" play that voices the grievances of the people very earnestly and indulges in a great deal of proletarian rhetoric may not have much impact on the lives of the people. It is dogmatic to assume that such a play is necessarily political because it adheres to Communist platitudes and stereotypes of socialist realism. What makes a play political is not its fidelity to the Party or to any model prescribed by Brecht or Piscator but its fidelity to a people whose oppression cries out to be enacted on stage.

While writing about the political theater in Bengal, I often asked myself a difficult question: For whom am I writing?—the Bengali reader who is intensely aware of my subject, the Indian reader who has never seen a play by Dutt or Sircar (though he may have heard of them), or the Western reader who has, in all probability, neither seen nor read anything about the contemporary theater in Bengal? I would like to believe that I have written for all these readers with varying degrees of success.

If I seem to have written exclusively for the Western reader, it is because I have assumed that the subject of the Bengali theater is totally unfamiliar to him. Consequently, there is a great deal of information in this book (particularly in the first chapter) which may seem platitudinous to the Bengali reader but which is absolutely essential for the Western reader. On many occasions, I have had to explain words and phrases, cultural activities and phenomena, which are taken for granted in India but which, I imagine, are foreign to most readers in the West. I hope that by elaborating on the minutiae of certain details I have not failed to confront the essential issues. It has been difficult to determine how much information is necessary for the Western reader and, more important, how this information has to be presented so that the facts of the Bengali theater are neither simplified nor distorted.

Facts are notoriously deceptive: they can be presented with any number of perspectives. The challenge for any writer of the political theater in Bengal is to organize and analyze these facts without succumbing to Western criteria of judging political theater. This does not mean that all Western criteria have to be summarily dismissed, even if this were possible. There is much to be learned from the models of political theater conceived by Brecht and Piscator. They are, in fact, greatly respected by the theater practitioners in Bengal. They cannot, however, be imposed on the political plays in Bengal, which have their own ways of dealing with their audiences and the political situation in India and the world. It is my hope that the political theater in Bengal will be judged, as it must be, by its own criteria of efficacy and entertainment.

One aspect of the political theater in Bengal that can be misconceived as a limitation is its "untranslatability." With very few exceptions, I doubt whether the productions discussed in this book can be successfully translated or staged in Western countries. If these productions were merely enactments of texts, they could, perhaps, be staged with the necessary adaptations, editions, and changes. But since most of them are not simply enactments but *activities* integrally related to the social and political milieu of Bengal—a milieu so turbulent and extreme that it resists comparisons with conditions of life in other parts of the world—it is unlikely that these productions can be performed with any integrity for audiences in foreign societies (particularly those with a developed economy and advanced technology).

The political theater in Bengal is essentially time bound. It is rooted in a particular soil and it addresses the needs of a particular community. To criticize the specificity of this theater as a sign of its insularity is to misinterpret its very strength. It is unlikely that the theater in Bengal has any "universal" significance, but it is, perhaps, for this very reason that it needs to be recognized, if not studied, by theater practitioners and critics in the West.

One problem with the concept of "universality" (and there are many problems which cannot be expanded on here) is its tendency to abstract a work of art from its historical reality and endow it with some mysterious essence that remains unchanging through the ages. Presiding over space and time as it were, eluding the irreversible process of history and the everchanging perspectives of people, it looms like a deity magically suspending a work of art in a timeless zone. This inherently mystical concept is far removed from the political theater in Bengal, which is rooted in a particular time. The strength of this theater is not that it can *last* forever, but that it *lives* so intensely in the historical moment of its creation that it has to constantly renew itself. In one respect, the political theater in Bengal is no different from the lives of the people it attempts to confront: it is desperately aware of its own mortality.

Canton, New York   RUSTOM BHARUCHA
1983

Acknowledgements

I would like to thank the Asian Cultural Council (formerly the JDR 3rd Fund) for sponsoring my studies at the Yale School of Drama. Without the friendship and support I received from Richard Lanier, Maureen Liebl, and Ralph Samuelson, I might never have written this book.

I thank Joel Schechter for first encouraging me to write an article about the political theater in Bengal for *Theater*. I am deeply indebted to him and to Stanley Kauffmann not merely for reading my manuscript so closely but for inspiring me to write about what I believed was important and necessary. I also wish to acknowledge the intellectual stimulation and support I have received from Robert Brustein, Richard Gilman, and Jan Kott.

Apart from my professors in New Haven, I would like to acknowledge the guidance I received from my mentors at Jadavpur University in Calcutta. I would also like to thank Samik Bandyopadhyay for providing me with many invaluable perspectives of the Bengali theater and for calling to my attention some unpublished documents and interviews. Naveen Kishore kindly arranged to send me this material from India. I owe a great deal to Dilip Kumar Chakravorty for assisting me on the translations of Bengali plays, articles, and pamphlets, and to Sakti Biswas for providing me with much valuable information on the People's Little Theater. Above all, I would like to thank Utpal Dutt, Sova Sen, Badal Sircar, and the actors of the Living Theater in Khardah, among other actors and directors in Bengal, who have stimulated me to write about the political theater in Bengal.

The production of this book would not have been possible without the expert editorial guidance of Damaris Kirchhofer and the
staff at the University of Hawaii Press. I thank them for their support.

Among my friends, I would like to thank Zarin Chaudhuri, who
first made me aware of the possibilities of theater; Bonnie Mar-
ranca and Gautam Dasgupta for opening me to many new ideas
and perspectives on performance and culture; and Nicholas Rand
who spent many hours listening to my crude thoughts on political
theater when he could have been working on Heidegger. My greatest debt of all is to my mother who sustained me with her strength
through a period of great stress and personal loss.

The title of my book is derived from Augusto Boal's concept of
"rehearsal of revolution," discussed in *Theater of the Oppressed.*
Most of the documentation on specific productions discussed in
chapters 2–4 was recorded by me during various performances.
Quotations from plays and critical references have been acknowledged in the notes at the end of the book. Dutt's *Towards a Revolutionary Theater* and Sircar's *The Third Theater* have been invaluable for the theoretical premises and biographical material used
in chapters 2 and 3, respectively. All references to chapter 1 have
been acknowledged in the notes. I am particularly indebted to
P. Guha-Thakurta's *The Bengali Drama* and Kironmoy Raha's
Bengali Theater for their lucid expositions of the early history of
the Bengali theater. The three sketches of Sircar's productions—
Sagina Mahato, Spartacus, Michil—that are inserted in chapter 3
are taken from *The Third Theater.* The photographs used in the
book are reprinted with the permission of Utpal Dutt, Badal Sircar, and Naveen Kishore.

1

Toward a Political Theater in Bengal

PROLOGUE

The Riot in Heaven

According to the *Natyashastra*, the ancient Indian treatise on dramaturgy and the art of acting, the first play that was produced in the cosmos ended in a fiasco. Performed in the presence of Brahma, the creator of the universe, the play represented the victory of the gods over the demons. The trouble started when the Daityas and the Vighnas (evil spirits), who were lurking in the background of the celestial theater, reacted violently to the enactment of their defeat. In a fit of indignation, they disrupted the performance by casting a spell on the actors, who could neither speak, move, nor remember their lines. The *sutradhara* (director) was powerless to control the situation since he himself was paralyzed. Audience participation became necessary in order to restore peace. The great god Indra, in whose honor the play was performed, entered the scene of action wielding a banner staff which he used to "beat" the evil spirits "to pulp."[1]

After this disastrous opening night of the Indian theater, the actors led by the sage Bharata requested Brahma for some means of protection. After all, it was Brahma who had imparted the knowledge of drama to Bharata in the form of the *Natyashastra* (also known as the *Natyaveda*). According to the legend, Brahma created the *Natyaveda* by borrowing elements from the four Vedas

—recitation from the *Rigveda*, music from the *Samaveda*, the art of representation from the *Yajurveda*, and sentiments from the *Atharvaveda*. What distinguished the *Natyaveda* from the other four Vedas was its availability to all people, including the Shudras, the underprivileged belonging to the lowest caste of society, who were denied access to the four Vedas. By creating a fifth Veda, Brahma hoped to win the support of all people regardless of their class.

After the disruption of the first performance in heaven, however, it seems that Brahma had second thoughts about theater as a popular art. He began to operate like a celestial censor. One of the first protective measures that he recommended to Bharata was the construction of a playhouse. He used his obvious influence on the other gods to ensure the safety of this building. The gods Chandra, Mitra, and Agni presided over the main building, the dressing room, and the stage respectively. Indra protected the hero of the play, Saraswati the heroine, Omkara the Jester, and Shiva the rest of the characters. Brahma also urged the actors to perform all kinds of rites and ceremonies in the *purvarangas* (prologues) to their plays. He wanted to make sure that the theater would function in the future without any interruptions or dissensions.

After ensuring the safety of the actors, Brahma turned to the evil spirits who accused him of favoring the gods. With the diplomacy of a master politician, he reassured the spirits that the theater would not discriminate against them. In an important statement, which may be viewed as the credo of Sanskrit classical drama, he said:

> In drama there is no exclusive representation of you or the gods: for the drama is a representation of the States of the three worlds.
>
> It will relate to the actions of men, good, bad, and indifferent, and will give courage, amusement, happiness as well as counsel to them all.
>
> The drama will thus be instructive to all, through actions and States depicted in it, and through Sentiments arising out of it.
>
> It will also give relief to unlucky persons who are afflicted with sorrow and grief or over-work. . . .
>
> There is no wise maxim, no learning, no art or craft, no device, no action that is not found in the drama. (Pp. 14–15)

It appears that the words of Brahma were so persuasive that the next play performed in heaven—*Amrita-manthana* (The Churning of the Ocean)—emphasized the harmony between the gods and the demons as they churn the ocean in order to obtain nectar. In the fourth chapter of the *Natyashastra*, we learn that the audience response was favorable: "the gods and demons were delighted to witness actions and ideas familiar to them" (p. 45). And from that performance on, it seems that Brahma convinced almost everybody that his vision of the theater was essentially benign, a reflection of his faith in the equilibrium of life.

Sanskrit Drama: Theater of the Ruling Class

There is a strategy underlying the divine origin of drama as described by Brahma. The riot in heaven and its divine resolution are too neatly contrived to be accepted as sacrosanct facts. In all probability, the narrative was written at a time when the authority of the Brahmins was dominant.[2] By designating Brahma, the creator of the universe, as the creator of drama, Bharata hoped to justify the propagation of Brahmanical principles through the medium of drama.

With the exception of a few minor dramatic forms like the *prahasana* (farce) and the *bhana* (one-act popular drama), where the deceptions of slaves, epicures, eunuchs, rogues, and mendicants were mildly ridiculed, Sanskrit classical drama was essentially a reflection of Brahmanical thought. Enjoyed exclusively by members of the aristocracy and the intelligentsia, it assumed that the sentiments of a play could only be perceived by the *sahridaya* (intellectually advanced). Besides, only a Brahmin could appreciate the intricacies of the Sanskrit language. Despite its occasional use of Prakrit dialects and popular conventions, the Sanskrit drama was essentially patrician. Sponsored by kings and ministers, it could not help glorifying the interests and ideals of the ruling class.

Even the most "popular" of all Sanskrit dramas, Shudraka's *Mricchakatika* (The Little Clay Cart), which dramatizes the revolt of a pretender to the throne in its subplot, cannot be said to challenge, even question, the aristocratic structure of ancient Indian society. The *vidushaka* (jester), who provides most of the commentary in the play, is a friend of the ruling class, and Sarvilaka, who begins the play as a thief, ends up fighting for the stability of the state. At the end of *Mricchakatika*, the pretender to the throne becomes the new king. He dispenses justice and everybody accepts his authority. The play ends with a benediction:

> May the people rejoice and the Brahmins be honoured
> May the virtuous kings tame their foes and rule earth![3]

In another Sanskrit classical play, Vishakhadatta's *Mudrarakshasa* (The Minister's Seal), generally considered the only historical play in ancient India, Chanakya, the most dynamic character in the play, conspires to overthrow a king only to support another king of his choice. This Machiavellian schemer is modelled on the legendary minister of Chandragupta Maurya (322–298 B.C.) who wrote a definitive political treatise on his emperor's reign entitled the *Arthashastra*. Though Vishakhadatta's Chanakya plots and schemes like his historical counterpart, he does not question the ultimate authority of the king. Nor does he provide any political analysis or commentary that contradicts the prerogatives of the aristocracy in ancient India.

The play is less inspired by the pragmatism and intellectual rigor of the *Arthashastra* than by the lively action of the *Brihatkatha*, that inexhaustible storehouse of popular legends and stories compiled during the Gupta era in India. There is no sense of threat in Vishakhadatta's intrigues involving kings, ministers, and spies, Brahmins disguised as Jain monks, and noblemen masquerading as snake charmers. The institution of royalty is never challenged. At the end of the play, all dissensions are resolved by Chanakya with theatrical aplomb and Chandragupta reigns in triumph and glory.[4]

Apart from the *Mudrarakshasa*, there is no play in the Sanskrit classical tradition that addresses a political situation or change in government from a historical perspective. Though there are many plays with references to wars and conspiracies and palace intrigues, they evade conflict by ultimately accepting the differences that exist between men and the equilibrium of the cosmos. It cannot be stressed enough that the Sanskrit drama was far removed from the pressures and turbulence of life in India, its civil strife, unsurpations, and invasions of foreign tribes. Sequestered in a rarefied world, it responded less to the everyday impulses of life than to the most intricate rules and patterns of dramaturgy prescribed in the *Natyashastra.*

By the time the Muslims invaded India around the tenth century, this drama had already exhausted its imaginative possibilities. Despite the efforts of Mughal emperors such as Akbar (A.D. 1556–1605) and Shah Jahan (A.D. 1627–1657), who appreciated Sanskrit literature and encouraged Persian translations of prominent works like the Upanishads and the *Bhagavad Gita,* there was no significant resurgence of interest in classical drama during the Muslim Age. In fact, the preeminence of Persian as the court language and the puritanical reaction of some of the Muslim rulers to art in general, contributed to the further decline of Sanskrit drama.

It would be safe to assume that by the time the British established their position in India by conquering Bengal in 1757, the classical drama had faded into oblivion. The only theater that existed in Bengal and other parts of India was folk drama, that anonymous tradition of people's theater that coexisted with Sanskrit drama and continues to thrive in various parts of India today.[5]

The Theater of the People: *Jatra* in Bengal

Contemporary Indologists are more or less convinced that a popular tradition of epic recitation must have existed before the emergence of Sanskrit classical drama. In fact, the two Sanskrit words for actor—*bharata* and *kushilava*—are inextricably linked to the more ancient profession of the rhapsode. On the basis of dramatic dialogues in the *Rigveda* and unobtrusive stage directions concealed within the texts of the *Ramayana* and the *Mahabharata,* we can assume that oral performances of the epics must have existed prior to staged performances of Sanskrit dramas. In all probability, these recitals were not very different from the chanting of the *itihasas* (legends) that flourishes even today in rural areas of India, where the recitation of the text in Sanskrit by the *pathaka* (reciter) is followed by commentary in the vernacular by the *dharaka* (interpreter). These recitations must have been the earliest instances of a popular theater in India.

Apart from the tradition of epic recitation, the renowned Indologist Sylvain Lévi believes that "before Bhasa and Kalidasa there must have flourished a Prakrit drama, already literary, yet closer to popular dialects than the classic Sanskrit drama."[6] He correctly points out that if the drama had been originally created in Sanskrit, it could have avoided using Prakrit as did the epic, the romance, the short story, and other literary genres. But, as every student of classical Indian drama knows, Prakrit is extensively used by the more robust and "popular" characters in Sanskrit drama such as the guards, the servants, the rogues, and the courtesans. This extensive use of Prakrit indicates the existence of a dramatic tradition earlier than the Sanskrit one we take for granted. It is unfortunate that this tradition is not available for our closer scrutiny and that it remains as hypothetical and nebulous as the oral tradition in India.

It is extremely difficult to speculate about the origins of the popular theater. Nor is it necessary to do so for the purpose of this study. Let us concentrate instead on the origins of the Bengali theater, notably its most ancient and cherished form of folk drama, the *jatra*. Operatic in form, this quintessential theater of Bengal (often referred to as the "people's theater") originated in the religious processions of the Krishna movement inspired by Chaitanya (A.D. 1485–1533).

The very etymology of the word *jatra* (which literally means "a march" or "procession" derived from the root *yâ* "to go") refers specifically to the processions of Chaitanya's movement.[7] It appears that this illustrious Vaishnava saint and religious reformer used the medium of *jatra* to propagate his teachings on *bhakti* (devotion) and love. He celebrated the glory of Lord Krishna by inspiring his devotees to participate in communal singing and frenzied dancing. These rhapsodic celebrations were the earliest instances of a popular theater in Bengal that actively involved the participation of the people.

The narratives of the early *jatras* were, for the most part, improvised around legendary stories of Krishna. Many of them focus on the time when he left his foster parents and sweetheart in Vrindavan and proceeded to vanquish his evil uncle, King Kamsa, in Mathura. Krishna's "march" to Mathura was the organizing principle of the early *jatras*. Though their performances between the sixteenth and the eighteenth centuries have not been adequately documented, we know that they were enthusiastically received by the people, who were intensely aware of the *jatra's* themes and characters—the sexual interplay of Krishna and Radha; the lyrical background provided by the nine *gopis*, companions to Radha; the tensions conveyed by Vrinda and Chandravali, Radha's rivals in love; the grotesquerie of Kubja, Krishna's hunchbacked wife; and the machinations of Radha's sisters-in-law, Jatila and Kutila.[8] Apart from the exploits of Krishna, the *jatras* dramatized Puranic legends, folk tales, and episodes from the *Ramayana* and the *Mahabharata*.

The enactment of the early *jatra* was operatic and hallucinatory, relying on songs and religious fervor for its effect. Performed in the open air or in the courtyards of temples, it conveyed the myths of the gods and the universe to the people with hypnotic immediacy. The conventions of the *jatra* and their relation to the political theater in Bengal will be discussed at length in the next chapter. For the moment, it is important to stress that this most intimate and popular theater of Bengal existed when the British emerged as a political power in India. Even though *jatra* passed through a period of decline as the contemporary theater in Bengal developed, it always remained particularly close to the people.

UNDER THE BRITISH RAJ

The Colonial Background of the Bengali Theater

Apart from the *jatra* and other minor dramatic folk forms, there was no significant theater in Bengal when the British gained supremacy during the second half of the eighteenth century. There were no playwrights, no playhouses, no professional actors. It is a startling fact that the first play in the history of the contemporary theater in Bengal was produced by a Russian—a certain Herasim Lebedeff, an adventurer of sorts, who came to India as a bandmaster toward the end of the eighteenth century. With the assistance of his Bengali tutor, Golak Nath Das, he translated two obscure European plays, *The Disguise* and *Love is the Best Doctor*, which were performed before a distinguished audience in a playhouse "decorated in the Bengalee style" on November 27, 1795.[9]

Lebedeff's attempts to "Indianize" these plays by adapting the characters and introducing excerpts of Hindusthani music were daring innovations. At that time, the only theater that existed in Bengal was exclusively British. There was the Calcutta Theater (supported by Warren Hastings) with a repertoire of *The Beaux Stratagem*, *The School for Scandal*, *Richard III*, and *Hamlet*, directed by a Mr. Massnick who had been sent to India by David Garrick. Another prominent theater personality was Mrs. Emma Bistow, the toast of English society in Calcutta, who directed musical comedies and entertainments at the Chowringhee Theater. It is said that when she left India in 1790 "for long Calcutta refused to be comforted" (H. E. Busteed, *Echoes from Old Calcutta*).

The English theater entertained officers, merchants, scholars, and clerks of the East India Company. It was so exclusive that even the ushers and doorkeepers were English. The first "native" who was permitted to enter an English theater was Dwarkanath Tagore, an enlightened aristocrat who was one of the founder-members of the Private Subscription Theater formed in 1813. His membership was a breakthrough that reflected the gradual easing of tensions between the British and the affluent members of Indian society.

A few years later in August 1848, a "native gentleman" named Baishnav Charan Adhya performed the role of Othello in a production at the Sans Souci Theater, the famous English playhouse. A letter in a contemporary edition of the *Calcutta Star* referred to him somewhat unflatteringly as "a real unpainted nigger."[10] While the racist implications of casting a "native" in the role of Othello are unavoidable for us today, Adhya's debut represented a significant triumph for the Bengali community. As the *Calcutta Star* reported, "His début has set the whole world of Calcutta agog."

By the 1840s, there was a demand for the theater among the people of Bengal. Popular theatrical forms like the *jatra*, the *panchali*, and the *kathakatha* had lost much of their appeal. With the spread of education and the reforms of orthodox Brahmanical customs and traditions, the people wanted to see a theater that would confront these changing attitudes in society. In addition, they wanted to be entertained. If the sahibs could go to parties and clubs and musicals, why couldn't they find their own means of recreation? In a way, the theater in Bengal emerged almost out of a sense of pride. It was a means by which the "natives" could assert their cultural heritage. The irony, of course, is that the theatrical heritage of the Bengali theater was intrinsically colonial. Before it could develop an indigenous tradition, the Bengali theater slavishly imitated the proscenium tradition of the nineteenth-century theater in England.

The most flagrant imitators were the Indian aristocrats and landlords who were fascinated by the techniques of the English theater—late importations of the lighting effects, scenic transformations, and magical disappearances that flourished in Drury Lane and Covent Garden. In extravagant attempts to out-English the English, these men of leisure organized elaborate productions of Bengali plays that were performed on temporary structures in their mansions.

Bidya Sundar was among the first of these private performances. It was produced at the cost of two lakhs of rupees (£13,000) in the house of Nabin Chandra Basu in 1835.[11] Staged in various parts of the house including the garden and the drawing room, the production relied heavily on sophisticated theatrical equipment imported from England. It was the scenic representation of this "environmental" spectacle that attracted the Bengal community more than the text of the play—a loose dramatization of *Annada Mangal*, a famous Bengali poem by Bharat Chandra.

As a play, *Bidya Sundar* was theatrically inept and derivative. But as a theatrical venture, it is of historic importance in the Bengali theater: it encouraged aristocrats like Jyotindranath Tagore and Pratap Chandra Sinha to patronize the theater by privately sponsoring performances of Bengali plays. Of course, these performances were as exclusive as the British plays in Calcutta. They were the diversions of an enlightened class of "natives" who attempted to assert their prestige by emulating their "masters." The early history of the Bengali theater reveals the cultural subservience of a colonized people.

Polygamy and the Sepoy Mutiny

The first original play in Bengali that was neither an adaptation of
a poem nor a translation of a foreign play was Ram Narayan
Tarkaratna's *Kulin Kulasarvasa*, a social play on the evils of polygamy. It was written in 1853 for a prize competition organized by
Kali Chandra Ray Chaudhuri, a philanthropic *zemindar* (landowner). The title of the play (which has been translated as "The
Top-Ranking Brahmin All-For-Prestige") refers specifically to the
orthodox Brahmanical practice of Kulinism that authorized a Kulin-Brahmin to marry a number of women.

In his play, Tarkaratna clearly sympathizes with the plight of a
Kulin-Brahmin girl who faced the unpleasant option of either remaining unmarried or marrying a polygamous male. Written in a
variety of dramatic styles, at once playful and acerbic, Tarkaratna
condemns the hypocrisies of matchmakers and the reduction of
marriage to a system of bargaining. While his criticism of polygamy is neither analytical nor particularly harsh, it must be remembered that *Kulin Kulasarvasa* was the first play in the history
of the Bengali theater that indirectly questioned the supremacy of
the Brahmins and the rigid structure of the caste system.

In 1867, Tarkaratna returned to the theme of polygamy in
Naba-Natak (The New Drama), which won the first prize in a
drama competition organized by the illustrious Tagore family. A
pithy summary of the plot only serves to highlight its innate melodrama: "Ganesh Babu marries a second time while his first wife is
still living. The son of his first wife leaves home, unable to bear the
cruel way in which his step-mother treats him. The first wife commits suicide. In the end Ganesh Babu dies of poison administered
by his second wife."[12] The death of Tarkaratna's polygamous hero
was regarded as a violation of one of the fundamental laws of Sanskrit classical dramaturgy, which stipulates that the ending of a
play must never be tragic. Apart from this innovation, Tarkaratna,
a learned Sanskrit scholar, assiduously obeyed the rules and structural principles of Sanskrit drama. The models for his "new drama" were Kalidasa, Shudraka, Harshavardhana, and inevitably,
the *Natyashastra*.

While one cannot deny the historical importance of Tarkarat-na's plays, they demonstrate the isolation of the Bengali theater from the political events in India. *Kulin Kulasarvasa* was first per-formed in the home of Ramjay Basak in March 1857, during one of the most turbulent periods in the history of British India. Eigh-teen fifty-seven, as every student of Indian history knows, was the year of the Sepoy Mutiny, a military revolt of feudal leaders often interpreted as the first national uprising in India. When one thinks of the injustices that culminated in the Mutiny—the British annex-ation of states and territories belonging to Indian princes, the lega-lized exploitation of India's natural resources, the crippling taxes and duties imposed on Indian landowners and manufacturers, the imposition of the English language, the total exclusion of Indians from decisions concerning the administration of their country—one cannot help feeling that Tarkaratna's plays on polygamy (pro-duced in 1857 and 1867) are not simply inadequate but almost redundant.

Another startling theatrical event was the sumptuous revival of *Shakuntala* in the house of Asutosh Deb toward the end of January 1857, shortly before the sepoys (native officers) of the East India Company decided to defy their officers. The romanticism of *Sha-kuntala* seems far removed from the violence and desperation of the political events. How does one justify the remoteness of the Bengali theater from the political atmosphere in the 1850s? It should be remembered that the Bengali theater had not yet emerged as a professional activity. The people were isolated from it and had no right even to see the plays sponsored by the *zemin-dars* and *babus* of their society. The system of buying tickets did not exist. Consequently, the views of the people could not be re-flected in a theater which remained essentially apolitical, if not unpolitical.

Had a playwright been emotionally roused by the Mutiny, it is unlikely that he could have written a play about its exigencies and its impact on the lives of the people. The Bengali theater was sim-ply not equipped to deal with the magnitude of the event. It was only beginning to confront its immaturity when the colonial ex-ploitation of the British provoked mass opposition and unrest.

Michael Madhusadhan Dutt (1824–1873)

Before the Bengali theater could confront contemporary events, it had to abandon the old strictures of classical Sanskrit dramaturgy. One of the earliest rebels of the Bengali theater, Michael Madhusadhan Dutt, began his career by defying the sacrosanct canons of the *Natyashastra*. This defiance was but one aspect of his larger rebellion against the values of the bourgeoisie in Bengal.

Madhusadhan identified himself with "Young Bengal," that first generation of Indians educated at the Hindu College and the Oriental Seminary, exclusive centers of English education in British India. The young men of Madhusadhan's generation were impossibly romantic: they read Tom Paine, despised the Tories, revered Byron, and rhapsodized about the French Revolution and the American War of Independence. Their earliest mentor was an inspired Eurasian teacher at Hindu College named Henry Louis Vivian Derozio, who formed a debating club called the Academic Association in 1828. There the students discussed "free will, foreordination, fate, faith, the sacredness of truth . . . the nobility of patriotism, the hollowness of idolatory, and the shams of the priesthood," among other weighty issues.[13] This tradition of freethinking and radical analysis of ideas continued in literary associations like the Society for the Acquisition of General Knowledge and political organizations such as the Society for the Amelioration of India.[14]

Madhusadhan responded passionately to his intellectual environment. A year before he left Hindu College in 1843 to become a Christian, he must have been inspired (like most young men of his generation) by George Thompson's series of lectures in Calcutta on westernization and the future of India. Thompson, the secretary of the British India Society and a renowned advocate of Indian rights, urged the members of the Young Bengal movement to become "the narrators of their own grievances." In a country with "foreign rulers, foreign councillors, foreign historians, foreign defamers, and foreign advocates," Thompson emphasized, "you offer no advice, you threaten no opposition, you recommend no modification." At the same time, despite his tentative criticism of colonialism in India, Thompson urged his audience to respect the history of England:

Judge not of our country by the acts of a few. Judge us rather by those deeds of universal charity, which have gained us an unsullied fame, even at the ends of the earth. Our national power has been abused—our honour too often tarnished—our resources too often prostituted—and our religion too often disgraced—but the heart of England has not been turned from the love of justice, nor her arm paralyzed in the cause of the poor.[15]

This rhetoric, specious as it may seem considering the pervasive injustices of the British Raj, was in all probability irresistible to Madhusadhan, who was infatuated by the eloquence of the English language. His greatest ambition was to "cross the vast Atlantic wave" and establish himself as an English poet recognized in England. Despite these delusions, Madhusadhan was no dilettante. After converting to Christianity, he acquired a thorough knowledge of French, Greek, Latin, Hebrew, and Sanskrit, while immersing himself in Milton and writing sonnets and heroic poems.

His first encounter with Bengali theater was his English translation of *Ratnavali*, a Sanskrit classical play, adapted by Tarkaratna for a private performance sponsored by the Rajas of Paikpara. It is said that, in a moment of bravado, Madhusadhan declared that *Ratnavali* was "worthless" and that he could write something better. In a few weeks, he wrote a play called *Sarmistha*, which was so daring in its use of the Bengali language that it caused a sensation.

Premchand Tarkabagis, among other orthodox pandits of Sanskrit literature, dismissed it as the product of "some English-educated young man of modern ideas."[16] Even Tarkaratna, the established playwright, suggested changes in the dialogue and style of *Sarmistha* that infuriated Madhusadhan. In a letter to his friend Gour Das Basak, the impetuous young playwright defended the European influence on his dramaturgy:

I am aware, my dear fellow, that there will, in all likelihood, be something of a foreign air about my drama; but if the language be not ungrammatical, if the thoughts be just and glowing, the plot interesting, the characters well maintained, what care I if there be a foreign air about the thing? Do you dislike Moore's poetry because it is full of Orientalism? Byron's poetry for its Asiatic air, Carlyle's prose for its Germanism? Besides, remember that I am writing for that portion of my countrymen who think as I think, whose minds have been more or less imbued with Western ideas and modes of thinking; and that *it is my intention to throw off the fetters forged for us by a servile admiration of everything Sanskrit.*[17]

These words convey a self-conscious bravura and lofty disdain of the commonplace that characterize the inimitable style of Madhusadhan's rebellion. In many ways, this style was inhibited in *Sarmistha* by the subject matter, a romantic episode from the *Mahabharata.*[18] For all his assertions of a "foreign air" about *Sarmistha* and his disregard of Sanskrit conventions and divisions of acts, Madhusadhan's first play is astonishingly similar to *Ratnavali* (the play he dismissed as worthless) in spirit and atmosphere. Both plays deal with the vicissitudes of love involving two women rivals and a vacillating hero; curses, interventions by sages, acts of repentance, and a happy denouement. Madhusadhan needed more immediate subject matter than a love triangle to dramatize his rebellious attitude toward traditional Hindu norms and dogmas.

Madhusadhan's Social Satire

It was not difficult to find this subject matter. The affectations of westernized Indians and their absurd adulation of everything European were too conspicuous to be ignored. As a connoisseur of Western art and literature, Madhusadhan was only too aware and, in all probability, embarrassed by the aping of Western manners and customs by English-educated Indians of his day. While he himself had responded somewhat ecstatically to English literature, he had assimilated his knowledge of Byron and Carlyle and Shelley. His westernization was no affectation; it was necessary as a stimulus for his imagination. Nor did he succumb to "intellectual anarchy," that dominant trait of the Young Bengal movement in the 1850s which inspired its advocates to "cry down the civilization of their own country."[19]

Madhusadhan was intimately acquainted with the vagaries of westernization exemplified by his *babu* friends and relatives. He exposed the pretensions of their world in a thoroughly engaging play called *Ekei Ki Bale Sabhyata* (So This Is Civilization!). Realistic in its minute observation of contemporary social attitudes and behavior, the play focuses on Naba Kumar, a quintessential *babu* of the 1850s, a pompous Anglophile who shocks his rich orthodox father by drinking, smoking, and swearing.

The casual arrogance of Naba as he orders his father to get him a glass of wine, his insolent attitude to his wife, whom he addresses as a courtesan, would be shocking (even today for a lower middle-class Bengali audience) if Naba were not also something of a fool. Perhaps, the most outrageous of his foibles is his attachment to a club called Jnana-Tarangini-Sabha (Society for the Promotion of Learning), an organization modelled on those exclusive societies frequented by the graduates of Hindu College. In the Sabha, Naba and his friends discuss female emancipation and widow remarriage while drinking, watching dances performed by *nautch* girls, and shouting slogans like "Be Free," "Let Us Enjoy Ourselves," "Jnana-Tarangini Forever," and inevitably, that most popular of cheers which survived the British Raj, "Hip Hip Hurrah."

While Naba's behavior is primarily a source of entertainment, it is also presented as a threat to the values of the orthodox characters in the play. Significantly, after discovering how his son spends his evenings, Naba's father retires to the holy city of Vrindavan unable to face the evils of westernization in Calcutta ("that sinful city" as he calls it).

Madhusadhan's attitude to Naba is ambivalent: he seems to enjoy his hero's failings while exposing their essential vacuity. In his next comedy, *Buro Shaliker Ghare Rom* (New Feathers on an Old Bird's Neck), the treatment of his hero is less equivocal. With unrelenting candor, he exposes the hypocrisies of Bhakta Prasad, an orthodox Hindu who indulges in surreptitious liaisons with women while advocating the sanctity of life. In the course of the play, Bhakta attempts to seduce the wife of his *rayat* (laborer) named Haniph. A seduction on the Bengali stage defied traditional conventions of propriety, but a seduction involving a Brahmin was even more scandalous.

Buro Shaliker Ghare Rom went even further in its provocation of orthodox Hindu norms. At a critical point in the play, Bhakta Prasad is beaten up by Haniph when the latter discovers his master's lechery. This humiliation of a Brahmin shocked many supporters of the status quo in the Bengali community including the renowned pandit Ramgati Nyayaratna, who condemned Madhusadhan's plays as "impure" and "filthy." Perhaps an additional source of controversy related to the fact that Haniph was a Muslim. While Madhusadhan does not pursue his criticism of Brahmanical hypocrisy with any rigor (at the end of the play, Bhakta repents and gives Haniph a gift of two hundred rupees), he was the first Bengali playwright to confront the social changes in Hindu society with a vivid sense of detail.

It is fatuous to dismiss Madhusadhan's social satire as harmless entertainment. When Utpal Dutt, the most prominent Marxist director in the contemporary Bengali theater, performed *Buro Shaliker Ghare Rom* in a village some years ago, he was stunned by the impact of the play on the villagers. Instead of laughing at Bhakta Prasad (as Dutt had imagined), the villagers were positively hostile to him. They viewed his hypocrisies and attempted seduction of Haniph's wife as signs of his oppression. They reacted to him less as a farcical character in a play than as a mythical class enemy who continued to dominate their lives. The impact of this production will be discussed in greater detail in the next chapter when we examine Utpal Dutt's plays. For the moment, it is necessary to emphasize that Madhusadhan's satire, circumscribed as it was by his bourgeois milieu, has a political undercurrent of which he was probably unaware.

The Phenomenon of *Neel-Darpan*

After Madhusadhan's comedies, the Bengali theater attempted to confront social and political problems in a more realistic manner. In fact, Dinabandhu Mitra's *Neel-Darpan* (Indigo Mirror), the first protest play in the Bengali theater to attack the tyranny of British indigo planters in India, was so realistic that it could not be produced when it was written in 1860.

As an employee in the British Post and Telegraphic Service, Mitra had toured the rural areas of Patna, Orissa, and the Nadia district of Bengal, where he saw the actual living conditions of the Bengali peasants, their poverty and exploitation by British planters who were pressuring them to grow indigo against their will.

Apart from mistreating the "natives," the planters brought false law suits against Indian landowners and laborers who refused to cooperate with them. There was also the system of *dadan* (advanced payment), which the planters used to lure Indians to work for them. Unfortunately, many illiterate and impoverished villagers failed to realize that the *dadan* was a subtle form of exploitation. By accepting it, they faced terrifying consequences if they happened to offend the planters in any way or if they failed to cultivate sufficient indigo.[20] The oppression had such an emotional impact on Dinabandhu Mitra that he was compelled to write a play about it: *Neel-Darpan.*

As an employee of the British government, he had to publish the play anonymously. After its publication, the play was immediately translated into English by Madhusadhan. Later, copies of the play were sent to influential people in England and Bengal by Rev. James Long, a prominent missionary in Bengal. The disclosure of facts concerning the outrages committed by the indigo planters created an uproar in government circles. The Landholders and Commercial Association of British India filed a suit against Rev. Long, who was ultimately tried and found guilty of treason against the British government. He was sentenced to one month's imprisonment and fined a thousand rupees. The fine was paid by Kali Prasad Sinha, a philanthropic member of the Bengali elite.

Neel-Darpan has been idealized by critics and practitioners of the contemporary Bengali theater. It is frequently viewed less as a play than as a phenomenon—the first instance of theater as a political force confronting the British government, the first attack on the Raj's commercial exploitation and, indirectly, its political tyranny and disregard of human rights.

The play itself is somewhat predictable as it sketches the total devastation of an Indian landowner and his family, victims of two malevolent planters named Mr. Wood and Mr. Rogue. At the end of the play, Golak Basu, the Indian landowner, hangs himself, his wife Savitri dies in a fit of madness, and their son Nabin Madhab succumbs to injuries after Rogue fractures his skull. More immediate than their suffering, which is expressed in melodramatic platitudes and stilted phrases, are the violent scenes, including one where two laborers refuse to accept *dadan* and are, subsequently, kicked and flogged by Rogue and Wood. In another scene, where the oppression of the "natives" receives its most lurid expression, we see Rogue attempting to rape Kshetromoni, a peasant girl.

ROGUE: Dear, dear, come to me.

KSHETROMONI: Sahib, you are my father, please let me go. . . . [*holds Rogue's hands and pleads*] Please let me go, you are my father.

ROGUE: I want to be the father of your child. Come to bed or I will kick your belly.

KSHETROMONI: Oh! My child will die. I am carrying. Have mercy, please let me go. I am pregnant.

ROGUE: [*tearing off her clothes*] I will see you naked. Only then you will be rid of shame.

KSHETROMONI: Sahib, I am your mother, don't make me naked. You are my son, don't take off my clothes. . . .[21]

While the melodramatic excesses of this scene are, perhaps, too blatant to need further emphasis (Kshetromoni sees Rogue as her "father" and her "son"), one can imagine the emotional power of this scene on an Indian audience in the nineteenth century. Even today, the rape of an innocent girl by a sahib would rouse cries of indignation in a rural or working-class Bengali audience. In many ways, a rape is a necessary element in the structure of any prole-tarian play in Bengal.[22] The violation of a woman is symptomatic of the violation of a country or an ideal or a brotherhood. Dina-bandhu Mitra's use of Kshetromoni's rape can be seen as a politi-cal strategy even though it was probably intended to represent the most heinous crime that a sahib could inflict on a "native."

The Assimilation of *Neel-Darpan*

Was it the realism and political fervor of *Neel-Darpan* that stirred the members of the National Theater to produce the play on a pro-fessional basis? Or was it the notoriety of the play that convinced them that it could be sold to an audience? If the play had been pro-duced when it was written in 1860, there could be no question of the daring and political commitment of the venture. But since the play was produced twelve years later, after the controversial facts it exposed had been assimilated by the Bengali community and grudgingly acknowledged by the British government, and after Dinabandhu Mitra had received the prestigious title of "Rai Bahadur" from the Raj, the first production of *Neel-Darpan* cannot be regarded unequivocally as a political act.

It is more legitimately remembered as the first play in the history of the Bengali theater that sold tickets to the public without discriminating against any particular social class or caste. Prior to *Neel-Darpan*, as we noted earlier, one had to be invited to the Bengali theater, which was monopolized by the intelligentsia and affluent members of the Bengali community. It is important to stress, therefore, that the first "political" production in the Bengali theater was also a resounding commercial success.

The sale of tickets from the first two performances (which were sold out) amounted to more than five hundred rupees, a substantial amount at that time. The reviews were unanimous in their praise of the production. Even the *Englishman*, the newspaper that supported the views of the British community, acknowledged the popularity of the play a few months after the first performance. In its issue dated April 19, 1873, we read:

> A special performance of this drama [*Neel-Darpan*] will, we understand, be given at the National Theater with a view to gratify the wish expressed by many Europeans to see it acted. The really conspicuous talent for histrionic art possessed by the Bengali cannot be seen to better advantage than in this drama.

Once the cause of a trial involving the British government, *Neel-Darpan* was now regarded as the best "native" show in town, deserving the attention of the English community. It was no longer a subversive play.

In one historic production of *Neel-Darpan*, however, performed by the Great National Theater in Lucknow in 1875, there was a disturbance in the audience involving a few British soldiers. We have a vivid description of this performance by Binodini Das, one of the most renowned actresses of the Bengali theater in the nineteenth century, whose autobiography *Amar Abhinetri Juba* (My Acting Life) is one of the most valuable documents of the productions, rehearsals, personality clashes, and gossip of the professional theater in Bengal. Binodini's description of the *Neel-Darpan* performance conveys more evocatively than any other I am aware of the essential naivete and amateur spirit of the professional theater in Bengal.

Well, the play started. The program note was printed in English and had a short outline of the story. At first we were uneasy but our fear disappeared as the play progressed and we started acting with enthusiasm.

Came the scene where Rogue Sahib tortures Kshetromoni. . . . As soon as that happened there was a commotion among the European spectators. They became agitated and crowded near the footlights. A few red-faced soldiers took out their swords and climbed on the stage. Others tried to hold them back. Oh, what a commotion! what running about! The drop curtain was immediately pulled down. I thought they would surely behead us.

Anyway, some of the *sahibs* went away but a few, still enraged, were on the stage. The Magistrate had meanwhile sent for a company of soldiers from the fort. The situation calmed down when they arrived. Magistrate Sahib stopped the play and asked for the manager. Everyone started looking for Dharamdas Babu but he could not be found. After a lot of searching, we saw him sitting motionless under the stage. Kartik Pal started pulling him by the hand but he would not budge. So the assistant manager Abinash Babu went to see the Magistrate, taking Ardhendu Babu along. . . . The women in the party then left for our boarding house. Scenery and costumes were all left behind in the custody of the police.[23]

It seems obvious from this charming passage, so unselfconscious in its exaggeration of minute details, that the Lucknow production of *Neel-Darpan* was less a political disturbance than a shindy. What Binodini in her panic failed to realize was the red-faced soldiers were, in all probability, drunk. Her fears that they intended to behead her colleagues cannot be taken too seriously. The very fact that the Magistrate Sahib offered the actors police protection indicates that the play was not politically offensive.

The Dramatic Performances Control Act

The commotion at this performance has sometimes been misinterpreted as one of the primary causes leading to the formation of the Dramatic Performances Control Act instituted by the British in 1876. Certainly, the phenomenon of *Neel-Darpan* as the first protest play of the Bengal theater could not be ignored by the British. But there were other less conspicuous, though no less troublesome, plays that could be described as more subversive. Many of the sporadic performances of these plays are not documented. Their scripts are lost. But we have some evidence of the emerging patriotic themes and songs of Bengali plays, notably *Bharat Bilap* (1873) or "India's Lament" where an actress representing Mother India appeared "dressed in rags, weeping and with dishevelled hair."[24]

Such patriotic plays, however, were not the immediate cause of the Dramatic Performances Act. Nor was the censorship a reaction to the irreverent pantomime-sketches of Ardhendu Mustaphi, a founding member of the National Theater and prominent actor of the Bengali stage, who appeared in an immensely popular farce called *Mustaphi Sahibka Pakka Tamasha* (Mr. Mustaphi's Great Skit), where he parodied the mannerisms of the British, singing verses like

> I am the greatest Englishman on earth
> None can be compared with me
> Mr. Mustaphi is my name
> Chattogram is my *Bilat* [England]
> Rom-ti-tom-ti-tom . . .[25]

Mustaphi's skit was a witty response to a vaudeville routine by an English actor named Dave Carson who advertised his mockery of the Bengali *babus* as *Debsahibka Pakka Tamasha* (Deb Sahib's Great Skit). Even if the British were offended by Ardhendu's satire of the Raj (and I am tempted to believe that they were amused by it), it is unlikely that they would have instituted a censorship law on account of its excesses.

What provoked the British to institute the Dramatic Performances Act was a farce called *Gajadananda O Yubaraj* (Gaja and the Prince) produced at the Great National Theater on February 19, 1876. In its irreverent way, the play criticized a prominent Bengali lawyer, Jagadananda Ray, who invited the Prince of Wales (on his visit to Calcutta in 1876) to visit his home and meet his family. What created a stir among members of the Bengali intelligentsia was that the prince had been permitted to see the ladies of the house, who welcomed him in traditional Indian style blowing conch shells.

The visit of the prince was mercilessly satirized in the Great National Theater production. Quite understandably, the British government could not permit a member of the royal family (the future emperor of India, Edward VII) to be caricatured on the Bengali stage. The police interrupted the second performance of *Gajadananda O Yubaraj*, and Lord Northbrook, the viceroy of India, issued an ordinance on February 29, 1876, which authorized the government of Bengal to "prohibit certain dramatic performances which are scandalous, defamatory, seditious, obscene or otherwise prejudicial to the public interest."

The members of the Great National Theater reacted to the ordinance by improvising a play called *The Police of Pig and Sheep* the very next day. This was too daring an action to pass unnoticed. On March 4, the deputy commissioner of police (appropriately named Stewart Hogg) stopped the performance and arrested eight actors. Significantly, the actors were condemned not for ridiculing British political authority but for producing *Surendra Binodini* (the main play that accompanied *The Police of Pig and Sheep*), which was considered obscene by the government. This charge could not be sustained in court and the actors were acquitted. Nonetheless, the Dramatic Performances Control Act was formally instituted later in the year.

Censorship is not necessarily a hindrance for the political theater. On the contrary, a certain degree of repression can be a stimulus for politically committed playwrights and directors: it compels them to explore more imaginative ways of conveying their message. A political theater that faces the opposition of the government is frequently more interesting than a political theater supported by the government. Unfortunately, when the Dramatic Performances Act was instituted by the British government, the professional theater in Bengal was only four years old. It was not equipped to deal with the rigors of censorship on a theatrical level. Besides, its practitioners lacked the commitment that was necessary to address the political situation in India.[26]

Girish Chandra Ghosh and the Professional Theater

For the most part, the plays of the Bengali theater between 1872 and 1912 included musicals, domestic comedies, sensationalized versions of mythological stories, and religious melodramas based on the lives of saints and devotees. Even historical subjects were pretexts for escapist entertainments that specialized in songs, dances, theatrical tricks, spectacular devices, and melodrama. The following playbill for *Ananda Raho*, a five-act historical play dealing with the Mughal emperor Akbar and his Rajput adversaries and allies, captures the spirit of the nineteenth-century commercial theater in Bengal.

Saturday, the 28th May, 1881

At 9 p.m., will be repeated with necessary improvements and additional grandeur that new and historical drama by Girish Chandra Ghosh

Ananda Raho or *Akbar*

This drama is no stale story, told in dull monotonous dialogue, nor is the work crammed with tremendous tiring octavo speeches and soliloquies. The greatest statesman and mightiest monarch Akbar is portrayed with a truly histrionic pen.

The dying speech of Rana Pratap will bring tears from every human eye!

The scene where Akbar suffers from the effects of poison, falling a victim to his own malicious machinations . . . this awfully grand scene we say will have an impression in the mind of the spectator never to be effaced, and impart a lesson illustrative of the Truth, that the crooked path of policy is always perilous!

Soul dissolving songs—where religion and love are harmoniously
blended together—will even for the instant inspire confidence and
love for God in the heart of the most ungodly! . . .[27]

Girish Chandra Ghosh (1844–1912), the author of *Ananda
Raho* and manager of the Great National Theater, was unquestion-
ably the most renowned figure of the Bengali commercial theater.
Often described as the Garrick of the Bengali stage, he was an
actor of exceptional versatility and naturalness who introduced a
psychological dimension to Bengali "character acting." He was
also the first director to emphasize the interpretation of characters
and the training of actors. During his career, he established prominent commercial theaters such as the Star, the Emerald, and the
Minerva. A prolific playwright, he is said to have written around
seventy plays. With the exception of *Abu Hossain*, a phantasma-
goric musical with a touch of the *Arabian Nights*, and *Siraj-ud-
daula*, his historical tour de force, few of his plays are revived
today. They are loosely structured works, episodic in form, full of
conspiracies, coincidences, and supernatural interventions that
rely on emotional climaxes and stirring songs for their effect.

Though Girish Chandra Ghosh claimed that Shakespeare was
his model, he was probably aware, after his production of *Macbeth* failed at the Minerva Theater in 1893, that the Bengali audience was not prepared to accept a play without songs, dances, and
bawdry. Consequently, he was compelled to "liven up" his serious
plays with a surfeit of songs, farcical interludes, and burlesques.
These plays included *Prafulla*, a melodrama depicting the vicissitudes and downfall of a prosperous Bengali family; *Balidan* (Sacrifice), which deals with the evils of the dowry system in Bengal; and
Sasti Ki Santi? (Punishment or Peace?), a social drama on the suffering of Hindu widows that questions their right to marry for a
second time.

Ghosh gradually lost interest in these social plays. He felt limited by their pedestrian issues and their appalling insularity. He
could not reconcile himself to the narrow visions of his bourgeois
characters. Turning to the heroes and saints of Indian history and
mythology, he ridiculed the middle-class morality of social plays in
Bengal.

Plays are written about human virtues and vices. But unfortunately, in Bengal, not to speak of virtue, one does not even come across a powerful enough vice. The crimes [the bourgeoisie] commit amount perhaps to cheating a minor, deposing falsely in court without being confounded by cross-examination, robbing a house after assaulting a couple of unarmed guards—such are their outrages. As for their sexual sins—may be keeping a mistress, or eloping with the neighbour's wife. As for their virtues, they may have fed some beggars in memory of their departed father, or subscribed a large sum to the Emperor's building fund, hoping for a title in exchange. You want me to abandon mythology, and write about these men? The so-called great men of Bengal are just vulgar schemers.[28]

Despite this devastating critique of the bourgeoisie, Ghosh himself was extremely cautious about his criticism of orthodox Hindu society. As a devotee of Ramakrishna, he believed somewhat naively that the corruption in his world could be surmounted by acts of goodness, nobility, and sacrifice. His idealistic vision of life inevitably colored his perspective of Indian history.

Ghosh's History Plays

In many ways, the historical plays of Girish Chandra Ghosh were no different from his mythological plays in spirit and form. The emperors Ashoka and Akbar were endowed with a grace and valor reminiscent of the heroes of the *Ramayana* and the *Mahabharata*. Ghosh deified the heroic deeds of his historical characters in narratives that celebrated the remoteness and grandeur of the past. Instead of questioning Indian history, Ghosh chose to idealize it.

Significantly, one of his first historical plays was entitled *Maha Puja* (The Great Religious Festival) where he represented Mother India, the goddesses Lakshmi and Saraswati, and the regal figure of Britannia in pageantlike episodes. It is tempting to interpret the allegorical figures of "Mother India" and "Britannia" as strategic personae that enabled Ghosh to dramatize British power in India while avoiding the censorship of the Dramatic Performances Act of 1876. But this would be too sophisticated an interpretation for Ghosh's naive and decorative use of these figures.

There was nothing ironic about his reading of history. For instance, when he commemorated the death of Queen Victoria in his play *Asru Dhara* (The Flood of Tears), he could not allùde to her without rapturously mythologizing her reign. Instead of restraining his histrionics by focusing on the facts of history, Ghosh succumbed to emotionalism and melodrama, focusing on the more sensational aspects of history such as personal feuds and acts of revenge.

Two of his most successful historical plays, *Siraj-ud-daula* (1906) and *Mir Kasim* (1907) are also his most factual. They dramatize the last years of Mughal rule in India and the emergence of the British as a political power in Bengal. Siraj-ud-daula, the *nawab* of Bengal who resisted the military aggression and duplicity of Robert Clive, is a legendary figure in Indian history. It was somewhat daring of Girish Chandra Ghosh to idealize his actions since he was inextricably linked in the minds of the British with the notorious Black Hole of Calcutta episode, where 146 Englishmen were incarcerated in an eighteen-foot by fourteen-foot space. Not surprisingly, the Dramatic Performances Act was imposed on *Siraj-ud-daula*. It was not that the British feared that the play would incite the audience to violence but that it would reveal the corruption, bribery, and blackmail that enabled the members of the East India Company to establish their supremacy in Bengal.

It is well known that the British won the Battle of Plassey by bribing Mir Jaffar, one of Siraj-ud-daula's principal generals, who betrayed his prince on the battlefield on June 26, 1757. Two days after the battle, Clive appointed Jaffar as the governor of Bengal and guaranteed protection to the state. In exchange, Mir Jaffar is said to have paid $3 million as compensation for the loss of Calcutta, $450,000 to the directors of foreign policy in Calcutta, and (unknown to the Company) $7 million to Clive in cash in addition to an estate worth about $90,000 a year.[29]

Apart from monetary "compensation," the British demanded the right to engage in personal trade without paying any duties to the Bengal treasury. It is interesting to note that the word "loot" is derived from the Hindi word for plunder. For even Percival Spear, the most genteel of European historians on India, is compelled to admit that, "The five years after Clive's departure may rightly be described as a period of open and unashamed plunder."[30] During this time, Mir Jaffar was deposed in favor of his son-in-law, Mir Kasim, who was courageous enough to oppose British oppression in Bengal. In the following letter addressed to the British headquarters in Calcutta, he exposed the corruption of the East India Company in unequivocal terms.

> Your gentlemen make a disturbance all over my country, plunder the people, injure and disgrace my servants . . . showing the passes of the Company, they use their utmost endeavours to oppress the peasants, merchants, and other people of the country. . . . They forcibly take away our goods and commodities for a fourth part of their value, and by the ways of violence and oppression they oblige the peasants to give five rupees for goods which are worth one rupee.[31]

This was the immediate historical background for Girish Chandra Ghosh's *Mir Kasim*. Panoramic in scope, the play focuses not merely on three generations of Indian rulers—Mir Jaffar, Mir Kasim, and Shah Alam, the titular emperor of Delhi—but it also represents prominent members of the Raj such as Vansittart, Holwell, Warren Hastings, as well as a French consul and some Armenian soldiers. Ghosh was less interested in exploring their motivations and perspectives than in presenting vignettes of their personal lives and political careers. While it would not be inappropriate to describe *Mir Kasim*, in the words of P. Guha-Thakurta, as "a thrilling tale of heroism, intrigue, and romance," one must not underestimate Ghosh's mastery of commercial theater techniques—the building of the climax, the momentum of the action, the bravura of the characters, and the boldness of the gestures.

These techniques are not merely virtuosic. As we shall see in the chapter on Utpal Dutt, they can be most strategically used to enhance the political awareness of the people. Dutt, who advocates a "revolutionary theater," openly declares his debt to Ghosh's historical plays. Melodramatic and blatantly commercial as they may seem to the critics, Dutt believes that they are orchestrated in such a way that the history of India acquires a vibrant immediacy. Ghosh's phenomenal rapport with his audience was possible not simply because he had grasped popular conventions but because he knew how these conventions related to the lives of the people.

He was aware that an Indian audience needed to be mesmerized by the magic of the theater before it could be made to think of historical issues.

It is not surprising that the popularity of *Mir Kasim* in 1907 greatly disturbed the British government in India. Though the play did not address the contemporary political situation either through allusion or allegory, the corruption of the British during the reign of Mir Kasim was only too familiar to Ghosh's audience. The middle-class Bengali community did not need a contemporary version of *Mir Kasim* to be reminded of British oppression in India: they were aware that this oppression continued to affect their lives. By glorifying Mir Kasim and giving him the best lines in the play, Ghosh created a hero whose patriotism was irresistible. Whether he was aware of it or not, Ghosh's rhetoric was more than a theatrical accomplishment: it was a force that roused the patriotic fervor of the Bengali community and inspired them to reexamine the struggles and glory of their national heritage.

Nationalism and D. L. Roy

Two years before Girish Chandra Ghosh wrote *Mir Kasim*, Lord Curzon, that most unpopular viceroy of India, announced the Partition of Bengal. This peremptory decision (by which the eastern half of Bengal was attached to Assam and the western half to Bihar and Orissa) served as a catalyst for the Swadeshi Andolan, a mass boycott of foreign goods and British manufactured articles, a protest movement involving the people and the bourgeoisie that had gradually developed since the formation of the Indian National Congress in 1885.[32]

The Partition was a deliberate attempt by the British to disrupt the equilibrium of life in Bengal. It was naturally defended by Lord Curzon as "a mere readjustment of administrative boundaries," so necessary for the good of the country. There could not be a more self-righteous vindication of British colonialism in India. In a letter to John Morley, Curzon asserted that he was

an Imperialist heart and soul. Imperial expansion seems to me an inevitable necessity and carries a noble and majestic obligation. I do not see how any Englishman . . . can fail to see that we came here in obedience to what I call the decree of Providence, for the lasting benefit of millions of the human race. We often make great mistakes here; but I do firmly believe that there is no Government in the world that rests on so secure a moral basis, or is more fiercely animated by duty.[33]

Curzon failed to realize that such sentiments could no longer be tolerated by the Indian people. By the turn of the century, the political enlightenment of educated Bengalis like Surendranath Bannerjee undoubtedly posed a threat to the Raj. Ironically, the British had contributed to the emergence of this enlightenment by providing Indians with a Western education. The political essays of John Stuart Mill, the fiery speeches of Edmund Burke on liberty and national freedom, the radical romanticism of Shelley, the patriotic aphorisms and writings of Mazzini and Garibaldi, had a tremendous impact on the minds of young Bengalis who could no longer endure the oppression of the British. They reacted to Curzon's announcement of the Partition by organizing processions, public meetings, and political conferences in the major cities and villages of Bengal, urging the people to boycott British goods and to fight for the freedom of India. The political enthusiasm of the people was so spontaneous that the British decided to reverse the Partition in 1911. Significantly, they shifted the capital of the Raj from Calcutta to Delhi.

In those early years of the nationalist uprising, the Bengali theater could not assume a militant stance on account of the restrictions posed by the Dramatic Performances Act. Besides, it was more interested in celebrating the escapist conventions of the commercial theater than in confronting the political situation of the country. Apart from Girish Chandra Ghosh's rapturously patriotic plays like *Mir Kasim*, *Siraj-ud-daula*, and *Chhatrapati Shivaji*, there were very few plays that responded even tentatively to the turbulence of the time. The most outstanding exceptions are the historical plays of D. L. Roy. More immediate than the plays of Girish Chandra Ghosh, they explored the past history of India in relation to the pressures and uncertainties of the contemporary situation in Bengal. Unlike the stock characters of the commer-

cial Bengali theater, Roy's characters were not operatic figures
who lost themselves in "soul-dissolving" songs and lachrymose
speeches: they were ideal representatives of a secular and humanist approach to life. They reflected Roy's particularly restrained
patriotism and rational assessment of British domination in India.

Roy was too cultivated a gentleman to indulge in chauvinism.
His assimilation of Western culture and rational attitude to life
enabled him to view Indian nationalism more objectively than his
contemporaries. He was always something of an outsider. After
returning from his studies in England (where he had published a
volume of English poetry called *The Lyrics of Ind*), he was ostra-
cized by many orthodox Hindus for his freethinking and indifference to traditional customs and taboos. Roy was not easily intimidated by their resistance. Apart from ridiculing all sections of
Hindu society in his first play, an irreverent farce called *Kalki Aba-
tar* (Kalki's Incarnation, 1895), he had the nerve to satirize Hindu
gods and goddesses and the obfuscation of the scriptures. Predictably, this farce was too offensive to be staged.

Roy made no attempt to stage it. His contempt for the professional Bengali theater was well known. Besides, as a district magistrate he did not have to rely on the theater to earn his living.
Unlike Girish Chandra Ghosh, who wrote plays, in his words, "out
of necessity," Roy wrote plays in his leisure hours. This does not
mean that he regarded playwriting as a form of indulgence. Ironically, by *not* writing for the professional Bengali theater, he could
take playwriting seriously and experiment with new forms and
ideas. By maintaining his distance from the stereotypes and debased conventions of the commercial theater, he could explore
more sophisticated modes of integrating historical material and
social commentary.

Roy's first important publication was *Rana Pratap* (1905), a historical play that dramatizes the struggle of the Rajputs to preserve
their independence. What is astonishing about the play is the validity and intelligence of its message. Instead of eulogizing the
heroes of Indian history and indulging in patriotic songs and emotional diatribes against the British, Roy questioned the possibilities
of Indian nationalism. With admirable insight, he observed that
Indians could only be politically free if they could abandon their
feudal values and moribund social priorities. To the chagrin of the

Brahmins, he pointed out that the British Raj was not the only source of oppression in India: there was exploitation *within* the Hindu structure of society. The caste system was responsible for dissensions and false hierarchies among the Hindus. Consequently, the national unity of India was a distant myth.

These ideas are expressed vividly in the following passage from *Rana Pratap* where Man Singh, the most illustrious of Rajput warriors, discusses the possibilities of freedom with the rulers of Gwalior and Bikaner.

MAN SINGH: Freedom, your Highness? If we had any national life, we might talk about freedom. We lost that life ages ago; and now the nation is rotting. . . . This endless inertia is certainly not a sign of national life. A Drābir Brahmin will not dine with a Brahmin of Benares. You lose your caste if you cross the seas. . . . The good old days are gone.

BIKANER: But they may come back if the Hindus are united.

MAN SINGH: That's impossible. The souls of the Hindus are so shrivelled up, have become so inert and isolated from one another that unity is out of the question.

GWALIOR: Will it never be possible?

MAN SINGH: Yes, but not till the Hindus freed from the bondage of lifeless, meaningless, outworn conventions get a new religion throbbing with living, magnetic energy.[34]

The "new religion" that Man Singh fantasizes about is brotherhood. Instead of supporting abstract conceptions like "patriotism" and "nationalism," Roy urged his countrymen to live harmoniously and love one another like brothers. This seemingly naive message was not understood by his contemporaries, who were victims of age-old prejudices and class distinctions. Toward the end of *Mewar Patan* (The Fall of Mewar), another play by Roy about the courage and solidarity of the Rajputs, two Rajput ladies discuss the virtues of manhood and love.

MANASI: Patriotism is greater than self-seeking, but manhood is greater than patriotism. . . . This nation shall surely regain its manhood.

SATYAVATI: But when?

MANASI: . . . The day when the people will cast off the age-worn scriptures and adopt a new religion.

SATYAVATI: What's that religion, Manasi?

MANASI: That religion is love. They will first have to forget themselves and learn to love their brethren, their race, mankind, and manhood.[35]

There are obvious similarities between these two sections of dialogue: a profusion of aphorisms, a question-and-answer mode of conveying ideas, a curiously turgid phraseology, and somewhat pompous humanism. It might be argued that in resisting the rhetoric of patriotism (exemplified by Girish Chandra Ghosh), D. L. Roy invented his own rhetoric which had many limitations. But at least there was an attempt to avoid the stereotypes of the professional Bengali theater that his contemporary, Kshirode Prasad Vidyabinode, exploited so skillfully. Not surprisingly, Roy's plays were destined to remain unpopular during his time while Vidyabinode's *Alibaba*, an operatic comedy with songs, dances, and farcical interludes, and *Alamgir*, a tragic drama on the last years of the Mughal emperor Aurangzeb, were resounding commercial successes. The Bengali theater had entered its most ignominious phase of commercialism.

Sisir Bahaduri

With the singular exception of Sisir Bahaduri, who starred in the premiere of *Alamgir* on December 10, 1921, there was no one who attempted to extend the possibilities of the Bengali commercial theater. It was not possible, of course, to even conceive of an alternative theater since there were no new voices, no radical playwrights, no startling visions. The plays of Girish Chandra Ghosh, Dinabandhu Mitra, D. L. Roy, and Vidyabinode were revived in tedious, ostentatious productions where the actors indulged in declamation and histrionic gestures.

It is not necessary here to describe those barren years. Let us, however, concentrate briefly on Sisir Bahaduri, the one exception of the Bengali theater whose mastery of technique and mesmeric power as an actor have been praised by Pudovkin, Cherkassov, and Dame Sybil Thorndike, among others. Bahaduri's performance in the title role of Vidyabinode's *Raghubir* has been eloquently described by one of his most ardent admirers, Sombhu Mitra. Mitra is himself unanimously considered the most outstanding classical actor in the contemporary Bengali theater.

> One had to see him to realize how a physical movement verging on the ridiculous can be transformed into the sublime. One was about to laugh when suddenly he drained all the laughter in the world by his unforgettable acting. I used to feel that he carried away my mind in a swift awesome flight and left me alone high up in the skies face to face with death.[36]

Apart from his legendary acting, Sisir Bahaduri was an innovative director who introduced a number of significant changes in the production of Bengali theater. As a former professor of English literature at Vidyasagar College, he stressed the virtues of authenticity and historical accuracy in the design of costumes and the construction of sets. He was also the first director in the Bengali theater to explore spatial levels and reject the use of footlights in favor of directional lighting from the wings. Although he worked within the framework of the proscenium, he occasionally attempted to break away from its confines by seating his actors in the audience and making them enter through the aisle. As early as 1927 he had criticized the limitations of the "picture frame" stage. With some bitterness, he observed that, "We have made the mistake of imitating the English models, of forsaking our own truth for the falsity of an alien import. We have to rectify the mistake and go back to the ways of our *jatra*."[37]

It is a pity that Sisir Bahaduri did not pursue this ideal. As a cultivated *bhadrolok* (gentleman), he was somewhat removed from the crudities and immediacy of *jatra*. Besides, his awareness of *jatra* as a primitive form of "people's theater" was minimal. He responded to it for purely aesthetic reasons. Even though Sisir Bahaduri was among the first directors in Bengal to appreciate Brecht, his own theater was ineluctably bourgeois. It is difficult to believe that his professional career coincided with the Noncooperation movement of Mahatma Gandhi: his plays scrupulously avoid any reference to the political unrest in the country.

As the years passed, his theater became increasingly redundant.

Unable to confront the poverty, famine, and communal riots of Bengal, it languished in a pitiable state of inertia and lassitude. Kironmoy Raha has written perceptively about the last days of Sisir Bahaduri.

> The terrible suffering of the common people was a kind of reality he had not seen or known at such close range before. Perhaps, he realized that the theater he had enriched and believed in was inadequate to cope with the maelstrom of socio-economic changes. It could neither portray the harsh reality of the lives of the common people nor provide wholly escapist fare. It could be that his sense of failure and frustration came from this realization.[38]

TRANSITION

To confront "the maelstrom of socio-economic changes" the Bengali theater would have to renounce its middle-class proclivities. Instead of dramatizing the lives of middle-class people for a predominantly middle-class audience, it would have to reach out to the working class by addressing the destitution of the tribal people and the oppression of laborers in factories, mines, and plantations. In order to examine the political movement in India with some accuracy and daring, it would have to abandon its insularity and fear of censorship.

The first Bengali playwright to assume a political stance in the thirties by defying the Dramatic Performances Act was Manmatha Ray. Generally underrated as a "transitional" playwright, he nonetheless deserves attention for his politically strategic use of allegory. Unlike Girish Chandra Ghosh, who interpreted mythological stories with unqualified literalness, Ray dramatized Hindu legends by selecting episodes that highlighted the political situation in India.

His allegorical intention in *Karagar* (Prison), for instance, which dramatizes a Puranic story concerning the birth of Lord Krishna in prison, was too blatant to be ignored by a Bengali audience in 1930. At that time, the prisons were full of Indian political prisoners who were arrested by the British because of their involvement in Gandhi's Civil Disobedience movement. Ray's play

referred specifically, yet insinuatively, to this situation. The underlying message of his allegorical drama was not difficult to read. It
required his audience to think analogically: just as Lord Krishna
ultimately vanquished the tyrant Kamsa, the Indian political prisoners would ultimately be able to overthrow their British masters.
Unfortunately, the analogy was more conspicuous than Manmatha Ray had imagined and *Karagar* was promptly banned by the
government censors.

It is necessary to sketch briefly at this point some of the most
turbulent political events in India around the time *Karagar* was
first staged. Though the Civil Disobedience movement was gaining
in momentum, it did not unify the various political factions and
parties that had burgeoned since the Swadeshi Andolan. One of
the strongest opponents of the Congress party was the Communist
Party of India (CPI), which was formed toward the end of the
1920s at the Tashkent Military School and affiliated to the Communist International a year later. The influence of the Soviet
Union on this party was so perceptible that in 1929 (a year before
Manmatha Ray wrote *Karagar*) the British Indian government
accused a number of Communists of conspiring to overthrow the
Raj with a Communist regime based on the Soviet model. This
accusation resulted in a trial that came to be known as the Meerut
Conspiracy Case.

Reaction to the trial immediately became a national issue.
Leaders of various parties and trade unions, notably Jawaharlal
Nehru (who was then the president of the All-India Trade Union
Congress), protested that the government was using the bogey of
communism to suppress the labor movement in India. If anything,
the Meerut Conspiracy Case intensified anti-British sentiments and
further enhanced the image of the Communist Party of India.
Attracting many intellectuals and students (primarily from the
middle class), the CPI actively supported strikes, disseminated
Communist literature, and was so outspoken about government
policies that it was summarily banned in 1934.

In February 1936, R. Palme Dutt and Ben Bradley, two fervent
supporters of communism, published an influential article entitled
"The Anti-Imperialist People's Front in India," which called for
the unity of all anti-imperialist forces in India. The article was so

persuasive that the differences between the various parties were temporarily forgotten, and the Communists were invited to join the Congress Socialist party. For a brief period, the myth of a United National Front prevailed. The Communists were particularly enthused by Nehru's anti-imperialist stance and declaration of socialism in his 1936 presidential address for the Congress party.

Gradually, however, tensions developed, since the Communists strategically used their position within the Congress Socialist party to dominate the trade unions and the Students' Federation. The possibility of any sustained rapprochement between the CPI and the other parties was completely destroyed when the Second World War broke out. Because the Russians were not immediately involved in the war, the Communists initially declared that it was an "imperialist war," but they later changed their position when Hitler invaded the Soviet Union. Automatically, the war became a "people's war" that had to be supported unconditionally, since it represented an international civil war against fascism. The Allied (and therefore Soviet) victory was more important to the Communists than the immediate independence of India. Unavoidably, this ideological stance totally contradicted the Civil Disobedience movement of Mahatma Gandhi and the militaristic nationalist policies of Subhas Chandra Bose.

The ferment of these differing political attitudes was so intense that it was not addressed by any playwright in the thirties and early forties. What was urgently needed, of course, was not an individual effort to assess the political situation but some kind of collective action among theater practitioners that would enable them to confront the increased militancy of the workers in India.[39]

The Progressive Writers' Association

Theater practitioners needed to organize as the writers had done in the Progressive Writers' Association (PWA), which held its first conference on April 10, 1936, in Lucknow. Inspired by numerous antifascist cultural organizations in Europe, notably the International Association of Writers for the Defense of Culture Against Fascism, which was supported by Romain Rolland, Maxim Gorky,

Thomas Mann, André Malraux, among other luminaries, the PWA assumed a militant stance against British imperialism and fascism. Even though its members (including famous Indian writers such as Mulk Raj Anand, Munshi Prem Chand, Sajjid Zahar) wrote in various Indian languages and disagreed about their modes and techniques of writing, they unanimously resolved that:

> The new literature of India must deal with the basic problems of our existence today—the problems of hunger and poverty, social backwardness and political subjection. All that drags us down to passivity, inaction, and un-reason, we reject as reactionary. All that rouses in us the critical spirit, which examines institutions and customs in the light of reason, which helps us to act, to organize ourselves, to transform, we accept as progressive.[40]

For the first time in the history of Indian culture, there was an organized attempt to abandon those debased qualities of Indian literature that the Bengali theater exemplified so egregiously. Some of these "qualities," which the members of the PWA were never tired of attacking, included "mysticism," "romantic sentimentalism," "feudalism," and "over-concern with the fate of the individual." Though the PWA was somewhat Marxist in its orientation, it could not advocate a truly revolutionary art. Most of its members were not prepared to think in terms of dialectical materialism. Their sense of history was limited by their bourgeois inheritance and by their idealized, often sentimental awareness of the people. Moreover, as writers, they were entrapped by bourgeois conventions and modes of communication that prevented them from representing the lives of the people realistically. Nonetheless, they genuinely attempted to confront these limitations and to work in close coordination as "progressive" writers.

After a vigorous start, the PWA passed through a period of disillusionment between the years 1939 and 1942. The signing of the Russo-German Non-Aggression Pact and the Soviet Union's invasion of Poland greatly disturbed the Marxist members of the group. The vacillations of the committee members reflected the political confusion in India at the outbreak of the Second World War.

On September 14, 1939, the Congress Working Committee issued an important statement declaring that:

> India cannot associate herself in a war said to be for democratic
> freedom when that very freedom is denied to her. . . . If Great Brit-
> ain fights for the maintenance and extension of democracy, then she
> must necessarily end imperialism in her own country.[41]

On the other hand, the supporters of communism in India staunch-
ly upheld that the British had to be supported in the international
war against fascism. It is not surprising, therefore, that the CPI
became a legal party in July 1942 when it refused to accept
Gandhi's "Quit India" slogan—the credo of the nationalist movement in its final phase.

The differences between the Communists and the nationalists
were so irreconcilable that there were no all-India conferences of
the PWA between 1939 and 1942. Most of the members faced an
impasse: they could neither support the British government after
nearly two centuries of colonial oppression nor could they condemn it for fighting fascism in Europe. On the other hand, they
were ideologically drawn to the Soviet Union but they could not
accept its rapprochement with Germany. Even the ideal principles
of Marx seemed to have succumbed to the evils of fascism.

This dilemma was resolved when Hitler invaded Russia. Immediately there was an upsurge of antifascist fervor, particularly in
Bengal where prominent members of the intelligentsia formed an
organization called the Friends of the Soviet Union. In March
1942, Somen Chanda, a young writer committed to the growth of
the Marxist movement in India, was murdered by "pro-fascist elements" in the city of Dacca. Within a month, the Anti-Fascist
Writers' and Artists' Union was formed in Calcutta. Its members
included the most prominent artists, novelists, and poets of Bengal
such as Jamini Ray, Manik Bandyopadhyay, Buddhadev Bose, and
Bishnu Dey.

Significantly, even though there were no prominent theater personalities in the committee, one of the first activities of the Union
was the performance of a symbolic play by Tagore called *Rath*
(Chariot). The action of the play centers on a *rath* that gets stuck in

the middle of a road. Despite the chanting of the Brahmins and the desperate efforts of the *bhadrolok* to extricate the chariot, it remains stuck. Then the Shudras arrive and effortlessly lift the wheels of the chariot from the mud. The play subtly indicates that the obstacles of life can only be removed with the assistance of the Shudras, the exploited class of people.[42]

The significance of the Anti-Fascist Writers' and Artists' Union was that it attempted to reach a class of people who had been previously ignored by the intelligentsia. Apart from issuing pamphlets on the evils of fascism, the Union organized a number of song recitals in the working-class districts of Calcutta, Howrah, the 24-Parganas, Rangpur, Dinajpur, Dacca, and Chittagong. The workers of jute mills, iron and steel industries, and the tramway corporations participated in demonstrations and rallies where fervent songs by Benoy Roy (that "untiring golden voiced comrade" of the Union) and the Bengali version of the "Internationale" received a tremendous response. When the Japanese forces threatened to invade the eastern region of India toward the end of 1941, the peasants responded by singing militant songs composed by Roy where the Japanese were stereotyped as "Fascist fiends," "grisly monsters," and "gangsters." I shall resist the temptation to quote English translations of these songs; their rhetoric is so absurd that it trivializes the obvious commitment and zeal of the members of the Anti-Fascist Writers' and Artists' Union.

One of the characteristics of political rhetoric is its predilection for metaphors that reduce calamities and states of emergency to banalities and the crudest of cliches. Nearly forty years after the Japanese threat of invasion in India, it is almost impossible to accept the anti-Fascist resolutions passed in the Union without suspending one's disbelief vigorously. Statements such as, ". . . the poisonous jaws of Fascism are straining to swallow our own dear country," and "If today Fascism is victorious, it would mean the permanent visitation of locusts on the world's fair field," are nothing more than rhetorical flourishes for us today.[43] They exemplify, in the words of Professor Hiren Mukherjee, one of the severest limitations of the cultural movement in India: "the over-exuberance of the pseudo-Marxist."

Professor Mukherjee, himself one of the more vigorous spokesmen of the political theater movement in India, was not able to resist such "exuberance" in his statements about the political theater. In his inaugural speech at the first conference of the Indian People's Theater Association (I.P.T.A.) in Bombay on May 25, 1943, he succumbed to perfervid prophesies and emotional exhortations.

> Come writer and artist, come actor and playwright, come all who work by hand or by brain, and dedicate yourself to the task of building a brave new world of freedom and social justice. And let us all remember, if we wish for a motto, that "the workers are the salt of the earth and to be part of their destiny is the greatest adventure of our time."[44]

The Indian People's Theater Association

One can accept the lack of restraint in Mukherjee's rhetoric when one considers the historical importance of the I.P.T.A. in the Indian theater. It was the first organized national theater movement in India, the first concerted attempt on the part of Indian theater practitioners to collaborate in an antifascist and anti-imperialist theater, and the first significant reaction to the "cheap commercial glamour," "pseudo-aesthetic posturing," and "sobstuff" of the contemporary theater.[45]

The model of the I.P.T.A. was the folk theater of India, that rich and diverse field of primitive theatrical forms including the *jatras*, the *tamashas*, the *kathakalas*, the *burrakathas*, and the *jarigans* that flourished in the rural areas of India. The members of the I.P.T.A. had noble intentions of learning the art of theater from the people but they faced many problems. In the first place, they had to confront their insularity as middle-class intellectuals who were ignorant of the conditions of life in the villages. Then there was a problem of language. The members of the I.P.T.A. had to learn the languages of the people, the dialects of the peasants in Rajasthan and Bihar and Andhra Pradesh, before they could hope to dramatize the lives of these people.

Most of the early plays of the I.P.T.A. (many of which are merely recorded without extensive description of either production or script) are predominantly urban in their perspective. There is nothing "folk" about them. The more memorable plays are appallingly abstract exposures of fascism and imperialism. In the opening ceremony of the I.P.T.A. in 1943, there was a presentation of short plays in Marathi, Hindi, Bengali, and even English (a one-acter entitled *Strange Meeting* by a Chinese playwright, Ting Ling). While the plays were on a number of significant themes, including the communal rivalry between Hindus and Muslims and the interaction of science and politics, their tone was too doctrinaire to qualify as "people's theater."

In one of the more dynamic plays, *Yeh Amrit Hai* (This Is Immortality) by K. Ahmad Abbas, a scientist who discovers *amrit* (immortality) is besieged by historical and allegorical figures including Beauty, John Bull, Religion, and Hitler. They attempt to seize *amrit* from the scientist in a series of verbose sketches. The committee of the I.P.T.A. criticized the play for its lack of coordination, its idealized and peripheral references to the working class, and its concentration on lectures rather than on theatrical action. Its facile treatment of fascism and imperialism was also roundly condemned.

> We are amused by Hitler and John Bull, we are not roused to deepest anger and a determination in our hearts to fight them, the enemies of culture and the basis of all culture, freedom. At this time, it is not enough to be amused by the enemies of all decent human values. We must fight them till they are completely destroyed.[46]

The criticism was constructive. In his next play for the Bombay branch of the I.P.T.A., Abbas avoided the trivialization of serious subjects inherent in the use of allegorical and abstract figures. He concentrated, instead, on the very immediate suffering of the villagers in the Malabar district during the cholera epidemic of 1944. Since anticholera vaccine was not easily available, hundreds of villagers died out of sheer neglect.

The protagonist of Abbas' play *Zubeida* was modelled on a Muslim girl of Malabar who had abandoned purdah in order to join the relief forces, only to die of cholera herself. Abbas was inspired by the heroism of this girl. His play, set in the United Provinces of India rather than in Malabar, captures the horror of the cholera epidemic through its eerie use of funeral dirges. It also evokes the very essence of Indian village life in its faithful representation of the *baithak*, the daily gathering of the village elders who discuss the tribulations of life while smoking the hookah and indulging in gossip. Such evocations of rural life made *Zubeida* intensely popular with the people. At certain open-air performances, there were as many as ten thousand spectators. It is of some historical importance that many of the spectators of *Zubeida* included women who had never seen a play in their lives.

The I.P.T.A. was responsible for changing the very structure and conception of theater in various parts of India. By performing for the masses rather than for limited audiences, it made theater more available to those sections of society who had previously ignored it, or had been prevented from seeing it. Though many of the productions of the I.P.T.A. were invariably hectic and hastily improvised, they succeeded in conveying the exigencies of the historical moment to their mass audiences.

The imminence of India's independence was so intoxicating to the masses that the I.P.T.A. had no difficulty in rousing their patriotic fervor and making them forget, if only temporarily, their caste distinctions. The enthusiasm of the mass audiences was more intense than the British government had imagined. It is, perhaps, for this reason that the Dramatic Performances Control Act, so conspicuous at a time when the productions of the Indian theater were scarcely subversive, was now incapable of restraining the inflammatory power of the theater in India. The theater was no longer a mere entertainment with some social and political significance: it had become the very forum of the people.

I.P.T.A. and the Folk Theater

Apart from raising the consciousness of the people by improvising plays on subjects such as police repression, the food crisis, strikes, and the life of a *kisan* (farmer), the members of the I.P.T.A. attempted to adapt the traditional forms of the folk theater in order to confront contemporary issues. In the southern state of Andhra Pradesh, for instance, the *burrakatha* (a popular folk form involving the recitation of a dramatic ballad) was revitalized in such a way that it acquired political significance.

The *burrakatha* is intrinsically Brechtian in structure. It involves two performers apart from the reciter of the ballad—a joker who ridicules the heroic deeds of the ballad by interrupting the narrative with bawdy asides and irreverent remarks, and a commentator who explains the intricacies of the narrative, clarifies the issues, raises questions, and urges the audience to reflect on the action. Both the joker and the commentator play an instrument called a *burra*, a makeshift stringed instrument with a long, narrow neck attached to the base of a hollowed pumpkin with hide stretched on its side. The instrument is as rough and sonorous as the performance. The *burrakatha* recitals were so popular with the people of Andhra Pradesh that there were as many as 375 performances during the year 1944.

In a particularly successful recital, Balurao, the son of a poor peasant with Communist leanings who was jailed during the most repressive period of the British Raj, urges the people not to be seduced by fascism in their opposition to the British. The joker interrupts his exhortations by playing the devil's advocate: he dismisses the entire narrative of the reciter (who assumes the role of Balurao) as an ingenious piece of British propaganda. The commentator then intervenes and reminds the audience that fascism poses a very severe threat to world peace. He narrates in vivid detail the rapes, murders, and crimes inflicted by the Japanese on the innocent people of China, Malaya, and Burma. With patriotic zeal, he emphasizes that the Indian National Congress has consistently supported the Chinese in their struggle against fascism. By juxtaposing the views of the reciter, the joker, and the commentator, the spectator of the *burrakatha* recital was politically educated while being thoroughly entertained.

Fascism was rambunctiously personified in yet another performance organized by the Andhra Pradesh branch of the I.P.T.A.: a play called *Hitler Parabhavam* (The Downfall of Hitler) written in the racy style of the *veedi bhagavatam* or "street play." From an eyewitness report of this performance at the All-India Kisan Conference in March 1944, we learn that Hitler was presented as a braggart, a *miles gloriosus* figure, surrounded by "an entourage of yes-men."[47] Two prosperous farmers and their wives repeated all his words mechanically, thereby ridiculing his peremptory statements. The most outrageous comedy in the play occurred when Mussolini and Tojo lamented their fate and placed their heads on

Hitler's shoulders, sobbing like children. It is unlikely that the audience learned anything about fascism in the course of the play; they were too busy laughing at Hitler.

Another popular performance of the I.P.T.A. was Gopal Krishnayya's bravura enactment of the "medicine man." It is fairly common to see religious mendicants in Andhra Pradesh wandering the streets and selling medicines rather like the mountebanks of Renaissance Italy. The selling of the medicine, which is at once the pretext and object of the performance, is more than a business transaction, it is a virtuosic act. In order to utilize this act as a means of commenting on the social condition of India, Gopal Krishnayya reinterpreted the nature of the illness to be diagnosed. Instead of providing medicines to cure coughs and colds, he claimed that he could eradicate social diseases and national problems. Clad in the traditional costume of the mendicant and armed with his bow and arrow, he prescribed pills and powders concocted by Lenin, Stalin, Gandhi, and Nehru that could exterminate the Nazis and purge the imperialists.[48]

This method of propagating nationalism to the masses was undeniably naive, but it cannot be dismissed as trivial. The audience responded to Gopal Krishnayya's prescriptions for national unity with loud cheers and rounds of applause. This reception indicates that the naivete of political theater is not necessarily a limitation. More often than not, it embodies the very strength of political theater.

Bijon Bhattacharya

Unlike the Andhra Pradesh and Maharashtra units of the I.P.T.A., which explored the social possibilities of folk forms with considerable success, the Bengal branch of the I.P.T.A. failed to exploit the indigenous theater familiar to the Bengali peasants such as the *jatra*, the *kabijan*, and the *kirtan*. Its most significant contribution to the Indian political theater movement was its production of Bijon Bhattacharya's *Nabanna* (New Harvest) directed jointly by the playwright and Sombhu Mitra and first produced in October 1944. Radical in form and content, terrifyingly honest in its depiction of suffering, and daringly innovative in its use of language and stagecraft, *Nabanna* is another landmark in the Bengali theater as significant as *Neel-Darpan.* In many ways, its ambition and courage have never been surpassed. The subject of the play was nothing less devastating than the deaths of five million peasants during the Bengal famine of 1943–1944, one of those horrifying calamities that defy description and annihilate the imagination.

In a memorable interview toward the end of his life, Bijon Bhattacharya recalled the difficulties and contradictions he faced when he attempted to dramatize the appalling conditions of life during the famine.

> I saw the people dying like cats and dogs in the streets of Calcutta muttering, fumbling. . . . Could I reach my ears forth to them? This was my only thought. I would go to many places and sit thinking: What to write? What to do? How to do? Just to gauge the depth of their suffering? While going on like this, I thought that if I wrote a drama and actually produced it, would it be worthwhile? . . . I was not a dramatist, not a writer, nothing. But the effort was there. Then on hearing, knowing, and understanding the people, and being one among them in the parks and streets, I became sorry to see that the art-form was not strong enough to convey the depth of their suffering, their tragedy, their crisis. Thus I went on when I suddenly felt, if the people could speak for themselves, I could perhaps talk in their own terms, for I know the people very well, how they talk and laugh and think and convey their emotions. I know how to react like them. . . .[49]

It was this instinctive sense of being with the people that enabled Bijon Bhattacharya to write with such astonishing insight about their acute suffering. He always maintained that his masters were neither Aristotle nor Michael Madhusadhan Dutt but the villagers, farmers, *bauls* (a sect of itinerant singers), boatmen, and hunters he had come in contact with through his life.

Born in the village of Khankhanapur in the district of Faridpur (now in Bangladesh) on July 17, 1915, Bhattacharya had lived for many years in the villages of Khulna, Jessore, Basirhat, and Satkshira before coming to Calcutta, where he studied at Ashutosh College. He did not exaggerate his contact with the people. As a child, he had enjoyed the company of the most vagrant and impoverished class of people, including the fakirs and the *bauls.* He would go to their dens and listen to their music and folklore, which were invariably accompanied by the wild beating of drums. He also mixed with certain classes of village artisans who were associated with primitive handicrafts. He observed them at work and learned about their superstitions and faith in particular deities and omens.

Bhattacharya discovered that the people had their own versions of the *Ramayana*, the *Mahabharata*, the Vedas, and the Upanishads, which reflected their robust temperament and resilience to the harshness of life. For instance, they represented the elephant god Ganesh with teeth protruding behind his trunk—a visage that contrasted sharply with the toothless, more genial, appearance of the Ganesh worshipped by city people. In addition to deities, Bhattacharya was fascinated by the ritual signification attached to the dog, the horse, and the snake by the villagers of Bengal. He witnessed a number of stirring ceremonies involving animal worship where he discovered the vibrationary power of *mantras* (sacred words). With a childlike sense of awe, he marvelled that sound waves could affect the behavior of animals.

In all his observations of rural life, Bhattacharya was not embarrassed to reveal his idealization of the people. He honestly believed that they were endowed with a "sixth sense" that enabled them, for instance, to forecast the weather by smelling the wind. There is something almost Wordsworthian in his awareness of how the lives of the people are interrelated with the forces of nature. He was particularly responsive to their sense of tradition, their "mythical hunches" as he once described it. In an impassioned statement, Bhattacharya claimed that:

> The strifes of the people are no less than those of any heroes of our time, any of the Greek gods. Dionysian rituals are still performed in our land, it awaits an eye to see it and to project it on the stage. Therein lies my strength. . . . A snake-charmer or a boar-hunter or a boatman on the River Padma with all his troubles seems to be glorious. Project him, and he will sail down the river in Greece, even down the Clyde into the sea, yes, he can. I greatly admire a man's anscestry. I try to depict it. . . .[50]

Such rhapsodic statements about the people were not entirely convincing to those members of the Bengali theater community who viewed the predicament of the people in doctrinaire Marxist terms. Bhattacharya was very honest about his resistance to Marxist dogma as well as to European theories of political theater. Despite his admiration for Brecht, for instance, he was aware that, as an Indian who had never seen a performance of the Berliner Ensemble, his knowledge of the "epic theater" was purely theoretical. He strongly believed that Brecht's views of the theater emerged from a consciousness that was "essentially German." He felt estranged from its intricacies. In addition, Bhattacharya believed that Brecht's "assimilation" of Marxism (which is problematic even for Western theoreticians of the political theater), was also colored by a specifically German world view that emerged from an acute awareness of social conditions, processes of work, technological developments, and labor-management relations in postwar Germany.

Dismissing European models of dramaturgy and characterization, Bhattacharya admitted that, "If I have to do anything Indian, I must know that I can't entertain a German or an American spectator, an English or a Soviet artist without the [Indian] people."[51] Taken out of context, the statement lends itself to criticism. Bhattacharya seems to be appallingly insular in his adherence to the "people." However, a more accurate way of interpreting his point of view would be to see his adherence to the people as a relationship so intimate and steeped in the minutiae of their lives, that it defies translation into another language or theatrical tradition.

This brings us to one of the central aspects of Bijon Bhattacharya's political art. It cannot be translated. The difficulties are not merely technical, though the dialects of his plays are almost impossible to translate even into standard Bengali. (When he lived in the villages, Bhattacharya noted that the dialects of the people changed "mysteriously" after every two miles.) But apart from the twists and turns and hidden resonances of dialects, there is a more fundamental problem with the translation of Bhattacharya's plays. It has to do with his absorption in the lives of the people, his surrender of an urban, Marxist perspective to the myths and folklore of rural Bengal.

One is constantly struck by Bhattacharya's reluctance to teach people how to live their lives according to principles and stan-

dards alien to them. Instead, he prefers to question their beliefs
and taboos by working within their social framework. Only after
presenting their way of life with the intimacy of a participant does
he begin to expose its inner contradictions and limitations, its dissensions and areas of corruption. This ability to think with the people is Bhattacharya's greatest gift as an artist. Consequently, when
he criticizes any particular aspect of their lives, he is neither doctrinaire nor condescending. Rather, his criticism of the people is
rooted in a very genuine concern for their exploitation and impoverished state of being.

Nabanna (New Harvest)

The process of learning embodied in the action of Bhattacharya's
plays is unobtrusive. His characters (or "people" as he prefers to
call them) learn about the conditions of their lives with quiet
strength. In Nabanna, we see a group of peasants, anonymous victims of the Bengal famine, passing through a series of crises. They
represent in microcosm the five million peasants who died in the
famine, yet these characters are more than emblems. They are
human beings with particular fears and desires who gradually
realize that their only resilience to suffering lies in their collective
strength. We see them achieve this awareness toward the end of the
play after they have left their famine-stricken village only to be
reduced to the most abject poverty in Calcutta, where they develop a political awareness of their suffering.

It is now widely acknowledged that the Bengal famine was not
a natural disaster but a man-made one. The terrible irony about
the famine is that it was not caused by any significant shortage of
food. On the contrary, the per capita availability of food supply
was 9 percent higher in 1943 than in 1941, which was not a famine year.[52] The problem was that this food was not made available
to the peasants and laborers in the rural areas of Bengal. Instead, it
was exported by the British to feed its armed forces fighting in
Europe and Japan.

The indifference of the British government to the horror of the
famine is one of the most unpleasant memories of the British Raj in
India. The characters of Nabanna seem to be aware of this indifference. They learn that the famine is not a calamity inflicted on

them by the gods; it is a disaster that could have been averted if the administrators of their country had some humanity and concern for the oppressed. Bijon Bhattacharya makes his "people" survive their destitution and return to their village with a renewed awareness of their rights as human beings. It is significant that the play is entitled *Nabanna* or "New Harvest." It looks toward the future with unconcealed courage and hope.

What saves the play from tendentiousness is the vibrant quality of its life. Enacted with fierce commitment and a burning sense of injustice by young members of the Bengal I.P.T.A. (including six Communist party organizers with no theatrical experience), the first performances were revelations for Bengali theater audiences who had reconciled themselves to the sensationalism and melodrama of the professional theater. They discovered for the first time in *Nabanna* the extraordinary impact of realism in the dialects and street cries of the actors, the minutiae of their gestures, movements, and responses, and the stark simplicity of the set and the costumes. But apart from these technical innovations, it was the unquestionable validity of the production that stirred thousands of spectators in Bengal and other parts of India. *Nabanna* proved that it was possible for the Bengali theater to address the devastation of the famine without minimizing its extremity or trivializing its terrifying impact.

The compassion of Bijon Bhattacharya for his countrymen, his belief in their humanity despite their impoverished existence, was undoubtedly the underlying strength of *Nabanna*. In a seminar on the Bengali political theater held in Calcutta in 1977 shortly before he died, Bhattacharya revealed the source of his inspiration for *Nabanna*.

> I spotted in a Calcutta street a crawling baby fumbling over the corpses searching for its mother's breast. The mother was already dead. Even while we organized gruel kitchens to feed the starving people, I felt the need to do something meaningful. Only when I wrote my play *Nabanna* and staged it, did I have the feeling that I had at last become a mother to that hungry child even as I mothered my play to make it grow into a performance for the people. That image of the crawling child has haunted me ever since. Whenever in my creative quest I miss the crawling baby, I shift my position endlessly till the child comes to view again.[53]

Three Plays

Despite this perspective of the playwright as a mother figure, which may seem melodramatic to the Western reader, there is nothing sentimental about Bijon Bhattacharya's awareness of the people. In order to protect their rights as human beings, he makes them confront, and eventually, reject those superstitions and primitive beliefs which are largely responsible for their exploitation. However, it must be emphasized that the rejection of the old way of life in Bhattacharya's plays is never brutal. The learning process of his characters is profoundly moving.

In *Garbhavati Jananee* (The Pregnant Mother), a group of villagers collects herbs for a living. Their work is not simply a job that provides them with a meager income; it is a faith that they have inherited from their ancestors. Their knowledge of the medicinal and life-nourishing properties of nature sustains them in all their suffering. It even gives them a sense of pride. Quite instinctively, these villagers regard themselves as healers of men. Bhattacharya disturbs the equilibrium of their world gently, yet firmly: one of the villagers is poisoned by a snake while he is collecting herbs. This is an evil omen and the villagers are confused. Desperately, they try to heal their comrade by using all kinds of folk medicines, antidotes, and potions handed down from the past. They exhaust their folklore and traditional sources of wisdom. Their efforts are futile. The villager dies. The morale of the community is shattered as the villagers lose faith in the restorative power of herbs. They realize that their blind adherence to the maxims, taboos, and prescriptions of their forefathers can only perpetuate their state of ignorance. They prepare themselves for a change in their way of life and in their modes of perception.

In the course of this astonishingly powerful and economical play, we recognize the emergence of a consciousness: the villagers realize that before they can be healers of men they have to learn how to protect themselves. The process of this education is convincing precisely because it emerges from within the villagers. There is no education campaign in *Garbhavati Jananee*, no teacher apart from the people themselves. At the end of the play, we see the lives of the villagers in a state of transformation. We can feel them questioning the assumptions of their livelihood and their relation to the past. The questioning is suggested rather than stated. There is no explicit confrontation between the dogmas of the past and the ideals of the future in *Garbhavati Jananee*. There is simply a death, an ebbing of faith, and a silent retreat from the past.

In contrast, Bhattacharya's *Devi Garjan* (The Roar of the Goddess), which deals with the oppression of landless peasants by a ruthless class of landowners, is militant, loud, and violent. Unlike *Garbhavati Jananee*, where the villagers are victims of their own beliefs, the peasants of *Devi Garjan* are victims of external agents —mercenary landlords who think of life solely in terms of trade and profit. The conflict of *Devi Garjan* is more explicit, more political than the subtle confrontation of values in *Garbhavati Jananee*.

In the climactic scene of the play, the villagers actively resist the authority of the landowners, who are represented by two figures embodying power: Prabhanjan, the landowning custodian of the *dharmagola* (paddy store of the temple), and the village priest, whose inexorable reverence for tradition makes him a political reactionary and a supporter of the status quo. Significantly, Bhattacharya concentrates the attack of the peasants on the landowners within the sacrosanct precincts of the temple.

MANGLA: What I say is open up the *dharmagola*, distribute the paddy stored in the temple.

PRABHANJAN: Impossible. This is blasphemy. *Dharmagola* paddy belongs to the Goddess—to no one else. Only after it is offered to the Devi in *puja* can it be distributed as *prasad* to the poor.

DIGAMBAR: For two years running we had drought and famine. We had to miss the *puja* and the big feast, no? So why not perform the *puja* now? Well, revered priest, how about it?

PRIEST: Hm. The suggestion is good. But this is not the auspicious season for Devi *puja*. You must follow the almanac.

DASARATH: For Devi's worship all seasons are auspicious—each and every day is auspicious. Open up the *dharmagola*.

PRABHANJAN: No, I will not.

MANGLA: Open up, I say.

PRABHANJAN: No.

MANGLA: Open up. For the last time we say, open up.

PRABHANJAN: No.

> [*They attack—turmoil—shouts—Prabhanjan is beaten up—the doors of the paddy store are broken down*][54]

The violence of the revolt is crystallized in the central image of the play, the roar of the angry goddess. By entitling his play *Devi Garjan*, Bhattacharya emphasizes that divinity is on the side of the peasants. The goddess Devi does not punish the villagers when they enter the *dharmagola*. On the contrary, she becomes emblematic of their revolt.

The juxtaposition of the mythological and the realistic is one of the central characteristics of Bhattacharya's dramatic art. In *Haanskhalir Haans* (The Ducks of Haanskhali), for instance, we are presented with two levels of reality. We see a group of beggars involved in a construction operation, the digging of an underground railway that symbolizes, for Bhattacharya, "technological progress and change."[55] In startling contrast to the beggars ("a mass of the lumpenproletariat" as Bhattacharya describes them), there is Bonbibi, the forest goddess, who complains to her elder sister, the Earth Mother, that the beggars of Calcutta are hopelessly exploited. The Earth Mother reacts tempestuously and with tragic consequences: the earth trembles and one of the vagrants, Bhishma, is buried in the ground. His colleagues accept his death with resilience and a renewed awareness of their situation. While Bhishma is carried away to the morgue, they continue their work with greater zeal, resolving to dig the ditch to Haanskhali through the swampy, impenetrable area of the Sunderbans district.

Bhattacharya admitted the extreme difficulty of concretizing the "enormous" vision of *Haanskhalir Haans*. He blamed his *bhadrolok* actors for not being sufficiently responsive to its subtleties. Perhaps, he needed to admit that his vision of the earth rising up in protest against the oppression of the masses was larger than his play could sustain. It was also more contradictory than he imagined. How, for instance, does one interpret the accidental death of Bhishma? Surely it is somewhat ironic that he should die even as the earth protests on his behalf. He seems to be at once a scapegoat and a sacrifice to the gods. Is the silence of his colleagues a form of indifference to his death? Or are they so downtrodden that they simply accept his death without protest?

Another contradiction in the play concerns the beggars' persistence in digging the ditch. Does it signify a certain confidence that their oppression will cease one day or is it a gesture of futility? Bhattacharya fails to state or even suggest how the workers will surmount their oppression. Consequently, the ending of his play is ambivalent. While seeming to assert the strength of the people's will, he can also be criticized for failing to provide a solution to the people's problems.

It is precisely this ambivalence that makes Bijon Bhattacharya so exceptional in the political theater movement of Bengal. As early as *Nabanna*, he refused to write doctrinaire plays where good and evil, capitalism and slavery, freedom and oppression were treated unequivocally. Moreover, he resisted the rigors of the party line much to the annoyance of the Communist members in the I.P.T.A. He defended his nonpartisan attitude by asserting that, "The country and its people were our subjects. Our job was to prepare the soil; it was the job of the political people to sow the seeds. We were preparing and enlightening the people from a broadly humanistic point of view."[56]

Perhaps this is the fundamental reason why the politicians of the Bengali theater are somewhat apprehensive of Bhattacharya's efficacy as a playwright. They fail to realize that his awareness of the people in rural Bengal was so intimate that he did not need political doctrines in order to write about them. All he needed to do was absorb himself in their lives. This absorption was so intense that one could say that Bijon Bhattacharya wrote with the people rather than about them.

After *Nabanna*

The schism between the "political people" and the "artists" of the Bengal I.P.T.A. was most conspicuous after the production of *Nabanna*. In a report by the secretary of the I.P.T.A., we learn that the "artists (notably Bijon Bhattacharya and Sombhu Mitra) did not have much confidence in the capacity of the Party to give them any guidance where Art is concerned."[57] Their emphasis on "technique" and "absolute freedom for expressing their talents" were responsible for their "drifting away from the Party." The "rigid loyalty" of the political members of the I.P.T.A. to the Party, however, proved to be counterproductive to "the artistic and cultural front." The two factions fought, quarreled, argued, and indulged in vicious diatribes and character assassinations. The Bengal I.P.T.A. could not sustain the onslaught of their attacks. By 1945 it had ceased to function as a coherent organization.

The splintering of the I.P.T.A., however, was not a calamity for the Bengali theater. On the contrary, it was a stimulus for the non-professional theater movement that emerged in the fifties. As early as 1948, Sombhu Mitra, who had codirected *Nabanna*, formed a prestigious theater company called Bohurupee.[58] The artistic autonomy of the group and its explorations of poetic drama were obvious reactions to the regimentation and political orientation of the I.P.T.A. Many amateur theater groups proliferated in Bengal following the example of Bohurupee. The more recent and significant of these groups, notably Nandikar, Theater Workshop, Chetana, and Theater Unit, will be discussed in a later chapter. Now let us concentrate on the political theater of Utpal Dutt, who is unanimously considered one of the most talented and controversial figures in the contemporary Bengali theater.

2

The Revolutionary Theater
of Utpal Dutt

Utpal Dutt is a phenomenon in the contemporary Bengali theater. His stamina bewilders his colleagues. Even his most outspoken critics have often wondered at the sheer momentum of his activities. In the course of a month, Dutt is capable of writing, directing, and acting in a revolutionary play for his group the People's Little Theater; improvising a street-corner play on some topical issue concerning the elections or the future of Indira Gandhi; rehearsing a new *jatra* production for performances in villages, tea plantations, and industrial areas; compiling his notes on Brecht, Piscator, and German classical drama; writing vicious reviews of contemporary Bengali plays; acting in commercial Hindi films where he specializes in cameo roles, notably villains and buffoons. From rehearsals to political meetings to film studios, Dutt moves from one disparate experience to another revelling in the contradictions of his life. A Marxist director who is also an acknowledged and accomplished ham, a spokesman of equality and freedom of choice who directs his plays like a tyrant, an amateur scholar of Hegel and Marx who is also a pamphleteer and polemicist—Utpal Dutt embodies all these oppositions. They constitute his being.

THE EARLY YEARS

Like most revolutionary intellectuals, Dutt was once a member of the bourgeoisie. He began his career in the political theater by "betraying," in the words of Aragon, "his class of origin." At the age of twenty, Dutt reacted violently to his Jesuit education and his

familiarity with the Western classics. The fact that he could recite
Virgil and Shakespeare dismayed him. During the late 1940s, he
was appalled by his isolation from the people and the political turbulence of post-Independence India. He felt the futility of acting
and directing plays by Shakespeare in English that he produced
for the Little Theater Group. His mentor at that time was Geoffrey
Kendall, the director of the Shakespeareana International Theater
Company, which toured India in 1947.

Dutt's participation in this tour was his first encounter with the
professional theater. He learned the tricks of the trade from Kendall, a regular trouper who emulated the tradition of Henry Irving
and who was never reluctant to beat his actors if they neglected
their duties.[1] Kendall was Dutt's self-appointed guru. Not only did
he teach Dutt how to project his voice, how to fence and strike postures of grief, how to change his facial expressions, he instilled in
the young actor a sense of responsibility and discipline. Early in
his career, Dutt learned to take the theater seriously.

After the Shakespeareana troupe left India, Dutt returned to the
Little Theater Group with a renewed awareness of the craft of theater. He disciplined his actors in vigorous productions of Shakespeare. Every month there was a new play—*Othello, A Midsum-
mer Night's Dream, Twelfth Night, Hamlet.* While the acting of
the company became clearer, the blocking more defined, the sets
and costumes more detailed, the actors of the Little Theater Group
began to wonder why they were doing Shakespeare.

In March 1948, the Communist Party of India was banned.[2]
The Little Theater Group responded by printing a political article
in their program protesting violently against the ban and the subsequent censorship of the I.P.T.A. The irony, of course, is that the
production accompanying the article was nothing less inflammatory than *Romeo and Juliet.* Miriam Stark, the principal actress of
the company, raised the question that was on everyone's mind: "If
we really believe what we've written, then why are we staging the
classics and for whom really?"

The members of the Little Theater Group realized that they
could not presume to be radical so long as they continued to perform plays exclusively for a minority audience, the westernized
intellectuals of Calcutta. In order to make their theater more relevant, they dutifully staged the plays of Clifford Odets *(Waiting for*

Lefty and *Till the Day I Die*) and interpreted *Julius Caesar* somewhat predictably as a study of fascism, with Caesar appearing as a timeless dictator, Antony a Fascist orator, and Cassius an extremist revolutionary. These timid revolutionary gestures did not satisfy Dutt. He felt more isolated than ever from the fighting in the streets, the political rallies in Hazra Park, Bowbazar, and Dibrugarh, the oppression by the police, and the Prisoners' Freedom movement in India.

The I.P.T.A.: A Brief Encounter

In 1950, Dutt joined the Bengal unit of the I.P.T.A. and discovered for the first time in his career the intensity and tumultuous excitement of the people's theater movement in India.[3] After performing traditional proscenium theater for an urban audience, it was an intoxicating experience for him to face twenty thousand workers in a field or a street. The open space, the mobility of the performance, the exchanges with the audience, the rough immediacy of the acting, the singing of the "Internationale," the possibility of police intervention, the tension in the air, all these elements contributed to a theatrical experience that was unlike anything Dutt had imagined.

It was invigorating just to watch the members of the I.P.T.A. at work: Mrinal Sen (now a famous Bengali film director) experimenting with shadow plays, Hemanga Biswas composing Bengali folk songs, and Tapas Sen focusing spotlights on makeshift scaffolds. Perhaps the most valuable of all contacts for Dutt was Panu Pal, the creator of the *pathnatika* (street-corner play) in Bengal. It is said that Pal interrupted a rehearsal of the I.P.T.A. one evening and urged his colleagues to improvise a play on the imprisonment of Communist leaders by the very next day. *Chargesheet* was written overnight and feverishly rehearsed for a couple of hours. By 5 P.M. the actors assembled in Hazra Park and performed the play on a lecture platform for thousands of workers. Later, the play was performed a number of times from Jalpaiguri to Canning in markets, fields, squares, and most frequently, on trucks.

The mobility of this form of theater and its direct transmission of political issues appealed to Dutt. In fact, he continues to write and perform such plays, often expanding them to full three-hour performances. These plays will be discussed later, especially *Din Badaler Pala* (Play of Changing Times), but it is important to stress Dutt's awareness at this stage in his career of the most naive and rough form of political theater as the most effective medium of propaganda. Dutt also realized that a *pathnatika* is not simply an illustration of a political message: it is a theatrical activity that incorporates particular strategies and modes of communication. It is politically effective only insofar as it is theatrically immediate.

Though Dutt's association with the I.P.T.A. was enlightening, it was not without problems. Dutt was a member for only ten months before he was blacklisted by the more doctrinaire members of the Party. His production of Tagore's *Bisarjan* (one of the few Bengali classics Dutt has ever staged) was dismissed as threateningly reactionary. In addition, Dutt was accused of drunkenness, arrogance, opportunism, even abusive language (he addressed a member of the group as "bitch").

More offensive to the puritan Party members was Dutt's freethinking and irreverent questioning of Marxist dogma. When the twenty-one-year-old Dutt marched into the Party office on 46 Dharamtala Street with a copy of Trotsky's *Permanent Revolution* in his hand, he was asking for trouble. On being questioned about this dissidence, Dutt explained to the older men that Stalin could only be understood once Trotsky and Bukharin had been mastered. This was an outrage to the Party members whose knowledge of Marxism was so minimal that they dared not participate in any kind of ideological debate.

Dutt has openly dismissed these men as "ignorant windbags," but he also emphasizes that "their officiousness and high-handed methods have nothing in common with the Party's thinking."[4] In recent years, his attachment to the Party has become more vocal.

> I am not one of those frustrated intellectuals of the West and their empty-headed Indian imitators, who equate Party guidance with regimentation, bureaucracy, Zhdanovism, and what have you. My relations with the Party in my country have been intimate and long, and I have never met a single Commissar of Mr. Koestler's imagination who has tried to bulldoze me and my colleagues into some kind of Party-line.[5]

Dutt's critics would be inclined to respond to such passages with some cynicism. They would emphasize that he protests too much to his advantage. They would snidely point out that Dutt has recently received substantial financial assistance from the CPI(M) party (the ruling Marxist government in West Bengal) for his new projects. Despite these allegations, Dutt is, to my mind, honest when he asserts his independence as an artist. In matters of the theater, he accepts no laws but his own.

In this respect, one should mention his resistance to the Marxist plays of the I.P.T.A., which religiously follow the party line. What Dutt finds so insufferable about these plays is their relentless boredom exemplified by the platitudes of the proletarian hero, who is invariably presented as an embodiment of goodness. With pungent humor, Dutt exposes the bourgeois impulses underlying the creation of such creatures.

> The Communist Hero appears as a superhuman Captain Marvel without a blemish in his character, advocating war or peace according to the current Party-line. . . . And one comes to the conclusion: this man is not even subject to sexual desires, or a cough or cold. He does not even fart. He is, therefore, a walking tribute to the bourgeois society which has produced such perfections.[6]

Most astutely, Dutt views the morality of this hero as intrinsically Gandhian.

> Our revolutionary heroes are often Gandhian ascetics; it is the villain who smokes, drinks, and leads a rich sensuous life. If the revolutionary hero were shown too poor to buy himself a cigarette, that would be all right, but he proceeds to moralize, and castigate bodily comfort as a bourgeois sin. It sounds apparently revolutionary, but is its opposite: it is repetition without thought of the counter-revolutionary rodomontade of M. K. Gandhi.[7]

It is impossible not to be entertained by such passages. But alongside the humor there are a number of sharp observations. When one speaks of a perfect proletarian hero, Dutt argues, one assumes that the revolution has been successful and that there is nothing to strive toward. By presenting an impossibly consistent hero in a utopian world where everything works with clockwork efficiency, the playwright only succeeds in isolating even the most fervent members of the Party, who are, of course, aware of the imperfections in their society and, more vulnerably, of their own human failings (they drink, smoke, swear, make love).

If the proletarian hero does not isolate the audience, then the playwright achieves something even more insidious: he rouses a false sense of complacency in the spectators by making them believe that their Marxist government is the true revolutionary state. What a production of the I.P.T.A. invariably failed to stress was that, despite the growth of the Communist movement in West Bengal since Independence, the constitution of India remained fundamentally reactionary. By etherealizing communism and projecting "oversimplified, anemic, spiritless symbols of revolution," the I.P.T.A. succeeded only in confusing its audiences, or else numbing them into a kind of blind, self-righteous submission.

When Utpal Dutt left the I.P.T.A., he was convinced that political theater could only be effective if it entertained the audience. Lectures on dialectical materialism and sermons on illustrious comrades were of no use to a working-class audience. He realized that the Bengali laborers were prepared to see their imperfections reflected on stage. At the same time, they wanted to see their enemies—the sacrosanct figures of the ruling class—humiliated, lampooned, and ultimately crushed on stage. Instead of emulating the perfect proletarian hero, so distant from the confusion and squalor of their lives, they wanted to participate in a fight with their most familiar oppressors.

Even in the most abstract plays of the I.P.T.A., Dutt was amazed to see how spontaneously the audience responded when an oppressor came on stage—the moneylender, the landlord, or the police officer. A villain, Dutt realized, was indispensable for a political play not only because he had to be crushed (thereby providing the play with a thrilling climax), but because he provoked the audience to jeer at him. Perhaps, this explains Dutt's penchant for boisterous villains and winningly eccentric tyrants. They are his scapegoats. He makes use of them as butts of ridicule and then ceremoniously kills them. We shall examine these figures later but, for the moment, let us return to the year 1951 when Dutt left the I.P.T.A.

The Little Theater Group

Going back to the Little Theater Group was Dutt's only option. It must have been difficult for him to face a production of *Mrs. Warren's Profession* after his turbulent experience with the I.P.T.A. However, he resolved to make radical changes in the philosophy, structure, and repertoire of the Group. In no time, he had convinced the company that they should only stage plays in the Bengali language for a predominantly working-class audience. The non-Bengali members of the group were disheartened to realize that they were no longer useful to the company. Many of them came from the most prosperous and westernized Jewish families in Calcutta. Essentially British in their education and culture yet Indian in their status, they could not "betray their class of origin" and attachment to the English language as easily as Dutt had renounced his bourgeois heritage. They left the Little Theater Group, however, believing in the validity of Dutt's revolutionary ideals.

With the production of *Sangbadik* (The Journalist), an adaptation of Simonov's *The Russian Question*, the Little Theater Group announced its status as a Bengali theater group committed to the revolutionary struggle of the people. It did not, however, abandon its aesthetic standards by immediately producing a number of agitprop plays. That would have been somewhat juvenile. On the contrary, it resolved more ambitiously to perform the classics for the people in much the same way that Roger Planchon has staged the plays of Racine and Molière for the working-class community at Villeurbane.

Two notable productions of the Little Theater Group were Tagore's *Achalayatan* performed for thirty-five thousand spectators in Wellington Square, Calcutta, and Jyotindranath Sengupta's translation of *Macbeth*, which toured several villages in remote areas of the Bengali countryside. While Dutt has many misgivings about producing Tagore for a mass audience (he has complained about the maestro's "extreme sophistication" and "overindulgence in poetic twists and abstruse symbols"), he has always responded to the robust quality of Shakespeare's plays. His early book *Shakespearer Samajchetana* (Shakespeare's Social Consciousness) could not have been written without the insights he had gained as an actor performing Macbeth for rural audiences in Bengal.

The responses of the villagers to an Elizabethan classic seemingly alien to their social and economic situation were revelations to Dutt. He marvelled at their instinctive understanding of Macbeth's impulses and vacillations, their fearful response to Sova Sen's demoniac portrayal of Lady Macbeth's ambition, their jocular, yet wary, acceptance of the supernatural. He realized that the villagers grasped the intricacies of the narrative in *Macbeth* because they responded to it on the level of myth. They could not have done so, however, if Dutt had adhered to the time-bound conventions of the proscenium theater that he had inherited from Geoffrey Kendall. It was only by immersing *Macbeth* in the ritual world of *jatra* and by transforming Shakespeare's language into a bold, declamatory form of incantation that the Little Theater Group could reach a Bengali working-class audience with an Elizabethan classic.

Dutt is convinced that any production of a classic for a mass audience has to be magical in its presentation. It has to invigorate the workers with tempestuous action, violent deaths, and passionate love. The action of the drama has to be played for all its worth —loud voices, extravagant gestures, bold expressions, assertive entrances, and thunderous exits. This theater has no patience with nuances and subtleties of characterization. It ignores rationales and motivations.

The more fastidious among Dutt's critics complain that his dramaturgy is too crude and simplistic to be taken seriously. The more enlightened assert that he does not present his spectators with choices. By immersing them in a panorama of action so compelling and sensational that it is impossible to resist, he seduces them into a blind acceptance of his spectacle. He does not permit his audience to choose how they can change their lives. He dictates their way of life. This criticism is legitimate but it applies more accurately to Dutt's later revolutionary plays than to his production of *Macbeth*. Dutt's conception of staging Shakespeare for the masses may have been crude but it was, in all probability, closer to the guts of the Elizabethan theater than most European revivals of Shakespeare's plays in recent years.[8]

Apart from touring villages with *Macbeth*, the Little Theater Group revived a number of classics in the nineteenth-century Bengal theater, notably Girish Chandra Ghosh's *Siraj-ud-daula*. Dutt never fails to reiterate how much there is to be learned from this historical play even though it is generally underrated by scholars as a melodrama that distorts crucial facts relating to the emergence of the British Raj in India. Dutt responds to those very elements of Ghosh's dramaturgy so distasteful to the purists: the random structure of action, the accumulation of tense episodes, the series of climaxes, the vast canvas of historical figures, the treatment of villains and heroes as archetypes, the patriotic sentiments, the unabashed emotionalism. While he acknowledges Ghosh's idealized interpretation of history and religiosity, Dutt emphasizes that, "The Siraj-ud-daula myth fired the imagination of the revolutionary youth. What the historians could never do, the playwright [Ghosh] did almost overnight: he created a focal point for the revolutionary-patriotic fervor of the Bengali masses."[9]

Siraj-ud-daula provided Dutt with a model of a historical play that is also a commercial extravaganza. He has perfected this model in recent years, investing it with a political consciousness not to be found in the plays of Girish Ghosh. In fact, he has come to rely on it so inexorably that he seems to be restricting his growth as a revolutionary artist. But this is to anticipate the later career of Dutt, which will be discussed toward the end of this chapter. In the 1950s, however, the positive influence of *Siraj-ud-daula* on Dutt cannot be denied. It shaped one of his fundamental beliefs about political theater, namely, its reliance on entertainment, the noblest of functions in the theater, once described by Brecht as that "business which always gives [theater] its particular dignity."

Another playwright of the nineteenth-century Bengali theater whom Dutt reveres is Michael Madhusadhan Dutt. They are not related, though they share family names and some traits of character—a certain meteoric brilliance, an infectious arrogance and outspokenness, and an absolute disdain of petit bourgeois norms. It is no coincidence that one of the landmarks in Dutt's career as an actor is his uncanny impersonation of Madhusadhan in his recent play *Darao Pathikbar* (Stay, Passerby).

When the Little Theater Group was exploring the tradition of
the Bengali theater, it was only natural that they should stage at
least one play by Madhusadhan. His plays may not be revolutionary (Dutt admits that they are "limited in vision by the essential
backwardness of the colonial bourgeoisie"), but they are the earliest and most succinct critiques of bourgeois corruption and hypocrisy in nineteenth-century Bengali society.

The Little Theater Group decided to stage *Buro Shaliker Ghare
Rom* (discussed in the previous chapter) thinking that it was nothing more than a farce with some social significance. Certainly,
there was no attempt on Dutt's part to politicize the protagonist,
the feudal lord whose sexual exploits and economic oppression are
unassailable. He chose to play the role in "a bald wig with a stub-
born wisp of white hair standing in a desert," hoping to disengage
himself as a performer from any criticism of the character. One
performance in a village, however, changed his perspective of the
role so drastically that he was compelled not merely to alter his
performance but to reexamine his awareness of the audience as an
integral factor in the creation of political theater.

>   Stunned silence greeted the first bout of horseplay. These peas-
> ants were seeing something which is their daily life, being evicted
> for non-payment of rent, being whipped, their women seduced by
> pimps of the lord. They were not laughing with me at my part, they
> were hostile, balefully looking on at their class-enemy, hating me. It
> was no laughing matter to them.
>   I believe it was this miasma of hostility that drove me to a defen-
> sive pose. . . . I felt the hatred out in the dark field, and wanted to
> defend the part I was playing, wanted to defend myself, and assert
> the evil lord's own logic to hit back at the grim faces. And the part
> changed—then and there. The horseplay disappeared, the slapstick
> was abandoned. If the audience was not going to laugh with me,
> they would see how terrible their adversary could be. The seduction
> of the peasant's wife was no longer funny, but the lord's maniacal
> revenge on his class-enemy. At the end of the performance, we felt
> we had supped full of horror. We had misread the play and my part.
> We had underestimated the dramatist, ignoring the economic basis
> of the lord's lusty doings. Sex was his way of getting back at these
> dishonest peasants who cheated him of what was to him, his due by
> British dispensation. . . . The play was not a farce at all, it was a

frightening chronicle. And my purely external approach to the part, merely interpreting it as a clown, was shaken, by the Audience reacting on the basis of their own experience of life.[10]

I have quoted this description at length not only because it is so vivid but because it conveys Dutt's temperament as an actor and his ability to learn from the most immediate experience. It also illustrates an issue that is often idealized in the political theater: the debt a revolutionary artist owes to the people. The vigorous audience reaction to *Buro Shaliker Ghare Rom*, however, cannot be exaggerated. It was one of those fortuitous accidents in an actor's life that changes the course of his career. Its impact on Dutt was electrifying, not unlike his discovery of a historical model in Girish Chandra Ghosh's *Siraj-ud-daula*. It made him aware that the suffering of the people can never be taken for granted in the political theater. It demands to be reflected on stage.

Gradually, however, with his increasing political involvement in street-corner plays, such as *Passport, Naya Tughluq, Saurin Master,* and his energetic participation in the Communist election campaigns, Dutt began to realize that it was not sufficient merely to reflect the suffering of the workers. It was important for a revolutionary playwright to alter the suffering and depict it passing through a process. The workers in the audience had to learn how to convert their suffering into anger. They had to be taught how to use that anger as a force against the ruling class. It was not sufficient to sympathize with the workers and observe them from a safe distance suffering in slums, factories, and mines. It was not enough to chant lamentations for the dead, the innocent Party workers shot down by the police. Such a theater could only be progressive. A revolutionary theater had to do more than evoke the suffering of the workers: it had to concretize the destruction of the system that was responsible for such suffering.

THEATER AS REVOLUTION

Angar

These views on revolutionary theater did not crystallize, however, until after Dutt had written and staged a definitive progressive play—*Angar* (Coal). As much as Dutt tends to disown this play,

which ends in "a mere wailing of laborers," one cannot underestimate its importance not only in Dutt's career but in the history of
the Bengali theater. Produced in December 1959 at the Minerva
Theater and performed to packed houses for 1,150 performances,
Angar is remembered even today as a spectacle, a technical tour
de force that showed workers drowning in a mine flooded with
water. What Dutt criticizes about his own play is not his sensational use of suffering as a theatrical device but his decision to end
the play on a note of such utter despair that no revolution was possible.

Certainly, the action of the play contained immense possibilities
for stirring revolutionary theater. A group of coal miners are exploited by their employers, who are prepared to drown them by
flooding the mines rather than suffer any material loss from fire.
Early in the play, two workers are killed in a mine explosion resulting from accumulated poisonous gases. In order to evade their
responsibility for the deaths, the owners of the Sheldon Colliery
arrange for injuries to be inflicted on the bodies of the slain workers and then to have them removed from the mine and left on the
Grand Trunk Road.

In the court case that follows, the counsel for the union uses a
postmortem report to expose the management. He accuses the
company of deliberately distorting evidence of its crime and attempting to avoid payment of compensation to the families of the
deceased. The manager of the company blandly contradicts these
statements by saying, "If I might make a guess, My Lord, the
Indian worker has been known to hide and send his wife to claim
compensation." The judge is convinced that the accusation of the
counsel for the workers' union is an unwieldy hypothesis, a mere
fabrication. The court is adjourned and the judge is invited to the
company director's bungalow for lunch.

In the course of this scene, so pithy and ironic in its manipulation of detail, Dutt exposes the devious machinations of a system.
While the management of the Sheldon Colliery is powerful and
corrupt, it is not invulnerable. Dutt prepares us for a direct confrontation between the workers and the company in the next
scene, which opens on a deceptively casual note—workers gos-
siping and idling away their time, seemingly indifferent to the po-

litical slogans painted on a wall. The scene erupts into a frenzy of action as groups of workers storm out of the mine protesting
against their dangerous working conditions. Despite the wheedling
reassurances of Mr. Dutta, the assistant manager of the company,
the workers unanimously resolve to strike.

The next scene dramatizes the effects of the strike on a particular family. We see Binu, the most fearless and idealistic of workers,
confronting the starvation of his mother and sister while attempting to remain faithful to his revolutionary principles. The threat of
the company increases when Mr. Dutta returns to negotiate terms
with the workers. He magnanimously offers a special bonus of five
hundred rupees and compensation to the workers' families in the
eventuality of death or injury to the workers. Despite resistance
among a militant section of the workers, the union agrees to accept the terms of the company.

The consequences are disastrous. There is a massive explosion in
the mine. The scene of devastation is theatricalized through details
such as the haze of smoke, the intermittent flashing of searchlights
and lanterns, the rescue team dragging out corpses from the mine,
the barbed wire surrounding the smoldering pit. The relatives of
the workers still trapped in the mine hover anxiously in the background. When it becomes impossible to enter the pit, the authorities order the rescue team to flood the mine. This is accomplished
with businesslike efficiency while the relatives of the workers are
urged to maintain peace in the area and to accept the failure of the
rescue operation. The impact of the tragedy on the survivors is so
overwhelming that there is no possibility of protest. They leave the
stage in silence.

The last scene is a coda, an epiphany of grief—seven workers in
the dark interior of the mine desperately try to find a way out.
After their efforts fail and their panic subsides into an eerie calm,
they accept their imminent death. Binu, who is among the entrapped workers, imagines that they are destined to be transformed into fossils one day. Many centuries later, he fantasizes,
excavators will discover the remains of a class of highly intelligent
subhuman creatures who chose to live buried in the earth because
they could not endure the wind and the rain.

As he fantasizes, the water begins to creep in. In a moment of utter futility, one of the workers writes a note he hopes will be read by men in the future: "Men on earth, do not forget us. We descend into the womb of the earth to collect treasures for mankind. There is no arrangement for our lives here. Craving for treasures transforms a man into a devil, and these devils have mercilessly killed us. Let us die, there is no harm, but make sure that no other man dies in this way like a rat."[11] Within seconds, the water gushes in and sweeps the workers away.

It is understandable why Dutt responds to *Angar* with some embarrassment. It does not seem very different from those spectacles of calamity that Hollywood specializes in, even though its purpose is ostensibly more serious—namely, to raise the consciousness of the Bengali community about the exploitation of the workers in industrial areas. What is disturbing about *Angar* is not that it fails to achieve this purpose but that it seems to exploit human misery as a source of entertainment. There is something perverse about staging a calamity as a spectacle and applauding the climax where workers are shown drowning.

It might be argued, however, that the context of the scene (the suffering of the workers) ultimately determined the response of the spectators and that it directed them how to view the presentation of the scene (the lighting effects, the music, the screams of the actors). But if eyewitness reports can be trusted (and they are more reliable than the ecstatic reviews of the production), what actually happened was that the presentation proved to be so immediate and novel for a Bengali audience in the fifties that it dominated any examination of the context. It seems that the audiences of *Angar* responded to the final scene not because it reflected the defeat of the revolutionary struggle but because it depicted a scene of horror with meticulous detail and awesome stagecraft.

While criticizing Dutt's dramatization of human suffering, one must stress his concrete awareness of spectacle in the theater. As an advocate of theater as a total art form, he is a pioneer in the contemporary Bengali theater. His production of *Angar* relied extensively on the music of Ravi Shankar and the spectacular visual effects of Tapas Sen, the foremost lighting designer in the Bengali theater. This emphasis on the technical aspects of the theater at the expense of political analysis was criticized by some leaders of the

I.P.T.A. Dutt, however, was confident that the Bengali theater had to develop technologically if it intended to interpret the social and industrial conditions of workers in post-Independence India.

He rejected the simple sets of the I.P.T.A. productions, the wooden boards, the rough canvas backdrop, the domestic interiors, and thought primarily in terms of massive structures—iron girders, bridges, wagons, trains, and factories. *Angar* was the beginning of an expansive vision. From then on, Dutt could think of revolutionary theater primarily in terms of magnitude and quantity. A revolutionary theater had to be performed for thousands of workers. It had to be produced a number of times. "Until a play is done a thousand times," he emphasized in an interview with A. J. Gunawardana, "you don't know how the people accept it." Dutt also realized that, in order to preach revolution to the people, it was necessary "to heighten the visual properties of the theater to a point where the theater itself would cast a spell on the audience."[12] It is significant, however, that Dutt continued to produce street-corner plays, which, by the very nature of their structure and presentation, did not need elaborate productions.

Despite the commercial success of *Angar*, the Little Theater Group resisted the lures of the commercial theater. It continued to believe in the validity of agitprop performances such as *The Special Train*, a virulent play written on behalf of the striking workers at the Hindusthan Automobile Factory in Uttarpara. Fearlessly disregarding the threat of police intervention, the actors of Dutt's troupe exposed the alliance between the Birlas, the notorious owners of the factory, and the Congress government in West Bengal, which attempted to break the strike by sending a special train full of *goondas* (toughs) and scabs to Uttarpara. Apart from producing the play in Uttarpara, where the actors collected money for the strike fund, the Little Theater Group staged *The Special Train* a number of times in the busiest areas of Calcutta. Not only did it hope to raise public consciousness of the strike, it wanted, more strategically, to direct public anger against the corrupt practices of the Congress government in West Bengal.

The contribution of *The Special Train* to the Communist election campaign of 1962 was too conspicuous to be ignored by the ruling government. According to Dutt, his theater was attacked

twice by "Congress rowdies" who used the Sino-Indian border conflict as a rationale for attacks on all Communist centers. *Angar*
(which was still running to packed houses) was singled out by the
Congress party as the most subversive of Communist dramas. This
is ironic because the play is so general in its condemnation of capitalism, so discreet in its advocacy of communism, that it cannot be
said to take a firm stand either on the cultural revolution in China
or the Congress party in West Bengal. It is simply, in the word of
the playwright, a "progressive" play.

Kallol

Dutt's production of *Kallol* (Sound of the Waves) in 1965 can more
justifiably be termed subversive and communist. The central action of the play, concerning the Naval Mutiny of Bombay in 1946,
is not much more than a pretext for the real political issue of the
play—the conspiracy between prominent leaders of the British Raj
and illustrious members of the Congress party who plotted to overthrow the armed rebellion. It is not surprising that Dutt was impri-
soned during the run of the play. *Kallol* is a deviously formidable
attack on the colonial inheritance and repressive administration of
the Congress party in India.

Dutt insists, however, that his play has more than topical significance. He sees it as his first step toward a revolutionary theater
committed not merely to the exposure of facts but to the unveiling
of history. Dutt is notoriously contemptuous of facts unrelated to
the social turmoil of the working class and their participation in
the class struggle. What concerns him is not what he calls "bourgeois truth"—an objective presentation of facts presented with
absolute precision and pretensions of impartiality—but "revolutionary truth" (his term again)—partisan, shrewdly pragmatic,
and filled with hatred for the enemy—that succeeds only if a playwright is willing to distort the facts of history in order to change
the bourgeois consciousness of his society. For Dutt, a fact in itself
may be true, but if it is "unrelated to social conflict" and "the
struggle of the proletariat," it automatically becomes false.[13]

While Dutt emphasizes that he has done his homework on the
Mutiny (he mentions eyewitness reports and inflammatory pamphlets written by the revolting sailors), he loftily defends himself

against those "bourgeois" critics who condemn him for altering one crucial fact: the surrender of the mutineers. In *Kallol*, the guns continue to boom on the battleship *Khyber* until the curtain falls. Sardul Singh, the leader of the rebellion, refuses to accept the terms of the establishment unlike his historical counterpart. In the climactic scene, which is remembered by Bengali theater audiences as vividly as the catastrophic end of *Angar*, we see Sardul Singh holding out till the last, a figure of resilience in a revolutionary struggle that continues beyond the play.

SARDUL: Hello, Dhanaush. Hello, Khyber calling.

RADIO: Hello, Khyber. Have you heard?

SARDUL: No. What? Why are you firing?

RADIO: We have won. Comrades, we have won.

SARDUL: What do you mean?

RADIO: They have accepted six out of our eight demands. Talwar has just now called off the strike.

SARDUL: And you call this victory?

RADIO: There was no other way.

SARDUL: We did not fight for this.

RADIO: In this struggle, you have given us leadership. Accept our greetings, Sardul.

SARDUL: What do you mean "have given"? I am still giving it. It is not yet time for "greetings."

RADIO: Do you mean the fight will continue?

SARDUL: Yes.—No Surrender.[14]

Just as in Eisenstein's film *Potemkin*, in which the mutineers who revolt against the Czar's tyranny do not surrender (even though the actual mutiny on board the battleship *Potemkin* failed in 1905), Sardul Singh's resolution to continue fighting has a revolutionary significance. The crucial difference, of course, is that the *Potemkin*'s mutiny ultimately triumphed in October 1917, while it seems that Sardul Singh's battle cry has yet to have any effect on the revolutionary consciousness of the working class in India.

Is Sardul Singh an initiator of the revolutionary process in India as Dutt seems to imply? Or is he, more accurately, a dynamic hero

whose theatrical ancestry can be traced back to the Rajput warriors of the nineteenth-century Bengali drama? Dutt would, in all
probability, claim that Singh is both a popular hero in the commercial theater tradition and a symbol of resistance and courage.
What Dutt does not sufficiently acknowledge, however, is the lure
of a popular hero, his ability to distract a working-class audience
from all issues but himself. How can we be so sure that a mass
audience responds to Sardul Singh because of what he represents?
It is possible that they can respond to his bravura, his flair, his
physical appearance more than to any "revolutionary truth" they
may derive from him.

Part of the problem with Dutt's conception of the "revolutionary hero" has to do with the importance he gives to "empathy" in
the theater. Whenever Dutt is questioned about the revolutionary
principles of his heroes, he invariably stresses how loudly the audiences cheer the actions of his heroes. No one can deny that the
audience response to most of Dutt's heroes is vociferous: his spectators cheer like a crowd at a soccer match. What needs to be
stressed, however, is that there is a difference between merely establishing a rapport with a hero like Sardul Singh and learning
about revolution from him. Though one does not exclude the other,
all too often one feels that Dutt's audiences cheer his heroes not
because they validate any particular principle of ideology but
because they stimulate the emotions on a visceral level.

A very apt analogy to this emphathetic relation between Dutt's
heroes and spectators can be found in the commercial Hindi film
—the major cultural industry and most appealing form of mass
entertainment in India. Just as Dutt's audiences cheer his heroes
for outwitting the members of the ruling class, the working class in
India cheer their favorite heroes in Hindi films as they watch them
beating up landlords and pimps and sundry villains. This audience
reaction, wild and potentially violent as it is, does not appear to
have any revolutionary significance. Hindi film audiences do not
cheer the dashing Hindi film actor Dharmendra because he fights
for the downtrodden. They cheer him because he fights so well.
They respond less to his proletarian principles than to his fist, the
grimaces on his face, the sweat on his brow, the hair on his chest.

While it is possible to criticize the revolutionary pretensions of
Kallol, one cannot deny the ferocity of its attack on the Congress

party. The strength of the play lies in its topicality. By boldly declaring that the Congress party was nothing but an agent of imperialism, *Kallol* challenged many sacrosanct assumptions about the nonviolent noncooperation movement of Gandhi. Dutt has never lost an opportunity to condemn the "peacemakers" of India, their hypocrisy and betrayal of the revolutionary struggle, their predilection to compromise with the oppressors rather than fight them. *Kallol* exemplifies his contempt for Gandhian ethics.

The advocacy of violence and hatred of the enemy in the play disturbed even the more liberal political leaders, editors, educationists, and writers. Almost without exception, the newspapers in Calcutta, particularly the *Ananda Bazar Patrika* ("a particularly repulsive specimen of hack-writing," according to Dutt) published vituperative reviews and editorials demanding the "social boycott" of the play. Even the CPI party (the revisionist section of the Communist party in India, which had split in 1964) condemned the political opportunism of the play.[15]

This cumulative attack on *Kallol* did not, however, affect the box office. If anything, it was free publicity for the Little Theater Group. Even when the newspapers stopped accepting advertisements of the play (Dutt claims under the instructions of Congress leaders and police officers), the CPI(M) trade unions and peasant associations of Bengal distributed posters of *Kallol* to every major city and village. The play continued for 850 performances, much to Dutt's satisfaction. At last he had produced theater that was no longer attacked for its crude dramaturgy or vulgarity or sensationalism but for its political content. In his words, the Bengali bourgeoisie were "reacting to a political play politically."

Ajeya Vietnam

One of the ironies of political theater is that it thrives during the worst periods of repression. The more a group is attacked for its political audacity, the more its commitment to revolutionary principles increases. Dutt was not intimidated by the campaign against his theater even after spending six months in the Presidency jail. If anything, he condemned the Congress regime and the reactionary factions of the Communist party even more vigorously.

Apart from these topical issues, Dutt concentrated on one of the

most critical events in world politics—Vietnam. There is not, in
my view, a more blatant propaganda play condemning American
aggression in Vietnam than Dutt's *Ajeya Vietnam* (Invincible Vietnam). When Samik Bandyopadhyay, Calcutta's foremost critic of
the Bengali theater, was asked by an interviewer of the *Drama
Review* what Dutt's street-corner production of *Vietnam* accomplished, he rightly said:

> It is not a question of accomplishing. As far as Calcutta is con-
> cerned, we have had a long association with the entire Vietnam
> experience. . . . In 1946 when the French were occupying Indo-
> china, there were student demonstrations in Calcutta in support of
> the Vietnamese independence struggle. And students got killed in
> the streets for such a seemingly remote cause. So there has been a
> deep emotional connection with Vietnam.[16]

Among the innumerable Bengali poems and plays written in
support of the Vietnamese, *Ajeya Vietnam* was the most daring
and blatantly propagandist. Dutt enjoys narrating a story of the
time when a certain Mr. Clark of the *New York Times* confronted
him backstage after a performance of *Ajeya Vietnam*. "The American Army," insisted Mr. Clark, "cannot kill the unarmed Vietnamese villagers—from where did you get this news?" Dutt replied,
"From a newspaper published in Hanoi." Enraged by the heinous
representation of the American characters in the play, Clark protested, "It's false propaganda." Dutt responded, "We take for true
whatever the Vietnamese write or say, while you, the Americans,
are the world's No. 1 liars."[17] This short exchange demonstrates
how unequivocal the propagandist's view of a political situation
must be. For Dutt, the Vietnamese *cannot* lie. Even if he is aware
of certain inaccuracies in their information, he will use them strategically to intensify his attack on the Americans.

The integrity of a propagandist is always suspect precisely because his sense of good and evil is so inflexible. He is willing to lie,
sensationalize facts, create horrifying images, spread false rumors,
and whip up hysteria in the audience to make the "good" more
good, the "evil" more evil. Dishonesty is a propagandist's prerogative. He plays dirty only to uphold his sense of justice. His loyalty

to an oppressed people is more important to him than any objective scrutiny of facts.

There can be no question about Dutt's loyalty to the Vietnamese people in *Ajeya Vietnam.* It is embarrassingly fervent. Not only are they presented as fearless, intensely patriotic, and vigorous soldiers, they are endowed with all kinds of "civilized" virtues—generosity, genial humor, respect for old people, even an affinity for Western classical music and Walt Whitman. The Americans, on the other hand, are a depraved lot. Syphilitic and uncouth, they are presented as sadists who rape, torture, and kill the Vietnamese with clinical pleasure. Though Dutt borrows many stereotypes of the Americans and the Vietnamese from the tradition of propaganda, he is, to my mind, most skilful in his strategic manipulation of these stereotypes.

The play opens briskly with General Fitz-Coulton of the U.S. Army ordering four American officers to capture the Vietnamese village of Ho Bo. The general, who sits imposingly in front of a huge map of South Vietnam, bombards the officers with facts and figures ("The Viets have attacked us 1,23,000 times, killed 4,16,000, captured 70,769 weapons," he intones) and explicates the methods of torture (with hunting knife, barbed wire, flame thrower, or butt of rifle).

Not only does Dutt inform his audience about interrogation methods used by the Americans, he rouses them emotionally by concentrating on the equipment. The general speaks as much to the officers on stage as to the Bengali working class in the audience.

> GENERAL: Please note item number 12—an invention of the US Military Intelligence, the Stockton battery, for delivering electric shocks of variable intensity to humans. . . . These two electrodes will have to be fixed to—look at the chart, please—to nipples in case subject female, and penis in case subject male. Remark, necessary to get subject thoroughly wet before operation.[18]

Dutt is consciously aware that the impersonality of the statement makes it all the more horrifying. His general uses the most abstract of languages, occasionally interrupting his litany of facts with an offhand statement ("when you contain communism, you can't really be bothered with Genevas and things") or a brusque order ("I do not tolerate gum-chewing in my room").

What is ingenious about Dutt's characterization is the way he uses the general as a medium for conveying information against the Americans. For instance, in the midst of the instructions to the officers, the general suddenly asks them: "Open your files, page 22. One, do you have any venereal disease? Two, do you suffer from insomnia?" These questions are answered by the general himself, who tells the audience that "one American in every four has venereal disease" and that "the United States alone consumes two-thirds of the world's total production of sleeping tablets." These seemingly redundant facts succeed in alienating the Bengali audience from the Americans, who appear a wasteful and decadent people.

It should be stressed, however, that the general is not simply an information medium but a thoroughly entertaining character—as one of the officers mutters sourly, "The bastard can't resist theatricals." The general simply has to shout "Flooksy" to someone offstage and a chart entitled "List of War Gases" descends onto the stage. He intimidates the officers with relish as he warns them about the Castro Battalion, the Vietnamese guerrillas of Ho Bo, who are led by a formidable fighter called Trac. With a sudden change of tone, he introduces them to Madame Lan Huu, a mysterious veiled woman who is to guide them through the jungles of South Vietnam to the village of Ho Bo. A touch of melodrama is inserted by Dutt when Madame Huu informs the officers that her father, a rich landowner, was killed by Trac. "I believe I have a blood-debt to pay off, gentlemen," she murmurs rather like one of those victimized patrician figures in a novel by Pearl Buck.

The scene ends abruptly with the general losing his composure and gradually becoming a maniacal Hitler-like figure. His last speech is calculated to threaten the audience with its fierce images and relentless momentum.

GENERAL: Gentlemen, the War Department's orders are absolutely clear—kill all, burn all, destroy all. We know we'll never win this war out. But all the same we'll leave such a scar on the face of Asia, such a festering wound on her body, that the Chinese commies will quake in their shoes!

[*General's mouth begins to twitch and foam*]

Like in Indonesia. There they took even the children of the communists out and spitted them on the point of a sword . . . don't spare anyone . . . cut off women's breasts if you like, but don't spare anyone . . . tear out this country's guts.

[*On the map of South Vietnam gesticulates the black shadow of the mad general at Cu Chi*]

(Act 1, p. 7)

After this diatribe, which builds to the first of at least four climaxes in *Ajeya Vietnam*, we see the Vietnamese at work in a makeshift hospital at Ho Bo. Unlike in the first act where all movement was regimented, there is a bustle of activity in this act as Dr. Vinh and his nurses attend to their patients, victims of napalm bombing. Despite vivid scenes of horror depicting children suffering from poison gas, there is no sense of despair conveyed by the Vietnamese characters. A patient suffering from severe wounds argues belligerently with the doctor about returning to his post, and a seventy-five-year-old grandmother is cheered by the guerrillas when she shoots down an American plane.

The Vietnamese are presented as a robust community. They have no time for false sentiments or melodramatic platitudes. Note the following speech where the guerrilla Duyet bids farewell to his beloved, Nurse Nguyen Thi Mao.

DUYET: I'll tell you a story, little one. One day, a few weeks back, comrade Trac, Muon and I went patrolling into Cu Chi town, dressed like monks. We came to the American Officers' Club and it was so hot they had taken the barricade off a couple of windows and we looked in. Nailed on the wall were half-a-dozen dried, shrivelled, little things which looked like rotten leather pouches to me . . . On close examination we have established beyond doubt that they are women's breasts.

[*Mao gasps in horror*]

Does that startle you? Haven't you wiped out all weakness yet, comrade Nguyen Thi Mao? Women of Vietnam cannot afford to be startled any longer, my friend. The Americans cut off the breasts of the women they have raped and nail them up on the wall as trophies. . . . Goodbye, my beloved, we shall meet again, soon.

(Act 2, p. 18)

There could not be a more brutal farewell. Dutt subverts the familiar scene in most political propaganda (drama and film) that shows the two young lovers, glowing with life and revolutionary zeal, pledging their faith in the future. In *Ajeya Vietnam*, it is Grandma Kim who romanticizes about the future with an abundance of metaphors: "The rice-fields shall be full again, the mother's womb will be heavy with child and Ho Chi Minh's face, angry now, will once more be lit up with a smile."

Dutt never fails to use such rhetoric in the more reflective moments of his propaganda plays. He knows that the working class is easily wooed by such passages, appallingly bourgeois to the intellectuals in his audience. As Roland Barthes points out in his essay "Writing and Revolution," "The lower-middle-class mode of writing has been taken up by Communist writers because, for the time being, the artistic norms of the proletariat cannot be different from those of the *petite bourgeoisie* . . . [hence] the paradox whereby the communist mode of writing makes multiple use of the grossest signs of Literature."[19]

It must be stressed, however, that Dutt does not restrict himself to this highly rhetorical, almost precious mode of writing. Shortly after Kim utters the lines above, she encounters her grandchild Pupu, who has been blinded by poison gas. The language used in this encounter is less florid. It follows a question-and-answer pattern reminiscent of ballads.

PUPU: Won't I see Mama when they take off the bandage? Where's Mama?

KIM: Mama? But Mama can't come to you, my pet. Who killed your Mama?

PUPU: The Americans.

KIM: What will you do when you come out with me?

PUPU: Kill Americans.

KIM: That's right.

PUPU: If I kill Americans, won't Mama come and sing to me?

KIM: Yes, Pupu, if you kill many Americans, Mama will come and sing you to sleep.

(Act 2, p. 20)

The power of this scene is conveyed in the language, so elegiac and haunting in its use of the refrain that it almost makes an audience forget its insinuative propaganda.

In deliberate contrast to this quiet exchange, Dutt ends the second act with a collision of sounds. A Vietnamese harvest song on the radio increases in volume as bombs from American planes explode nearby. As the cacophony builds and the curtain closes slowly, Dr. Vinh shouts the final lines of the scene, which resound like the thundering chords of a symphony: "Communism against Imperialism! Civilization against barbarism! Science against cannibalism! Vietnam against America!"

In the third and last act of *Ajeya Vietnam*, the confrontation between the Americans and the Vietnamese is explicit and violent, building to a coup de theatre of stunning immediacy. The scene opens with the capture of the Vietnamese in the hospital. A battle of wits ensues between Dr. Vinh and Wheeler, the lieutenant colonel of the American troop, a cocky Harvard graduate, who refers to the Vietnamese as "Asian semihumans," "illiterate peasants," and "nigger gooks."

It is significant that the confrontation between the two men is not on political issues but rather on more peripheral subjects like music and literature. After burning a pile of books (which include tattered copies of the Bible, *Hamlet*, *War and Peace*, and Walt Whitman's poems), the Americans demonstrate their callousness to music. One of them refers to Vietnamese music as "bell-ringing and dog-howling" whereupon the civilized Dr. Vinh informs him that he enjoys listening to the "dog-howls" as well as to Beethoven, Bach, and Brahms. On hearing Chopin's *Revolutionary Etude* played by the People's Artist Lao-tien Ma on Radio Peking, Wheeler informs Dr. Vinh somewhat defensively that he had once contemplated a career as a concert pianist. He listens to the music appreciatively and then, suddenly, he picks up the radio, tears off its wires, and smashes it on the ground. Turning to Vinh, he says, "Chopin is absolutely thrilling. American cigarette, doctor?" It is through such encounters that Dutt creates an image of the Americans as uncivilized.

Another aspect of the Americans that Dutt theatricalizes with lingering detail is their sexual perversity. After searching the village for subversive literature and rifles, the GIs search the bodies of women "the American way." Nurse Nguyen Thi Mao is singled out for special treatment when she accuses the Americans of dissecting women's breasts. Dismissing her accusation as Communist slander, Wheeler and Captain Knight advance on her "with unabashed grins of lust on their faces." When she protests that they have women at home, Wheeler argues, somewhat speciously, "We have them, of course, but they are cadaverous, pale, bloodless. It is yellow that drives me mad. Guard, switch off the light." The stage is plunged into darkness as Nurse Mao is systematically raped by the Americans. "A revolving stage-light reveals snatches of the outrage" (according to the stage directions). The voice of an operator is heard in the darkness intoning, "Peyton Place calling Rolling Stone, Peyton Place calling Rolling Stone. . . ."

The specificity of detail in this scene, which may seem ludicrous to a Western audience, is calculated to fill a Bengali working-class audience with outrage at the enemy. A rape (as I mentioned in my analysis of *Neel-Darpan*) is an essential constituent of any proletarian play in Bengal. Nothing can rouse the anger of a Bengali audience more than to watch a woman brutalized on stage. It is difficult to elaborate on or rationalize this response because it is so instinctive, so immersed in a tradition of values that views a woman predominantly as a mother. The rape of a woman is not simply seen as a particular tragedy: it is considered a violation of life itself.[20]

Dutt, however, subverts these traditional associations by making Grandma Kim assert that "the true, faithful, chaste [Vietnamese] woman is she who has been raped by the enemy." This is somewhat daring on Dutt's part because he knows that his audience believes that there is no act more dehumanized than rape. Yet he makes a seventy-five-year-old character (his voice of reason in the play) urge the younger women to accept the indignity of rape.

KIM: When will you fight, dear daughters, if you brood on shame
and things? Maidenly honor and the dignity of women shall
return after we have won the war, because there is no chastity if
there is no freedom. When you are not free, you are violated
already.

(Act 3, p. 28)

In this speech, a relationship is established between rape and the
future of the country. Unlike *Neel-Darpan*, where the rape of Kshetromoni by Mr. Rogue is presented as the most glaring instance of
British oppression, the rape of Nurse Mao by the Americans is presented by Dutt almost as a condition for freedom. It would be
interesting to examine how the Indian women in Dutt's audience
reacted to such reasoning. There can be no doubt that most femi-
nist theater groups in Europe and America (even those with a
Marxist orientation) would not react to it favorably.

The tension of the scene increases as Mao is tortured for concealing information from the Americans. (She swallows a paper
disclosing facts concerning the U.S. Army.) Electrodes are placed
on her breasts, which have been sprinkled with water. Loops of
barbed wire are fastened around the necks of the Vietnamese men.
After Mao is tortured to death, Wheeler begins to cross-examine
Dr. Vinh about the paper. The deeper Wheeler drives a knife into
Vinh's stomach and the closer he brings a flamethrower to his face,
the more Vinh resists the torture, shouting out lines from Whitman's "Young Libertad." His hysteria mounts as he quotes a poem
written by the Vietnamese poet Tu Huu honoring the memory of
Norman Morrison (martyred through self-immolation). The recitation is excruciatingly painful even for the Americans, who extin-
guish the flamethrower of their own accord. Dr. Vinh speaks the
following lines with "dazed calm."

VINH: The children of my country call him Uncle Morrison. This
was necessary. We keep telling them Johnson and Wheeler are
not America. Uncle Morrison has given our children belief that
there are workers and Communists in America, that Paul Robeson is America, that Lincoln and Whitman were Americans.

(Act 3, p. 32)

Dutt uses here a technique that never fails to affect an audience (even those resistant to propaganda): the narration of memorable names. The mere sounds of "Morrison," "Robeson," "Lincoln," so resonant and charged with associations of humanity and goodness, have a lulling effect. They appeal to the broadest humanitarian feelings, a sense of being part of a world community that could exist if it were not for "gangsters" like Johnson and Wheeler.

Dutt, however, does not allow Vinh's statement to become a humanist assertion of the brotherhood of men. There is no possibility of loving the enemy in Dutt's propaganda plays. Consequently, there is no forgiveness shown to the American soldiers by the Vietnamese when the hospital is suddenly counterattacked by the guerrillas led by Madame Lan Huu, the official guide of the Americans. She turns out to be the deadly enemy of the U.S. Army—Trac. This is a coup de theatre reminiscent of American war films where an ineffectual ally suddenly metamorphoses into a deadly Fascist.

As the Vietnamese imprison the Americans with ruthless efficiency, Wheeler claims his rights as a prisoner of war. He pleads that, as a soldier, he is simply "obeying orders, nothing more." Dutt permits his audience some sympathy for Wheeler, who mutters under his breath, almost to himself:

> WHEELER: If it's forgiveness one asks for—what forgiveness and for whom? For what? What does one do when one arrives at the crossroads of big events? One probably turns to one's mother for a kind word, but my mother died last year.
>
> (Act 3, p. 38)

The mother figure on stage, Grandma Kim, however, has different views on forgiveness that reflects the attitude of her playwright to the Americans.

> KIM: To you Mark Wheeler, young enough to be my grandson, I should have liked to say, I forgive you. We who believe in the Enlightened One, and breathe the green air of this country have always forgiven, for so is it in the Three Sacred Books. But now, I cannot and will not forgive. I charge you with killing children and poisoning the air. I charge you with filling a peace-

ful, loving, forgiving people with hatred and the lust to kill. I charge you with destroying the springs of human kindness that have flown in this country for thousands of years. I charge you with bringing into the mud the fair name of America and filling each one of us, from here to Peking, with undying hatred for everything American. The smoke from your bombs has blackened the face of the Buddha and what was forgiveness is now divine benediction on revenge. [*After a pause*] I even thank you for it, Mark Wheeler. You've taught us how to hate and so we shall win the war.

(Act 3, pp. 39–40)

The power of this rhetoric, its reliance on exotic images and an aura of tradition ("the Three Sacred Books"), its vivid use of metaphor ("the blackened face of the Buddha"), its momentum through repetitions of phrases and words ("I charge," "forgive," "hate"), skilfully conveys Dutt's militant message by mixing the languages of mythology and the law. *Ajeya Vietnam*, however, does not end with so grandiose a speech. One of the last lines of the play is uttered by an American, significantly the only black character on stage. He whispers to Trac: "I believe in you. Vietnam is invincible. For the people of America, you must win."[21]

Din Badaler Pala and Teer

I have discussed *Ajeya Vietnam* at length because it exemplifies the techniques and strategies that Dutt exploits as a propagandist. The use of the climax, the visualization of torture, the momentum of action, the larger-than-life presentation of characters, the collision of sounds are some of the elements that recur in all of Dutt's plays. In *Din Badaler Pala* (Song of the Changing Times), an ambitious street-corner production that followed *Ajeya Vietnam*, there is a sudden reversal of action at the end of the play that shocks the audience almost as much as Madame Lan Huu's abrupt appearance as Trac.

Written specifically for the 1967 Communist election campaign, *Din Badaler Pala* is a courtroom drama featuring a young Communist party worker who is accused of murdering a police officer during the food riots. Almost till the end of the play, which lasts three hours, the counsel for the defence systematically destroys the accusations of the witnesses, who include two prominent members of the Congress party and the CPI, a government bureaucrat, and a landlord. Just when the audience is absolutely convinced of the prisoner's innocence, the Communist worker proudly declares during the prosecutor's cross-examination that he murdered the police officer in cold blood. "Such policemen should be shot like mad dogs," he asserts. Reversing the evidence against the worker had, in Dutt's words, a "double effect" on the audience: "shock at the realization that the boy had been legally guilty all along, and thrill at the challenge thrown at the state machinery."[22]

The impact of *Din Badaler Pala* on the Bengali working class was electrifying, particularly in areas where the food riots had resulted in violent clashes with the police. Dutt is characteristically modest when he denies that his play was primarily responsible for the defeat of the Congress party in the 1967 elections (as some of his enemies claimed). He states that his audiences were already smoldering with anger when they saw *Din Badaler Pala* and that his play merely succeeded in consolidating their emotions into a "collective rage" against the Congress government.

It could be that Dutt minimized the political efficacy of his play because he was so profoundly disappointed by the outcome of the elections. Although the Congress party was ousted, it was replaced by the United Front government, a coalition of opposition parties including the CPI, the "rightist" section of the Communist party. In *Din Badaler Pala*, Dutt had stressed that the representative of the CPI (one of the witnesses in the trial) was as much a part of the establishment as the other opponents of the Communist worker. One can understand Dutt's discomfiture when he saw the CPI firmly entrenched in the ranks of the United Front government.

The problem with this government was that its parties were not at all "united" on major issues. The CPI(M), in particular, had to accept the "bourgeois" leadership of the Bangla Congress party despite its antithetical policies concerning the revolutionary transformation of the parliamentary system. Tensions were particularly acute between Ajoy Mukherjee, the moderate leader of the Bangla Congress and the chief minister of the United Front government, and the CPI(M) leader, Jyoti Basu, who announced the government's decision to take over the Calcutta tramways without consulting Mukherjee. This announcement, which was hailed by the masses, intensified the rivalry between the two leaders and their respective parties.

Apart from threatening the leadership of the United Front government, the members of the CPI(M) were accused of extending their influence in the rural areas of the West Bengal by adopting a militant land policy whereby *benami* land (land registered under false names) could be distributed to the poor. The CPI(M) was also accused of misusing *gherao*—a practice that enabled workers, students, and employees of various establishments to assert their demands by physically "encircling" the representatives of these establishments (bosses, vice-chancellors, foremen, managers). Between March and August 1967, there were 1,018 *gheraos* in 503 establishments resulting in considerable tension and a decline in productivity.[23]

Interpreting *gheraos* as terroristic tactics, the central government of India clearly indicated its opposition to the United Front in West Bengal. Instead of confronting this opposition collectively, the various parties within the Front continued to fight over socioeconomic and administrative issues. In 1968, President's Rule was instituted in West Bengal, provoking mass resistance. When the Second United Front government was formed in February 1969, its members were determined to resolve their earlier differences. But once again, when Ajoy Mukherjee received the chief and finance ministerships and Jyoti Basu functioned as the deputy chief minister in charge of police and administration, tension mounted.

It was not long before the CPI(M) established itself as the dominant party. Its land policy, conceived by Harekrishna Konar, was so successfully implemented that the rights of sharecroppers were protected in many rural areas of Bengal. In addition, 300,000 acres of land illegally held by landlords and rich farmers were recovered; 230,000 acres of land were distributed to peasants; and as many as 800,000 workers from various plantations and industries received higher salaries and increased benefits amounting to 200 million rupees ($25 million).[24]

Not surprisingly, the CPI(M) was warmly supported in the rural areas. This resulted in intensely violent party clashes that caused an outbreak of strikes, disturbances, and a general break down of law and order. The situation was not facilitated when armed policemen stormed into the West Bengal assembly one day while it was in session and created an uproar by smashing furniture. Perhaps the reductio ad absurdum of the political situation was a mass *satyagraha* (accompanied by fasting) led by Ajoy Mukherjee in protest against the "murders, violent clashes, looting, *gheraos*, and forcible occupation of land" that his own government was unable to control. It was not long before the Second United Front government collapsed in March 1970.

The political situation in West Bengal between 1969 and 1970 was particularly turbulent. Significantly, Dutt did not write any major play addressing the political contradictions of this period. Instead, he focused much of his attention on the Naxalbari uprising by writing a play called *Teer* (Arrow).

In the spring of 1967, a peasant rebellion broke out at Naxalbari in West Bengal, which was hailed by the Communist party of China as "the spring thunder over India." Months later in August 1967, there was yet another uprising of the peasants against their landlords in the Srikakulam region of Andhra Pradesh. These uprisings had a tremendous impact on the extremist members of the CPI(M). Believing in the validity of armed guerrilla resistance, these members eventually formed their own party —the CPI(M-L)—on May 1, 1969. By this time, the Naxalite movement had already gained momentum in the rural areas of Bengal.

The Maoist leaders of the movement—Charu Mazumdar and Kanu Sanyal—demanded nothing less than an armed insurrection of the people, a rural-based mass movement relying on guerrilla warfare that would ultimately lead to an overthrow of the bourgeoisie and the armed forces. The immediate opponents of the movement were the feudal landlords and *jotedars*. By eliminating them, the Naxalites believed that they could set up "liberated zones" in the countryside that could be used to encircle and finally capture the cities.

Though the Naxal leaders claimed that the revolution had to be won through an alliance of the working class with the landless peasants, many Naxalites were predominantly middle-class youths. Some of the most brilliant students in Calcutta University were actively involved in the movement. More militant than the French students participating in the revolt of 1968, the Naxalites avoided the rhetoric and symbolization of political activities in which the French students indulged. They applied their ideology more vigorously. Certainly, they did not succumb to what Susan Sontag has described in *Styles of Radical Will* as the European tendency to "talk revolutions away." The Naxalite movement did not fail because it talked too much. One could say that it fought too fiercely for its own survival.

In recent years, Dutt has criticized the excesses of the Naxalite movement: its politics of terror, its indiscriminate slaughter of police officers and CPI(M) members, its perversion of the doctrines of Marx, Lenin, and Mao. However, in 1967 Dutt was too emotionally involved in the movement to be aware of its limitations. In a rare moment of candid self-criticism, Dutt has admitted that the Naxalites appealed to his "inherent extremism," his "own petty-bourgeois arrogance," even his "hidden desire to be a politician."[25] These are the admissions of a middle-aged radical able to look back on his mistakes with some humor.

While irresistibly drawn to the Naxalites, Dutt produced his play on the Naxalbari uprising—*Teer* (Arrow)—which focused on a violent incident in the village of Prasadujot where ten women were ruthlessly killed by a police force. In preparation for his play, Dutt visited various villages in the area where he interviewed militant peasants and their wives. Despite its political commitment, however, *Teer* satisfied neither Charu Mazumdar, who believed that the play merely "dabbled in democratic slogans," nor the members of the CPI(M), including many of Dutt's friends, who believed that the play grossly exaggerated the role of the Naxalites in the class struggle.

The *bhadrolok* members of Dutt's audience, of course, were predictably appalled by the production's lurid scenes of violence. It must have been quite traumatic for them to watch the police kill the womenfolk of the peasant guerrillas on stage, and then to leave the auditorium and face the violence in Calcutta: the deserted streets, the muffled explosions of bombs, the burning buses and trams, the beheadings of landowners, and the slaughter of police officers.

Calcutta was an inferno of revolutionary activity at the time, and the rights and values of the middle class were never more vulnerable. *Teer* did not attempt to analyze the trauma afflicting the middle class. It concentrated entirely on the armed struggle between the peasants and the police and depicted the activity of the guerrillas with graphic literalness. Even more explicitly than the Vietnamese in *Ajeya Vietnam*, the peasants of Naxalbari demonstrated to their audience how a guerrilla unit had to be organized. *Teer* appealed directly to the activists in the audience to learn the tactics and strategies of the revolution. As Dutt once remarked, "It's not enough to have a rifle in one's hand—one must know how to fire it and must hate the enemy enough to fire it."[26]

AFTER THE REVOLUTION

Despite such fervent revolutionary statements, Dutt realized that he could not participate in the Naxalite movement without abandoning his innate theatricality. He has written with considerable wit about the Naxalite phase in his career, when he was pursued by the police for producing *Teer*. If we can believe Dutt, who frequently lives life like a character in a detective novel, he avoided the police for a couple of months, disguising himself during rehearsals of *Teer*, flying to Bombay (where he had accepted a major role in James Ivory's *The Guru*), moving surreptitiously from hotel to hotel, running down corridors to escape plainclothes policemen, and even encountering a smuggler called Mr. De Silva, who was supposed to hand over weapons to Dutt "for the revolution." I quote Dutt's description of his confrontation with the police in an elevator not only because it demonstrates his sense of humor but because it provides a theatrical perspective on his revolutionary ideals.

In the cramped quarters of the lift, I did a bit of Orson Welles [*The Third Man*]. "I have been expecting you, gentlemen." I began and kept declaiming all the way to Secret Police Headquarters at Crawford Market, where, attempting a particularly effusive greeting to the Deputy Commissioner, I knocked my head resoundingly against a lintel and paused in my oration. As soon as I began again, the Deputy Commissioner said, "Shut up! Don't try your tricks here." I was overwhelmed with gloom at this inartistic behavior. . . . When they began interrogating me, I searched my memory for a good part I could play in the circumstances, and decided on Julius Fucik before the Gestapo. But it did not work. The Deputy Commissioner and his officers refused to conform to the scenario, and you cannot very well perform by yourself. They refused to torture, to yell, to tempt, and do the hundred other things expected of them. . . . They made it clear to me that they thought of me as a misguided fool. However, there was an Inspector, lean and hungry-looking, who seemed to appreciate theater as much as I did, and he gradually took over the questioning. He threatened and yelled as theater commands, and I had the satisfaction of playing grotesque heroics.[27]

This encounter with the police, which resulted in Dutt's second term of imprisonment, makes one wonder whether Dutt views politics more theatrically than he views theater politically. Despite all his affirmations about the "Party," and the "class struggle," and the "revolutionary struggle of the people," Dutt is fundamentally a comedian who is fascinated by the theater. In my first meeting with him, to add a personal note, he told me quite bluntly, "Listen . . . I'm a hack, a professional interested in the commercial theater." When his colleagues protest that they do not know when he is serious, he snaps at them: "Damn it, I *am* serious, only my expression, independent of me, runs into theatrical devices, and I start smelling of greasepaint." Even Dutt acknowledges that he "cannot resist theatricality" and that he often "does everything with an eye to audience reaction."[28]

At this point, it is necessary to raise a few questions. Does Utpal Dutt's theatricality as a person and artist undermine his commitment to the "revolutionary struggle of the people"? Is politics incidental to his vision of the theater? Does his outrageous sense of humor trivialize his analysis of proletarian issues? How does one reconcile Dutt's hilarious yet self-deprecating description of his encounter with the police with perfervid statements such as, "The day I cease to participate in political struggle I shall be dead as an artist too"?

I turn to these questions next, though I must prepare the reader (if he is not already convinced) that these ambivalent aspects of

Dutt's personality and dramaturgy cannot be easily reconciled. While acknowledging that Dutt overdoes his revolutionary rhetoric and his political posturing, I cannot deny the immediate impact of his plays on the working-class audiences in Bengal. It seems that Dutt's theater is most true to its revolutionary principles when it is also blatantly theatrical. Like his mercurial personality, it is an odd combination of absurd histrionics and passionately partisan political feelings.

Jatra: The People's Theater

Between 1967, when *Teer* was first produced, and 1970, when the Little Theater Group left the Minerva Theater, Dutt learned much about his function as a political artist. His interest in the Naxalite movement waned once he realized that he had isolated himself from every leftist group in the country. Disenchanted with his "private revolutionary theater," Dutt turned to the *jatra*, the traditional folk theater of Bengal, to discover new structural devices and modes of communication that could be used to rejuvenate the "people's theater."

The political possibilities of *jatra* had already been explored by Mukunda Das during the early years of the independence movement in India. He was the first artist in Bengal to realize that the *jatra* did not have to rely on traditional subjects based on stories from the *Ramayana*, the *Mahabharata*, and the *Puranas*. He also realized that the *jatra* had languished since the nineteenth century because it had retained a sacrosanct aura despite the loss of its religious significance. In order to preach nationalism to the villagers of Bengal through the medium of *jatra*, Das rejected this aura and concentrated instead on the dramatic structure of *jatra*—its operatic conventions, melodramatic gestures, and hypnotic songs, all of which unfailingly captivated a rural audience. The structure of *jatra* was so resilient that it was able to incorporate radical alterations in its subject matter and adopt a contemporary idiom.

With Mukunda Das's pioneering work, topical political figures and situations gradually crept into the mythological framework of the *jatra*. The gods and goddesses became freedom fighters and patriots. The devils and villains were transformed into members of the ruling class. An actor playing a British officer, dressed in tight trousers and brandishing a tin sword, gesticulated like a demon character in traditional *jatra*. The chorus continued to sing devotional songs but for different reasons. Theirs was a political litany rather than a meditation on the cosmos.

The people responded enthusiastically to these changes of content, and gradually the *jatra* became political during the last years of the British Raj. Despite severe opposition from the government, *jatra* troupes continued to perform in rural areas. The significance of these performances cannot be denied. While politicians failed to communicate with the people about abstract issues like nationalism and imperialism, the *jatra* actors could rouse their patriotic emotions with a song. Even after Independence, *jatra* continues to thrive in rural areas, where villagers are now quite accustomed to seeing Marx, Lenin, and Mao appear in the coveted roles of the heroes.

Utpal Dutt's contribution to the politicization of *jatra* is immense. He has a canny understanding of its mechanics and conventions. They appeal to his Elizabethan sense of the theater. The rough trestle stage surrounded by an audience on all sides, the prominence of the musicians and the chorus, the absence of unnecessary props and technical devices, the flamboyant costumes— these are conditions of the theater that stimulate an actor to display his art.

Though Dutt has a healthy respect for the tradition of *jatra*, he has rejected some of its requirements, notably the enactment of female roles by male actors. If Dutt compromises on some of the conventions of *jatra*, it is not necessarily that he wants to but that his audience demands certain changes and omissions. A *jatra* audience is notoriously assertive. There might be twenty thousand workers from tea plantations, mines, and steel plants at a single performance. Since many of the workers have to work a shift next morning, they do not have time (as their ancestors did in the nineteenth century) to watch twelve-hour *jatra* performances with over twenty-five songs. Consequently, Dutt has to minimize the number of songs and restrict, to his disappointment, the entrances of Vivek—a Morality-like character, the conscience of the play, who interrupts the narrative to comment on the action, externalize the emotions of the characters, and raise appropriate questions. He functions in his own time zone that clashes with the action of the *jatra*. Vivek operates like an alienation device in much the same way as the *juri*, another convention of the *jatra* that Dutt has attempted to revive.

It appears that in the second half of the nineteenth century when *jatra* became increasingly dramatic, many of the actors were not used because they could not sing. The convention of the *juri* was introduced, which allowed musicians to sing on behalf of the actors. A character tossed the first line of a song to one of the singers and the chorus completed it for him. The musicians, dressed in long black coats and turbans, sit on stage through the performance and observe the action. At climactic moments, they stop the action and distance it by singing about it. After watching a murder, for instance, they may confront the villain and remind him in no uncertain terms that he will not be able to escape the consequences. At such moments, the *jatra* is transformed into a mock trial where the *juri* functions as judges and the members of the audience serve as witnesses.

The conventions of the *juri* and the Vivek no longer appeal to mass audiences in Bengal, and it is interesting to speculate why. Apart from the fact that they both rely on a potentially tedious surfeit of songs, they blatantly impede the momentum of the action. They break the spell of the *jatra*. In this sense, they function as primitive Brechtian devices that direct an audience to view the action of the play more objectively. This is intolerable for most Bengali working-class spectators, who demand sustained dramatic action with frequent climaxes. Reflecting on how fundamentally alien Brecht is to the people's theater in Bengal, Dutt remarks that:

> The Brechtian style interferes with our people's responses because they are used to another kind of theater, and all forms must come from the people's understanding. . . . As I understand it, epic structure advances the action to a certain point and then halts, cuts it entirely and proceeds with another episode, or with the same episode in a different light. This directly contradicts our people's expectations. They're accustomed to the dramatic atmosphere getting thicker and thicker, until it becomes almost unbearable.[29]

This is a very perceptive comment on the Bengali theater audience, particularly the working-class audience that watches *jatra* so passionately.

What is riveting about a *jatra* performance is precisely the evocation of its atmosphere, so tumultuous and intoxicating that it is impossible to resist. The spectator is carried along in a *jatra* production by its endless murders, love scenes, Machiavellian soliloquies, and anguished scenes of repentance. According to Dutt, these actions move in a series of "convulsions." The very structure of *jatra* compels a spectator to submit to its violent momentum. Experiencing *jatra* is like being immersed in a crowd on one of Calcutta's busy streets, where one's body acquires an automatic mobility. In this street you become one among thousands of people. Your body becomes part of a mass of bodies and your life becomes absorbed in a cluster of experiences. Just as one loses one's identity in a crowd, one tends to lose oneself in the expectations of a *jatra* audience. It is difficult to respond to *jatra* as an individual; one can only respond as part of a mass of people to the spectacle on stage. Perhaps this is the reason why Dutt believes that *jatra* is truly the people's theater of Bengal.

The language of *jatra* is so immersed in popular folklore that even majestic political figures like Mao Tse-tung have to yield to its power. Dutt envisions the *jatra* character of Mao as "the Good King who lives in caves," illustrious, saintly, and invulnerable to the attacks of Chiang Kai-shek, "the Evil King who suffers from epileptic fits." The idiom of *jatra* is timeless. Dutt sees Chiang Kai-shek ranting at Chairman Mao just as Aurangzeb, the most fanatical of Mughal emperors, cursed and raged at Shivaji, the "mountain rat," in traditional *jatra* performances.

Dutt marvels that *jatra* can reflect the political impulses of the people in the present while evoking historical resonances of the past. In his production of *Sanyasir Tarabiri* (The Sanyasi's Crusade), which dramatizes the Sanyasi rebellion in eighteenth-century British India, he was amazed to see how instinctively his audience grasped the contemporary political implications of the play while responding to the corruption in the rule of Warren Hastings. The ultimate crushing of the Sanyasi rebellion and the systematic destruction of the Naxalite movement in Bengal were not isolated historical events for Dutt's audience. Though separated in time by almost two centuries, these two events affected his audience simultaneously during the performance of the *jatra*. Dutt believes that *Sanyasir Tarabiri* would have been less effective if it had settled for a more conventional dramaturgy. It was the timeless, mythical quality of *jatra* that gave the play its particular immediacy.

Surya Shikar

Dutt's first professional contact with *jatra* was his production of *Rifle* in 1969—a play that skilfully related the revolutionary activity of the Bengal rebels in the thirties to the emergence of Indian independence. Instead of sustaining the patriotic ideals of his working-class audience, Dutt challenged them by emphasizing that the "collaborators" of the British in 1930 had become Congress ministers in 1947.

Dutt believes that it is important to provide the people with necessary historical information that has been denied to them. Occasionally this information relates to the ancient history of India and may not refer specifically to the contemporary political situation in Bengal. For instance, in his play *Surya Shikar* (Hunting the Sun), which was originally written for a professional *jatra* company, Dutt dramatizes the confrontation between the Hindu king Samudragupta (A.D. 330–375) and a learned Buddhist monk named Kalhan, a Galileo-like figure who challenged the premises of the Hindu scriptures with his scientific discoveries. This spectacular historical play (perhaps the least tendentious of all Dutt's plays) epitomizes the kind of entertainment that a *jatra* audience craves.

When Kalhan asserts that the earth revolves around the sun and that the moon and stars are not gods (as mentioned in the Vedas) but "matter," it is thrilling even today for villagers in Bengal, who have inherited innumerable superstitions and taboos from their forefathers. The heretical force of Kalhan's observations is conveyed directly in the language: "There is no afterlife, no heaven, no hell, no sun, no virtue, no gods, no God. There is nothing. Nothing."[30]

In distinct contrast to the finality of these words, Dutt makes

Samudragupta speak with all the seductive rhetoric one associates with heroes of *jatra*. He woos the audience to accept his point of view by speaking beautifully.

> SAMUDRAGUPTA: Can you imagine a world without gods, *yakshas, gandharvas, apsaras*? Without nymphs and fairies and monsters? What then will the poet write about, what will man dream with? They wish to turn the brutal light of truth into all the dark corners of our cherished childhood and spirit away all our beautiful lies. How can I breathe in a world of harsh realities? How can a person live without the ecstasy of falsehood?
>
> (Scene 3, p. 13)

Even villains speak eloquently in *jatra*. Samudragupta uses more metaphors than any other character in the play. As God's emissary on earth, he believes that Kalhan deserves to be condemned for "usurping the king's prerogative of hunting the sun." At the end of the play, he cuts out Kalhan's tongue so that it appears to the masses that the Buddhist heretic has recanted. This is a significant action because it silences Kalhan. Samudragupta's triumph in the play is a matter of words rather than actions. As the desperate Kalhan vainly attempts to deny his recantation, the emperor goes up to him and speaks these words with lethal eloquence.

> SAMUDRAGUPTA: It's no use, Maharshi, you can't fight me. You try to say there is no God. Very well, we shall make *you* a god. You gesture wildly with your arms to say man needs reason not faith. Very well, we shall fall at your feet and worship you, and make *you* a monument of blind faith against reason. You wanted to hunt the sun, old man; that was rash. This is how the sun is hunted. We shall make you, the mortal enemy of religion, a temple for the propagation of religion, just as we have turned Buddha, the enemy of Vishnu, into the tenth incarnation of Vishnu.
>
> (Scene 7, p. 24)

Destiny, however, has the final word in *jatra*. In much the same way that the texts of Brecht's Galileo survive his recantation, the books of Kalhan's foremost disciple are smuggled out of Samudragupta's capital. We are told in the last lines of the play that "the world will find out the truth, if not today, then tomorrow, a century, a millennium later." Kalhan will be remembered as that "courageous old man who lit a lamp to dispel the darkness of the world." He is apotheosized.

The confrontation between the King and the Buddhist is more subtle and ideological than most conflicts in *jatra* between the Good King and the Evil King. Indeed, there is a certain finesse about Kalhan's statements when he emphasizes that "falsehood is a relative term" and that "the scriptures were true when they were written." But Dutt cannot develop these ideas since his play relies so extensively on the conventions of the popular drama in Bengal —the palace intrigues, the spectacular crowd scenes, the torture of slaves, and, above all, the intricacies of romance.

There are at least three characters in *Surya Shikar* who contribute to the sexual interest of the play. There is Mahasveta, a courtesan who repents her misdeeds and becomes Kalhan's disciple, only to betray him at the end of the play. More provocatively, there is Urmila, the lascivious queen, who attempts to relieve her boredom by sleeping indiscriminately with her husband's generals. Finally, there is the passionate love story involving Indrani, a fervent disciple of Kalhan (necessarily a virgin), and the sex-crazed Hayagreeva, a general of Samudragupta's army, who asserts that "a woman is simply flesh that he enjoys for a night."

Hayagreeva provides Dutt with different languages of love. Before he meets Indrani, he declaims with appropriately lustful images.

> HAYAGREEVA: Every night I suck the life out of a fresh body and the following morning toss the dry flesh on the dung heap and they have one more applicant for the cat-house. . . . There is no such thing as woman, only an exterior, a hollow effigy. Break it open and you have an armful of straw, earth, and wood.
> (Scene 1, p. 2)

After he is impossibly in love with Indrani, who rejects him as a "cowardly womanizer," he speaks another language—the stuttering, hopeless words of unrequited love.

HAYAGREEVA: Why do you smile when you see Hayagreeva grovel at your feet? Is that not pride? Why else do you store your beauty and love in a miserly casket out of my reach? . . . I do not know what love is. Is it a painful gaping wound? Is it tongues of flame within the head? If so, then I certainly love. And I offer it to you for what it is worth.

(Scene 3, p. 11)

These speeches convey, more vividly than any examples I am aware of in Dutt's oeuvre, the rough lyricism of *jatra*. I should stress Dutt's *jatra* because his occasional crudities, sensational details, and grandiloquence (reminiscent of Madhusadhan Dutt) have little in common with the idiom of authentic *jatra*. Dutt's critics claim that he does not belong to *jatra*. His perspective, they say, is much too urban, his language self-indulgently ornate. What needs to be emphasized, however, is Dutt's use of *jatra* techniques and dialogue for the propagation of ideas. He is not interested in reviving *jatra*. That would be appallingly antiquarian to him. Nor should he be criticized for catering to a new movement in the Bengali theater—the "urban *jatra*"—a blatantly commercial enterprise that relies on obtrusive scenic effects and titillating cabaret items for its box office. Dutt's use of *jatra* is more pragmatic and intellectually sound than the purists of the Bengali theater care to admit.[31]

Tiner Talwar

After its successful run as a *jatra* production, *Surya Shikar* was revived by Dutt for his new group, the People's Little Theater, which was formed after the Little Theater Group disbanded in 1970. Dutt is the unquestioned leader of the group. He continues to write, direct, and act most of the principal roles, not unlike the actor-managers in the nineteenth-century theater. He makes all the decisions. His presence is felt in the smallest detail of his mise en scène. Every grouping, every climax, every sound cue is orchestrated by him. As for the acting style of the company, it is well known that he directs the gestures, movements, and voice patterns of his actors with utmost rigor. Some of his actors simply imitate his most popular mannerisms, including his chortles, burps, and rolling eyes.

There can be no question that Dutt's personality dominates every production of the People's Little Theater. When I once asked him, somewhat tentatively, if he believed that a revolutionary theater group should operate as a collective, he chuckled, "We don't believe in these things . . . we believe in the dictatorship of the theater." Dutt plays the role of the theater dictator most engagingly both off stage and on. His performance as Benimadhab, the tyrannical nineteenth-century director of the Great Bengal Opera in his play *Tiner Talwar* (The Tin Sword), is a tour de force of comic acting. It also exemplifies, quite unconsciously, the art of self-parody.

The play opens with a hilarious confrontation between Benimadhab and a sweeper belonging to the lowest of castes. To the strains of a melody on the harmonium, the lights come up on stage revealing a huge poster advertising the latest production of the Great Bengal Opera, *Mayurbhan*. Benimadhab ambles onto the stage amiably drunk and squints as he observes the poster. The sweeper emerges from a manhole and mischievously throws some dirt at him. This is the first action of the play and it never fails to amuse the audience. The sweeper reveals a caustic sense of humor as he apologizes for his action: "I poured the shit of the poor on Babu's body."[32] Somewhat taken aback, Benimadhab asks him if he goes to the theater. The sweeper dismisses the theater as trash and ridicules its highfalutin discourse. He defiantly asserts that he does not understand the *babu*'s theater and has no time for it. Benimadhab's ego is more than slightly deflated. As "Bengal's Garrick," he tries to impress the sweeper with a flamboyant recitation of a verse by Michael Madhusadhan Dutt. The sweeper is not impressed. He dismisses the lines as "worthless." When Benimadhab asks if he will see *Mayurbhan*, the sweeper rails at him:

> SWEEPER: Why should I see it? You *babus* simply brag and flirt with market girls and speak a language we don't understand. [*pouring debris into manhole*] Our slum's *Ramleela* is much better. So, what is this *Mayur* play all about?
>
> BENI: Mayurbhan is the prince of Kashmir. The story is . . .
>
> SWEEPER: Hang your prince! Why do you play kings rubbing color on your faces and wearing red and blue silk garments? If you're

so learned, why do you do all these childish things with a tin sword?

BENI: Tin sword! Childish!

SWEEPER: Dress up as you are! Don't you see my body is smeared with shit and mud?

BENI: Alright, alright.

SWEEPER: Are you ashamed of showing that? Is that why you fake by putting on flamboyant dresses and artificial beards, by reciting gorgeous verses? Why can't you write a play about me instead of the prince?

BENI: Ah! Each sentence pierces me like a sharp sword.

[*recites in the style of Madhusadhan*]

SWEEPER: Go to hell!

BENI: Alright, alright.

(Act 1, scene 1)

This exchange of dialogue (more racy and pungent in the vernacular than in English) raises the most important issue of *Tiner Talwar:* the responsibility of the nineteenth-century Bengali theater to the working class. The "Tin Sword" is a particularly significant title because it evokes, in its very artifice and theatricality, the ineffectuality of Benimadhab's theater in relation to the political confusion of the time. The play, however, is only indirectly political because it concentrates more on the excesses and pretensions of the nineteenth-century theater than on the political situation in India. The anti-British sentiments of the play become clear only toward the end. Perhaps this is why *Tiner Talwar* is Dutt's most popular play with the Bengali intelligentsia. The politics of the play are neither threatening nor immediate. They are circumscribed within the nineteenth-century milieu of the play.

The entire first half of the play presents a backstage view of the Great Bengal Opera, a group that evokes a theater of bygone years —the historical spectacles of Girish Chandra Ghosh and the pantomimes of Ardhendu Mustaphi. We see the actors of Benimadhab's company, an eccentric lot of comedians, rehearsing and learning their lines in a cluttered room that contains all the paraphernalia of the commercial Bengali theater—painted flats, rickety pillars, gaudy masks, and tin swords. In this world of cardboard and tinsel, there is little reference to the real world—the disturbances, the riots, and the censorship of plays that ultimately resulted in the Dramatic Performances Act of 1876. The actors of the Great Bengal Opera seem to be secure in their theatrical delusions and feudal loyalty to Benimadhab.

The only concern of the group is its financial insecurity, its dependence on the patronage of Birkrishna Daw, the proprietor of the theater. Like most of Dutt's villains, Birkrishna is whimsical and loquacious. He loves to hear his own voice, interspersing his chatter with frequent asides to his servants, who serve him with wine and *pan* (betel nut). He also fancies himself as a connoisseur of the arts, waxing eloquent on *Shakuntala* without remembering the name of the author. In fact, his ignorance of dramatic literature is so colossal that it becomes excruciatingly difficult for Benimadhab to flatter him. Needless to say, there are some excellent literary jokes at his expense.

The patron is also something of a womanizer. This aspect of his character is not entirely a laughing matter. It leads to a central conflict in the play when Benimadhab literally sells one of his actresses to Birkrishna in order to obtain ownership rights to his theater. The actress is Moyna, once a street girl, later transformed by Benimadhab into a captivating actress. (The first act of *Tiner Talwar* deals extensively with the maestro bullying and disciplining Moyna rather like Henry Higgins. He teaches her how to pronounce the Bengali consonant "sho" just as Higgins instructs Eliza how to pronounce her vowels.) When Moyna finds herself sold to an ageing, dissolute aristocrat, she protests violently. The maestro defends himself petulantly by saying that she does not exist for him as a person. She is his creation and, therefore, he can do anything with her.

This authoritarian attitude enrages Priyanath Mullick, the angry young playwright who serves as the catalyst in the play. He disturbs the equilibrium of the Great Bengal Opera with his radical views on a socially relevant drama. As *Tiner Talwar* proceeds, he tries to persuade Benimadhab to abandon the outmoded dramaturgy and melodramatic platitudes of the commercial theater. But the maestro resists these "westernized" views obstinately. He is more interested in his box office than in patriotism.

There is a striking scene in the second half of the play with Benimadhab and Mullick sitting on either side of the stage. The young playwright urges the maestro to do his play on Titu Meer, the great peasant-hero who fought a disastrous battle against the British in 1831.[33] While Mullick speaks, the maestro sips his wine. In the distance that separates them, we see the shadowy outlines of the painted set used in *Mayurbhan*, the proscenium arch decorated with mythological figures, the canvas backdrop with its perspective design. Benimadhab's theater seems totally redundant.

Gradually, however, with the burgeoning of patriotic plays in the Bengali theater and the subsequent arrests of actors like Amritlal Basu, Benimadhab cannot remain indifferent to the turbulence of his age. He decides to stage the heroic saga of Titu Meer. In his decision, we see the evolution of the Bengali theater from its mythological, fantastic, and romantic beginnings to a more concrete, historical, and patriotic form. Dutt captures this transition most effectively by gradually removing the obtrusive nineteenth-century props on the stage. He begins to emphasize the spaces between the props and the starkness of the black backdrop. While the Great Bengal Opera rehearses *Titu Meer* there are sporadic announcements by British officers positioned in the audience prohibiting any kind of protest against the government. Succumbing to these repressive measures, Benimadhab abandons the rehearsals of *Titu Meer*, much to the dismay of his company, and continues to rehearse Dinabandhu Mitra's *Sadhabar Ekadasi*, a social play that could not possibly offend the British.

Benimadhab, however, is disturbed by his own cowardice. In the final scene of *Tiner Talwar*, while performing his role in *Sadhabar Ekadasi*, he is suddenly roused by a British officer in the audience who laughs at him. Gradually, the lines of *Titu Meer*, which he had suppressed in his subconscious, begin to surface. The audience becomes aware of his erratic metamorphosis from a harmless character to a political rebel. Benimadhab silences their catcalls with a stirring performance as Titu Meer. He immerses himself in the role of the peasant-hero, his voice trembling with emotion.

BENI: *Sahibs*, why did you come to our country? We didn't harm you in any way. We were living in peace, in intimacy with our

brethren, in close bond irrespective of Hindus and Muslims. . . .
Coming to this country from thousands of miles away, why did
you trample your boots on our freedom?

(Scene 8, p. 127)

As the patriotic rhetoric gets more intense, the British officer
becomes increasingly disturbed. He ceases to laugh condescend-
ingly at Benimadhab when he sees his own death enacted on stage.
The killing of a British character by Titu Meer is the most violent
and naturalistic stage business in the entire production of *Tiner
Talwar.* We are taken aback by Benimadhab's ferocity as he stabs
the officer a number of times saying, "Take this, you British enemy!
Take this, you rapist British pirate! Take this little gift for what you
have been giving my country for years!" After this ritual killing of
the British government and a rousing patriotic song, *Tiner Talwar*
comes to an end. Benimadhab acknowledges the applause in the
role of Titu Meer "with a smile of triumph on his face."

The revolutionary message of *Tiner Talwar* is conveyed through
Titu Meer, the play within the play. This is an interesting strategy
because it enables Dutt to make a political statement within the
nineteenth-century framework of the play. But it is also for this
very reason that the politics of *Tiner Talwar* can be safely ignored;
they seem somewhat remote from the exigencies and contradictions of the contemporary world of politics.

Barricade

Dutt was, perhaps, aware that *Tiner Talwar* was not provocative
enough to popularize his views of the revolutionary theater. In his
next play, *Barricade*, which ostensibly dramatizes the rise of Hitler
in Berlin in 1933, the historical facts are inextricably linked to the
most immediate political events in Bengal, notably, the murder of
the eighty-year-old leftist leader Hemanta Basu and the rigging of
the 1972 West Bengal state elections by the Congress party.

Dutt realized that it would be dangerous to dramatize these
facts literally, so he settled for an allegorical framework whereby
the rigging of the 1933 German elections by the Nazis took on a
timely significance for the people of West Bengal in 1972. The

Congress party members in particular were most affected by Dutt's ingenuity. In an interview with Vijay Tendulkar and Kumud Mehta, Dutt describes their discomfiture with his characteristic blend of candor and cunning:

> Somehow the Congressmen in Calcutta think it is a terrible insult to them. They even tried to break up a show of ours. I asked them, "Do you admit then that you rigged the election?" They said, "Certainly not." I said, "Why are you so furious then? We are only showing how the Nazis rigged the elections."[34]

Apart from rigging the elections, the Congress party started a campaign against the CPI(M) members (significantly on the eve of the elections), accusing them of murdering Hemanta Basu, a much respected political figure in West Bengal. In *Barricade*, the Nazis accuse the Communists of a similar crime: the murder of a certain Judge Zauritz, an intellectual with no particular political affiliation. The circumstances and political exploitation of these two murders had immediate resonances for a Bengali audience in the early seventies.

Despite the "Germanness" of *Barricade*, (the Bengali actors look like Nazis in their blond wigs and black uniforms with prominent swastikas), the play never fails to relate to the political situation in Bengal either through suggestion or subtle innuendo. The prologue of the play directs the audience how to view the seemingly foreign subject matter, the emergence of nazism as a political force in Germany. *Barricade* opens with the *sutradhara* (stage manager) singing a song of the Red Force. A Bengali laborer, nondescript and casual, asks him why he sings "foreign songs in Calcutta."[35] He suggests that the stage manager should sing the revolutionary songs of Nazrul, the great Indian patriot. The stage manager retorts that there is nothing foreign about either "revolutionary songs" or the activity of "revolution" itself. The laborers of Tanzania, China, and India are all united in their oppression and their resistance to the exploiters. With considerable cunning, he points out that the weapon the laborer holds in his hand is "Made in Germany" and that the pamphlet in his pocket is written by Lenin. Somewhat enlightened, though disgruntled, the laborer asks what play will be performed. The stage manager announces *"Barri-cade."*

Without wasting any time, Dutt presents the audience with cru-cial facts that re-create the atmosphere of the political situation in Berlin of 1933. He does not use the doctrinaire convention of the lecture. Rather, he presents a cross-section of the characters in *Bar-ricade*—a Nazi officer, a doctor, a judge, an editor, a reporter, and the widow of Judge Zauritz—who appear behind cardboard cut-outs. The effect is at once grotesque and startling. The stage man-ager moves from one cartoonlike figure to the next, questioning them about their occupation and ideology.

During the course of the play, these simplistic two-dimensional figures become complex human beings. (The Nazi officer is the only exception; he simply becomes more grotesque, succumbing at one point in the play to epileptic fits.) The doctor, however, who is a middle-class intellectual devoted to the works of Schopenhauer, Hegel, and Kant, learns that politics denies a humanist attitude to life. The judge faces the ineffectuality of justice in a corrupt and authoritarian state. The editor, perhaps, learns that the "truth" of journalism is more complex than he imagines. The reporter con-fronts his disengaged attitude to politics. And finally, Ingeborg Zauritz, an ordinary housewife who metamorphoses into a mother figure, realizes that she cannot be indifferent to politics. Unlike the learning process of the other characters, which is implied rather than stated, Frau Zauritz becomes a fervent spokesman for the Communist workers at the end of the play. Her transformation is complete.

The most dynamic character in *Barricade*, however, is neither Frau Zauritz nor Bruno (the extremist leader of the Communists who appears in the second half of the play) but Otto, the reporter, who eventually exposes the Nazi involvement in Zauritz's murder. He faces tremendous resistance from Lunt, his editor, who blindly accepts the official statement of the Nazi party that Zauritz was murdered by Hutig, a Communist party worker. Instead of ques-tioning the statement, Lunt orders Otto to substantiate it with "spicy" details.

For Lunt, the "truth" of journalism (a standard he constantly upholds) is what the Nazi party decrees. Otto, on the other hand, is

more skeptical and proceeds to investigate the case by interview-
ing Communist workers. Drinking beer with them in a tavern,
Otto finds out that the Communists no longer address one another
as "comrade." Instead, they use the word *"genosi."* This is important evidence for him since Frau Zauritz had testified in court that
she had heard the murderers use the word "comrade." She had
immediately associated the word with the Communists and no one
had doubted this association in court.

In a crucial hearing of Hutig's trial, Otto destroys her evidence.
He also reinterprets another statement made by Frau Zauritz that
had been used against the Communists. Apparently, while the
murderers were stabbing her husband, Frau Zauritz had heard
them shouting, "Communist Party Zindabad" ("The Communist
Party Will Conquer"). Quite reasonably, Otto points out in court
that it does not make sense for the Communists to implicate themselves in a political murder so openly. He also indicates that one of
the clues—a communist leaflet confiscated from the Party office—
had obviously been forged because it had been signed by a Party
secretary who had resigned a year ago. "It can't be that the Communists don't know the name of their General Secretary," Otto
asserts, "it's not convincing." The Judge and Ingeborg Zauritz are
increasingly convinced that the murder was not committed by
members of the Communist party but, in all probability, by the
rival party.

Just when Hutig is about to be freed, the Nazi officer Lippart
dramatically intervenes in the trial. He announces that Hutig has
been taken away by the Central Force and, consequently, his fate
lies beyond the jurisdiction of the state court. Judge Fosse reacts
indignantly and voices his skepticism that peace can be maintained with Nazi interference on a judicial level. In the next court
hearing, Lippart announces that Fosse has been replaced by a new
judge. When Frau Zauritz protests that the case cannot proceed
without Fosse, she is curtly informed by Lippart that the judge has
been shot by two Communist suspects. There is silence in the court
and only Frau Zauritz has the nerve to ask, "Did these people also
cry 'Communist Party Zindabad'?" The terrorism of the Nazi
party becomes formidably clear to the characters on stage.

In the last scene of the play, Frau Zauritz joins the Communist boys behind the barricade. She is a maternal figure; she brings them food and urges them to take care of themselves. But she is not sentimental. Like Brecht's Pelagaya Vlassova, she asserts her willingness to participate in the Communist struggle against nazism. "I have not come to convey peace," she says, "I have come to give you swords." As she speaks, the sounds of firing and the explosions of bombs are heard in the distance. The Communist party workers continue to defend the barricade. We see their fighting postures silhouetted against the cyclorama. The red flag flutters as the curtain parts slowly.

Barricade dramatizes individuals caught in a vicious political system. It concentrates, however, more on the system, its inner workings and corruption, than on the psychological development of each individual. Apart from early scenes, hushed and Chekhovian, depicting Frau Zauritz in a state of mourning, the rest of the play is aggressively loud. The action is explicit and external. There are no private musings, few reflective moments. Significantly, most of the action takes place in the courtroom where all the gestures and statements of the actors are boldly asserted. Dutt strategically places the witness box center stage and makes the witnesses speak directly to the audience. The judge looms behind them. We see no profiles in Dutt's most rigorously directed scenes. The play is acted out toward the audience. There are no nuances, no distracting facial expressions, no hints of inner turbulence. Dutt directs *Barricade* with matter-of-fact efficiency.

It is difficult to believe that such a tightly knit production was rehearsed in less than a month. *Barricade* is unanimously considered the most staggering spectacle in the contemporary Bengali theater. A huge shadow of Hitler gesticulating like a madman, intricately choreographed street fights, a balletic Red Flag sequence, meticulously timed bursts of deafening music, constructivist scenery with stark outlines, the jury sitting with their backs to the audience in the orchestra pit—these are some of *Barricade*'s memorable theatrical effects.

What is striking about these effects is their essential economy. The frenetic shadow of Hitler, for instance, is created simply by an actor gesticulating in front of a powerful spotlight. At times, Dutt borrows his effects quite unashamedly from an old production by Piscator or Okhlopkov. His multiple staging and use of a massive newspaper as a backdrop in addition to the inevitable red flags and hammer and sickle are undeniably derivative. Nonetheless, Dutt never fails to infuse these familiar conventions with his own touch of eccentricity.

His use of music, in particular, is appallingly tasteless but resoundingly theatrical. You can hear the 1812 Overture, martial music that could be Russian or Chinese, excerpts from Beethoven, and film music, like the theme song from *Lawrence of Arabia*, all in one production. More often than not, Dutt's choice of music has nothing to do with the play. The court scene in *Barricade*, for instance, is interrupted at climactic moments of the trial by bursts of background music from *The Magnificent Seven*. On a certain level, the choice is quite absurd, but when it is heard in relation to the emotional orchestration of the scene, this music seems most appropriate. (It should be pointed out that Dutt's audience would not be familiar with the theme music. They would respond to it without identifying its source.) It is thrilling to hear the actors shout in order to "top" the music when they want the action to proceed. Dutt uses music quite simply to amplify the intensity of his productions. In this sense, he is very different from Brecht who believed that music should not simply "highlight" or "illustrate" a play but "set forth the text" and "take up a position" in it.[36]

Dutt's dramaturgy may not be particularly subtle but it is unremittingly intense. It relies on a tremendous coordination of the various elements in a production. As long as *Barricade* functions like a machine, one does not notice the stereotypes of the Nazis and the Communists and the unwieldy use of details in the trial. One is simply stunned by the production's momentum. But when the machinery of the production breaks down, the play begins to creak. This was my experience when I saw *Barricade* late in its run. The costumes looked a trifle threadbare, the set changes were clumsy, the lighting unfocused and appallingly amateur (Hitler's shadow looked like a Walt Disney cartoon), and, greatest of all indignities in the political theater, the red flags were not ironed. They looked bedraggled and creased, quite unlike the first performances of *Barricade* (which I attended) where they filled the stage with their stark red color and bold swastikas. What was once an awesome spectacle was now a sorry sight.

Apart from the production, the performances lacked fire and

the violent grotesquerie one associates with Dutt's actors. It could well be that the actors were not in top form; but I believe there was a more significant reason for the general ennui of the production. It had to do with the fact that the political situation in Bengal had changed radically since 1972. What gave the production its particular edge early in the run was its assault on the Congress government. I can still hear the audience cheer the climactic moments of the trial and abuse the Congress government with gusto. In 1979, the audience watched the play complacently. There was nothing to fight about any longer. Since the ruling government of West Bengal was the CPI(M) party and the Congress party had lost its power, the rigging of the elections by the Nazis no longer had the same political resonance. As for the murder of Hemanta Basu, most people in the audience had in all probability forgotten about it. Consequently, they viewed the political maneuvering of Judge Zauritz's murder without anger.

Dushopner Nagari

Barricade demonstrates that a political allegory is essentially time bound. It loses much of its significance when it is revived. Its specificity of detail is at once its strength and limitation. When Dutt produced Dushopner Nagari (Nightmare City), he abandoned the allegorical framework. He referred to political events in Bengal, notably the murder of Communist workers by goondas (gangsters), without specifying the victims or aggressors. Unlike Barricade, which refers unequivocally to political events surrounding the murder of Hemanta Basu, Dushopner Nagari presents a much wider vision of terrorism and police brutality in Calcutta.

The characters of the play correspond to generalized types: the businessman who has connections with the central government in New Delhi, the disillusioned goonda who wants a job, the illiterate goonda who accepts his exploitation, the Communist worker pursued by the police, among other familiar figures in Calcutta. In fact, Dushopner Nagari is so immersed in the everyday life of Calcutta that it almost ceases to be a propaganda play against the Congress and the central government in New Delhi.

When the play was banned under Section 124-A on charges of

sedition, it was very difficult for the government to prove that the murders and political turmoil of *Dushopner Nagari* were fabrications of Dutt. The members of the People's Little Theater compiled a long list of witnesses (including police officers and a governor) who had, at one time or another, acknowledged the state of crime in Calcutta. According to Dutt, one piece of evidence was particularly valuable, that of an inspector general who had virtually confessed that "the murder of policemen in Calcutta should be attributed to union rivalries and not to the Naxalites or the CPI(M)."[37] This evidence was, perhaps, too strong for the prosecutor, who began to postpone further hearings of the trial. Moreover, Indira Gandhi announced a state of emergency in the country and all political theater was more or less suppressed.

Dutt believes that his production of *Dushopner Nagari* was more than a play. It was a political phenomenon, a cause célèbre in the Bengali theater. He enjoys counting the number of times his play was "attacked" by "Congress gangsters." One early performance at the Star Theater had to be abandoned after "an army of the worst criminals in north Calcutta" severely beat up the stage crew, smashed the sets, knocked the lighting designer down on the street, and even "dragged an actress by her hair down the road."[38] Dutt relishes these details. They make his theater more daring and subversive. As he once said, "A revolutionary theater is noted by the number of attacks it has faced from the agents of the ruling class." Though this is a somewhat questionable premise, it cannot be denied that *Dushopner Nagari* was attacked for political reasons and even defended on one occasion by the CPI(M) members of South Calcutta who actually barricaded the street surrounding the theater in order to prevent any police disturbance.

To see the people fighting for his theater was a unique experience for Dutt. The very purchase of a ticket for *Dushopner Nagari* at that time acquired a political significance. It would be dramatic to say that people were risking their lives to see the play, but they were certainly protesting against the repressive measures of the Congress government by attending clandestine performances. Mr. Siddharta Shankar Ray, the chief minister of West Bengal (once described by Dutt as the "playboy of Mrs. Gandhi and her clique") reacted to the disruption of *Dushopner Nagari* by saying, "Political plays will naturally be dealt with politically." Dutt's audience reacted to this bland statement without speeches or rallies; they simply went to the theater.

After the Emergency, *Dushopner Nagari* was (and continues to be) a tremendous commercial success. In many ways, it is Dutt's most intricately structured play. It contains sections of political satire, physical violence, vaudeville routines, melodrama, and farce—a conglomeration of disparate events that Dutt orchestrates with professional skill. He uses contrasts to great effect in this production, particularly in the montage sequence that precedes the play.

The first image of *Dushopner Nagari* is the silhouette of a policeman standing on the top of a high platform. To the strains of loud melodious music, the lights brighten and twenty to twenty-five characters enter casually and walk around the ramps and levels on stage. It is like a film sequence of life on one of Calcutta's busy streets. We recognize familiar types of people in the swirling mass of characters. We see intellectuals, clerks, executives with black briefcases, lovers, beggars, *goondas*, a blind man. The music changes abruptly, the characters freeze with their hands raised, and the police (hitherto immobile figures in the background) suddenly break into action. They rush downstage and surround a young couple sitting on a bench. They hit the man and throw the woman on the floor. After this eruption of violence, the tranquil music returns and life continues in Calcutta. The characters move around the stage in a kind of stupor, seemingly oblivious to the violence that surrounds them. There is yet another interruption when the music becomes sinister and discordant. The characters raise their hands automatically, not daring to move. But this time it is the police who are attacked by the *goondas*. One more policeman murdered, yet another day in Calcutta.

Dushopner Nagari. Nightmare City. The montage leads into a passionate song about Calcutta that protests against the title of the play. Swapan, the CPI(M) worker who sings the song directly to the audience, claims that it is the exploiters who assert that Calcutta is a "Nightmare City." "For us, the people of Calcutta," he sings, "the city is beautiful."[39] It is the agents of the establishment who have "prostituted" the city. The song ends and the first words of the play are spoken by Lakhan Palit, a formidable businessman, black marketeer, and employer of *goondas*, who is the arch villain of the play. But Palit himself is simply a representative of a more anonymous and deadly enemy, the central government in New Delhi, which has consistently and ruthlessly discriminated against the people of West Bengal by not providing them with adequate food or financial aid.

Dutt plays Palit with lofty arrogance as he puffs on a cigar and surveys the audience with contempt. The performance is at once threatening and farcical. Palit speaks the most outrageous doggerel while uttering the direst threats to the Bengali people.

> In such crises
> Keep your damn work in your pockets—
> Don't you know me? If I just raise my little finger
> The tails of all jackals will be severed.
> Every first week of every month the checks I sign
> Do you think they are just for charity?
> If you're of no use to me, why the hell should I support chaff
>   like you?
>
> (Act 1, p. 2)

Dutt chooses this rough, jaunty mode of crude verse to introduce the lackeys of Lakhan Palit—a youth leader of the Congress (I) (Indira Gandhi's party) who ends all his speeches with a ridiculous refrain, "Jug jug jiyo"; a commissioner of police who is periodically morose and blustering; and an absurdly sanctimonious editor who wallows in all the bourgeois rhetoric one associates with popular Bengali newspapers like *Jugantar* and the *Ananda Bazar Patrika*. These representatives of the establishment are ruthlessly caricatured as they respond to all of Palit's orders with puppetlike submission. It seems as if Palit controls the entire economy and administration of Calcutta.

Juxtaposed against the world, there is the underworld of the *goondas*. Dutt introduces us to Manibhushan, a profoundly disturbed *goonda* who seems to be suffering from schizophrenia. Overcome with guilt for all the murders he has committed under Palit's orders, Manibhushan is nonetheless incapable of changing the course of his life. He disassociates himself from his crimes and yet continues to commit them mechanically for the money. This dilemma results in a kind of hallucinatory frenzy as he soliloquizes to the audience, using random images and perfervid symbols. (He sees "portfolios floating on a flooded field" and "blood oozing from the drenched leaf of a tree/Into the dirty flood water.")

It is interesting to speculate why Dutt wanted to present a sympathetic study of a *goonda*, generally considered a threat to society. Was this a political strategy? Was he pandering to a certain section of the *goondas* by making them believe that they were more sinned against than sinning? Did he hope to persuade them to support the CPI(M) party (for even the Communist party needs *goondas*)? Or did he want to vindicate those Communist *goondas* who had been accused of murdering policemen? These are some of the questions that come to mind when one thinks of Manibhushan's acute disillusionment.

There is, however, another *goonda*, named Girin, who appears later in the play. He is the terror of Belghoria and is presented as a bullying and illiterate gangster seemingly reconciled to his status in life. He is Manibhushan's antithesis. He has no conscience, no scruples, no discrimination. He kills when ordered to and does not reflect on his actions. But Dutt does not pit Girin against Manibhushan. Ultimately, *Dushopner Nagari* is Manibhushan's play. Girin is simply a threatening buffoon who succumbs to drunkenness and idiocy in the course of the play. He cannot be taken seriously.

Dutt directs our attention away from the predicament of the *goondas* by returning to the world of Lakhan Palit. This pendulum movement in the action is characteristic of the entire play. After the turgid verse of Manibhushan's agonized soliloquy, it is refreshing to hear the colloquial comments of Palit and his employees as they examine the photograph of a national leader. The situation is pure farce because the photograph is so dark that the leader cannot be deciphered. The photographer, who is employed by Palit for propagandist purposes, squints at the photograph inches away from his face and declares that the leader has vanished. Everybody attempts to "spot the leader" with hilarious consequences. Somebody points out a "round shape" that looks like the leader only to be informed that it is "the wheel of an aeroplane." What emerges from this farcical interlude is that there is *no* leader in India. The state of the country is almost as dark and confusing as the photograph.

Juxtaposed against this sequence, Dutt presents us with the false propaganda of the central government on the communications media. Palit interrupts his conversation by switching on a radio that blares the following message:

> RADIO: Although the standard of living in India is the lowest in the world, still it is true that India's development is remarkable. Although no one denies that during the last five years poverty has increased, still it is true that the campaign "Garibi Hatao" [Remove Poverty] has been immensely successful. Although the statistics of the U.N. show that almost 78 percent of the total population of this country do not receive adequate food, still who can deny that democracy and freedom of speech exist in India?
>
> (Act 1, p. 9)

Not content with deluding the people about democracy and *"Garibi Hatao"* (Indira Gandhi's catchy slogan), the media spreads false rumors about the repressive state of China hoping to divert the people's attention away from their real problems.

Dutt's use of the announcement is strategic. It enables him to speak directly to the audience in a language that contrasts sharply with the dialogue on stage. The action of the play literally ceases as Palit switches on the radio. The audience is compelled to concentrate on the words of the announcement. Dutt uses a propagandist device, the interruption of stage action by an announcement, in order to comment on the nature of propaganda itself, the devious logic and false promises of the central government.

After these announcements, the play returns abruptly to Manibhushan and his fantasies. There is a sudden intrusion in Manibhushan's hallucinatory world as a dapper figure clad in white pajamas and *kurta* (shirt) appears mysteriously from nowhere and introduces himself as Deb. It is only natural that this figment of Manibhushan's imagination should speak an appropriately ornate verse.

I am only yours, Manibhushan,
You have created me with every detail of your mind.
I am beside myself with joy at my own beauty—
Whatever you cherished and wasted is all within me,
You are my birth-giver, O poet of poets!
I am an imperishable allegory of your life-verse.

(Act 1, p. 13)

Deb is at once a model for Manibhushan and an apotheosis of his suppressed virtues. He is a possibility of what Manibhushan could have been. Not only does he provide a psychological dimension to Manibhushan's disillusionment, Deb is also a source of the most irresistible comedy. In the first place, Manibhushan refuses to accept his presence with equanimity. He scowls, glowers, and rages at Deb, who smiles mischievously at his alter ego rather like a playful philosopher. Manibhushan's discomfiture increases when he realizes that Deb is invisible to everyone but himself. Attempting to escape the tormenting, yet jocular, presence of Deb, Manibhushan goes to Palit's house.

There are at least three different theatrical styles in the confrontation between Palit and Manibhushan. First, there is an aggressive exchange of words as Manibhushan refuses to accept yet another criminal assignment, the murder of Swapan, the CPI(M) party worker who is pursued by the police in the second half of the play. When Palit's colleagues intimidate and blackmail Manibhushan, he extricates himself from the scene and speaks the following lines (ostensibly addressed to Palit) directly to the audience:

MANI: You found us oppressed by unemployment. Then you came and told us that we'd have to drive the CPM people out of the locality, and then you'd give us jobs. Day after day, we attacked them under police vigil. But still we didn't get jobs. Then you said, we would have to wait till the election. . . . My boys agreed and took to arson and fraud. We kidnapped the election-agents, changed the ballot boxes, guarded the election-booths with guns scaring away people, ransacked the booths, and stamped on false ballot papers. [shouting] But we didn't get jobs and are still burned by hunger.

(Act 1, p. 14)

This speech appeals directly to the sentiments of the audience. It is performed with all the conventions and gestures of pathos—the husky voice, the quivering lip, the trembling hand, and the occasional vibrato. Manibhushan attempts to persuade the audience (and in all probability succeeds) that he would not have been a *goonda* if he had been employed in some capacity or the other.

Turning to Palit, Manibhushan pleads for a job and affirms his desire to lead a different life. At this point, when the scene threatens to become either violent or melodramatic, Dutt inserts a touch of characteristic playfulness by making Deb, a silent onlooker for the first half of the scene, interrupt Manibhushan's statements to Palit. As Manibhushan gets increasingly annoyed by these interruptions, Palit gets increasingly disturbed by Manibhushan's responses to an invisible presence.

MANI [*to Deb*]:   Keep quiet. Don't interrupt what you don't understand.

PALIT [*to Mani*]:   W-h-a-t? What do you mean! Why are you abusing me this way? That's not right . . .

MANI [*to Palit*]:   I still didn't say if I would go or not [to murder Swapan].

DEB [*to Mani*]:   Your father will go.

MANI [*to Deb*]:   Watch it!

PALIT [*to Mani*]:   W-h-a-t?

MANI [*to Palit*]:   Damn you, I mean, not you, Sir. Our hunger is almost a whip in your hand. As you whip, we become your servants.

DEB [*to Palit*]:   Right you are. He can do anything for his stomach. His father was much the same.

MANI [*to Deb*]:   Don't abuse me by referring to my father. I'm warning you.

PALIT [*to Mani*]:   When did I refer to your father?

MANI [*to Palit*]:   No, Sir, you can't follow anything.

DEB [*to Mani*]:   Only you can!

MANI [*to Deb*]:   Now I'll slap you, just watch it!

(Act 1, p. 16)

The scene ends in a frenetic chase with Manibhushan attempting to attack Deb while a panic-stricken Palit runs wildly around the stage.

After this farcical sequence, the second half of the play begins on a seemingly somber note. We see a group of lower-middle-class people listening to a political speech with their hands raised. The speech, which exploits every rhetorical device in demagoguery, signifies absolutely nothing. One of the onlookers, a genial old man named Krishnachura asks the *goondas* and police surveying the scene if he can lower his hands. "I am not protesting," he claims with a disarming smile, "but if our hands are raised this way, people might think there is no democracy in this country, which is of course China's false propaganda." He continues to steal the limelight from the political speaker saying, "Moreover, according to medical science, if hands are raised for too long, the blood circulation is so badly affected that the ears begin to throb and it becomes impossible to hear lectures." This speech exemplifies the kind of humor and political satire that Dutt demonstrates in *Dushopner Nagari*. It is more wry and playful than the savage satiric humor of *Barricade*.

Krishnachura (played by Satya Banerjee, the most versatile actor in Dutt's company) is one of Dutt's most loveable creations. He exudes a middle-class warmth and geniality that are irresistible to a Bengali audience. He is just a man on the street with no particular political affiliations. He enjoys a good cup of tea and some lively gossip. With police oppression in Calcutta, however, he finds that he has to change his leisurely habits. He has to be more wary about whom he speaks to in his favorite tea shop and how he addresses the ubiquitous *goondas*. He also finds it absolutely necessary to place a telephone directory between his vest and *punjabi* (outer garment) in order to protect himself from the blows of the policemen. Though he is no revolutionary, Dutt makes him indirectly support the Communist movement.

In the course of the play, Krishnachura protects Swapan, the pursued CPI(M) worker, from the police on two occasions. At one point, Krishnachura improvises as a palmist, reading the hand of a Hindi-speaking policeman and prophesying all kinds of terrible calamities for him and his family. While the policeman is reduced to tears, Swapan escapes surreptitiously. On another occasion, Girin, the toughest of the *goondas*, chases Swapan into a tea shop. Krishnachura placates the *goonda*, flatters him, and makes him drink glass after glass of wine. In the meantime, Swapan disguises himself as the owner of the tea shop, wearing the kind of fake beard associated with *jatra* actors. All goes well till the real owner of the tea shop enters. Girin, in his drunken haze, believes that he is hallucinating when he sees the two bearded men. Dutt improvises on the situation with comic virtuosity, making Swapan and the owner of the tea shop enter and exit from a single door in quick succession. Double takes and gags abound with split-second timing. Krishnachura informs the bewildered *goonda* that the two bearded men are twins. As he continues to improvise with even greater vehemence, Girin passes out in a state of shock.

Undeniably, there is a great deal of farce in *Dushopner Nagari* that has no political significance. It is simply enjoyable for what it is. It does not refer to anything outside itself. Certainly, it is very different from the kind of "convulsion of the diaphragm" that Walter Benjamin talks about in the *The Author as Producer* that "produces better opportunities for thought than convulsion of the soul." Though Dutt directs the laughter in *Dushopner Nagari* against the agents of the ruling class, he frequently indulges in it without making a statement or stimulating a thought.

The farcical episodes in his play are important for structural rather than ideological reasons. Very often they highlight scenes that follow them. For instance, after Krishnachura reduces the Hindi-speaking policeman to tears, Girin and his gang enter the tea shop abruptly and search the place for Swapan. In the meantime, Swapan's brother, who is blind, enters the room oblivious to their presence. Without wasting any time, the *goondas* surround him and stab him to death. The murder is shocking more on account of its brevity than its intensity. It is performed in less than a minute, following a long farcical sequence that was leisurely entertaining.

In a similar way, Manibhushan's death follows abruptly after the second farcical episode involving the two bearded owners of the tea shop. Here again, we are lulled by the laughter provided by Krishnachura and Girin's drunkenness. Suddenly, we see Manibhushan, tense and overwrought, on the uppermost platform of the stage. The tonality of the play changes instantly. As Manibhushan waits to disclose incriminating evidence against the exploiters to a reporter, he rhapsodizes about what he could have been. "I could have created waves of questions in many new ponds," he fantasizes in the imaginary role of a learned professor with a large following. While he is in this delirious state, the police appear ominously and begin to converge on him. Manibhushan realizes that he has been betrayed by one of his closest associates, who has left him with a rifle containing no bullets. With predatory stealth, the police climb up to where he is and speak to him with quiet consideration. They ask him to go home. As he turns away from them and slowly inches his way downstage, the police fire. Manibhushan's body crumples onto the stage.

As the curtain slowly parts, two of Palit's employees, the editor and the Youth Congress leader, step in front of the stage and mourn Manibhushan's death in a hypocritically lugubrious manner. But the play does not end on this ironic note. Dutt concludes *Dushopner Nagari* with Girin terrorizing the helpless Krishnachura, who is predictably chastened and deprived of his wit. Just when we are preparing ourselves for a dying speech by Krishnachura, Dutt spares us the melodrama by making Swapan and his gang enter the scene of action and mercilessly thrash Girin. There is a scramble of activity onstage. Swapan steps forward and sings the concluding song of *Dushopner Nagari*, urging the people of Calcutta not to remain silent about their oppression but to resist the exploiters actively.

Despite this somewhat perfunctory conclusion, the play does not leave Dutt's audience craving for more action. After three hours of nonstop farce, violence, and political satire, they have received more than their money's worth of entertainment. But what does the play provide in terms of their political education? What does the audience learn in the course of the play? It seems to me that Dutt succeeds in merely confirming popular assumptions about the brutality of the police and the corruption of the central government. Though he attempts to show how the agents of the ruling class operate, the treatment (particularly in the second half of the play) is too farcical and simplistic to be taken seriously. Palit disappears after the first half of the play and the police become increasingly incompetent and dumb. If only Dutt could treat his villains with some complexity, his plays would provide more food for thought.

Dushopner Nagari does not even have a revolutionary hero of any significance. Swapan, the CPI(M) worker, does very little apart from sing two stirring songs. There is Manibhushan, of course, but his predicament is so romanticized that it is difficult to believe that he can conceive of anyone but himself. Besides, he is so victimized by the system that he does not operate with many choices. We are asked to take his dilemma for granted. *Dushopner Nagari* would be a richer play if Dutt's attitude to Manibhushan were more contradictory. It is not enough to present the *goonda* as victim. This may be an appropriate perspective for melodrama but it is not sufficiently complex for the "revolutionary theater" that Dutt advocates.

It seems to me that the play is ultimately limited by its commercial conventions. Its virtuosity overwhelms its message. It is too engaging to be effective. Though one cannot deny that Dutt evokes the politics of terror in Calcutta most vividly, one wishes that he would analyze the political turmoil in West Bengal more stringently.

THE PRICE OF ENTERTAINMENT

What is missing in Dutt's theater is precisely some form of sustained analysis of the political issues raised in his plays. Often dichotomies and oppositions are juxtaposed only too predictably. Dutt himself has lamented his predilection for creating "over-simplified, one-sided spectacles of Good versus Evil."[40] The problem with these spectacles is that there is nothing significant to be learned from them. Their outcome is inevitable. In addition, their dramatization of the people's struggle is so grossly simplified that it trivializes the intricate processes of revolutions in history.

In recent years, Dutt has acknowledged the necessity of providing a dialectical view of the revolutionary struggle, where the conflicts within the revolutionaries can be highlighted as much as their commitment to forming a "people's democracy." Unfortunately, very few productions of the People's Little Theater can be even tentatively described as "dialectical" in their visions of history and the class struggle. Even a play like *Sanyasir Tarabari* (which Dutt claims is a dialectical envisioning of the Sanyasi rebellion against the British) is essentially a historical extravaganza involving good and evil forces, where the "good"—the Sanyasis and Fakirs—commit a few dehumanized acts, and the "bad"—the British forces—have occasional moments of dignity and grace.

Dutt exaggerates when he describes these characters as "complexes of warring contradictions."[41] It is surely not "dialectical," as he imagines, to show the Indian soldiers fighting and betraying each other, and to depict one solitary English officer metamorphosing from an aesthete to a demagogue. Such transformations may be dynamic but they are very different from the contradictions that constitute the dialectically structured characters of Brecht.

This is not to say that Dutt should write characters like Mother Courage and Galy Gay (even if he could). In fact, he has argued very persuasively that Brecht's theater does not fulfill the expectations and needs of the working-class audiences in Bengal. He has also affirmed that the revolutionary theater of Bengal has to find its models in *jatra* and the historical plays of Girish Chandra Ghosh, not in the plays of Bertolt Brecht.

While this advocacy of indigenous models is surely pragmatic and intellectually sound, it is unlikely that the conventions of *jatra* or Ghosh's historical plays can be used to project a dialectical vision of history. These conventions—the climaxes, the songs, the religious iconography—are much too operatic and hallucinatory in effect to sustain any analysis of the contradictions in a historical situation. Relying on the principles of empathy and emotional amplification, the very structures of *jatra* and Ghosh's historical plays (so appropriate for the "revolutionary" spectacles of Dutt) seem to resist dialectical thinking.

If Dutt wishes to explore a more dialectical form of revolutionary theater, he needs to differentiate it more sharply from the agitprop theater he understands so well. In a dialectical theater, a specific political event is never examined for the sole purpose of rousing an audience to take an immediate political stance. On the contrary, the event is situated in a much larger historical perspective so that its contradictions are illuminated both in themselves and in relation to each other. As George Szanto has observed, a dialectical theater "attempts to demystify, by depicting separately, interactively, and always clearly, the basic elements which comprise a confused social or historical situation."[42]

Clearly, this theater is far removed from Dutt's "revolutionary theater," where emotion predominates and melodrama overwhelms commentary. In no play by Dutt can one seriously question the contradictions of his revolutionary heroes because they are simply not examined in any detail. Though he has clearly avoided the stereotypes of the "perfect proletarian hero" (examined earlier in relation to I.P.T.A. productions), he still tends to glorify his own more robust heroes in a somewhat simplistic manner.

Perhaps it is this idealization of his heroes that has prevented Dutt from writing a "proletarian myth of revolution," a fact that he grandiloquently acknowledges though not without asserting that he is working in that direction. Whether or not he will create a true "myth" (instead of a patriotic nineteenth-century saga with mythical figures) is open to question. It might be more practical for him to stop fantasizing about myths and concentrate instead on developing his own models of "revolutionary theater." If there is one issue that he needs to question with greater rigor, it is the function of entertainment in a theater that claims to "preach revolution" and "rediscover history."

Certainly, the entertainment value of Dutt's plays cannot be denied. We have seen how ingeniously he has exploited the commercial theater tradition in plays as diverse as *Kallol, Ajeya Vietnam, Surya Shikar, Tiner Talwar, Barricade*, and *Dushopner Nagari*. While a few of these plays (notably, *Ajeya Vietnam* and *Barricade*) exemplify the paradox that Dutt is most true to his revolutionary principles when he is blatantly entertaining, most of them do not quite sustain it. On the contrary, they entertain at the expense of enlightening an audience about its alienation and oppression, its position in the class struggle, and its relation to the processes of production.

At this stage in Dutt's enormously successful career, when his plays are regularly performed to packed houses, it is necessary to question his reliance on the entertainment provided by the commercial theater to raise the revolutionary consciousness of the people. While I believe that it is necessary, even essential, for the revolutionary theater to entertain, it can only do so with any integrity in the process of enlightening an audience. As Brecht states so succinctly in his essay "Theater for Pleasure or Theater for Instruction," "there is such a thing as pleasurable learning, cheerful and militant learning." Unfortunately, in most of Dutt's plays the "learning," if any, is scarcely pleasurable while the "pleasure" provided by the entertainment of his plays clearly dominates the learning process.

Dutt needs to reexamine the function of entertainment in his revolutionary theater. He needs to ask himself if this theater can develop within a commercial framework and to question whether he has exhausted the revolutionary possibilities of the commercial theater. Certainly, the commercial possibilities of the revolutionary theater in Bengal have never been more favorable. But it is for this very reason that Dutt ought to look beyond the commercial theater and search for new models of the revolutionary theater.

I do not doubt that Dutt is eminently capable of inventing these models. His talent is unique, his temperament inimitable, his theater unparalleled for its virtuosity and verve in West Bengal. But it should also be acknowledged that the recent productions of the People's Little Theater frequently follow a predictable pattern. Dutt seems to have come to the end of an extraordinarily active phase in his career. It is difficult to speculate in what direction he will move. One can only hope that he will continue to work toward the creation of a more rigorous and uncompromising form of revolutionary theater.

A scene from *Barricade*, with Utpal Dutt as Bruno (seated right)

Badal Sircar in rehearsal

Utpal Dutt at home

A scene from *Angar* (Coal) 1959

Bashi Khabar (Stale News) in rehearsal

Bhoma at Curzon Park

Dutt's *jatra, March to Delhi*

Spartacus at Angamancha

Michil at Curzon Park

3
The Third Theater
of Badal Sircar

An Alternative Theater

The emergence of the Third Theater is a significant development in the contemporary Bengali theater. Created by Badal Sircar, one of the most dedicated theater workers in India, it is a movement barely ten years old that challenges the premises of the commercial theater and indirectly questions the viability of the revolutionary theater practised by Utpal Dutt. It is the most rigorously noncommercial political theater in India today. Not only does Sircar believe that it is possible to work outside the commercial theater tradition, he feels that it is necessary to do so.

The Economics of the Third Theater

An extraordinarily committed man, who views his theater as a form of social work, Sircar is obsessed by its integrity. He firmly believes that he cannot be true to his principles by working within the economic structure of the commercial theater. His intense distrust of money makes him question seemingly innocuous procedures like publicity and the sale of tickets. The idea of "selling" a play to a bourgeois audience is repellent to him. Even more offensive is the thought of protesting against those very members of the establishment who sponsor the commercial theater. Sircar emphasizes that the Third Theater cannot rely on the establishment for its economic stability. He is only too aware of the compromises a political group has to make when it relies on managers, publicity agents, and grants commissioners to promote its theater.

Rejecting such temptations of the commercial theater as mass audiences, flattering reviews, and fame, Sircar advocates a "poor theater": "poor" not only in the sense in which Grotowski uses the word (when the theater is stripped of all accessories extraneous to the actor-spectator relationship), but "poor" in a very literal sense. A production by Sircar's group, Satabdi, invariably costs less than a hundred rupees (approximately thirteen dollars). The administrative expenses of the group are minimal. Since the plays are performed in rooms, Sircar does not have to rent one of the available theaters in Calcutta, which charge as much as twelve hundred rupees for a single performance. Consequently, he need not rely on government grants and expensive publicity in order to maintain his theater.

Sircar also has the freedom to reduce the cost of his tickets to one rupee (approximately a dime) and to waive this admission fee if a spectator cannot afford to pay it. This enables many people who do not generally go to the theater to see all the plays in his repertoire and, at times, see the same play more than once. Sircar knows that the poverty of his theater is its strength. Not only has it enabled him to survive when most theater groups in Calcutta are burdened by the rise in their production costs, it has enhanced his awareness of theater as a "human act." Defending his advocacy of "free theater," Sircar says:

> Free theater attracted us, not merely because our countrymen are poor and can ill afford the price of admission, but also because we came to the belief that in theater both the performers and the spectators should have equal status. Theater is a human act, hence all human beings involved—whether as performers or as spectators— should be free in their relationship with one another, and no external factor should affect that relationship. When admission is charged, the spectators automatically get the role of buyers, and the performers that of sellers, even though the receipts may not be for private profit.[1]

Whatever the validity of Sircar's rationales for a free (or almost free) theater, it must be emphasized that the majority of the people who see his plays in Calcutta are predominantly middle class and

can well afford to pay a rupee for a ticket. The buyer–seller relationship persists in Sircar's theater despite the minimal cost of the
ticket. In fact, without the system of tickets, his theater would not
be able to function. Since his plays are performed in rooms that
seat fewer than a hundred spectators, there has to be some organizing principle by which the number of people entering the room
can be restricted. Most performances are sold out.

The popularity of Sircar's theater, which lacks any publicity
apart from word of mouth, is the source of much resentment
among Bengali theater groups in Calcutta. Utpal Dutt in particular has referred snidely to Sircar's theater on many occasions,
emphasizing that, "Their apparent poverty and disinterest in publicity are a camouflage which fools many honest intellectuals.
They [the Third Theater] are a movement supported by the reactionary *kulaks* [*sic*] in New Delhi, to oppress the powerful political
theater in Bengal. Their object is to confront the political theater
with confusing intellectual acrobatics."[2] Referring to such statements, Sircar quietly asserts that theater practitioners like Dutt
are suffering from a "guilt complex." "Satabdi," says Sircar, "has
proved that it is possible to do theater without grants or money. It
is more free than other theater groups and, consequently, more
honest."[3]

The Aesthetics of the Third Theater

"Aesthetics" may be too grand a word for the totally unpretentious
dramaturgy of the Third Theater. Spartan in its simplicity, it dispenses with almost all the accessories one associates with the commercial theater—sets, lights, costumes, sound, and makeup. When
I once questioned Sircar about the "techniques" of the group, he
responded sharply, "We don't think about techniques. We think
about what we have to communicate and what is the best way of
communicating what we have to say."[4] Though this response is
somewhat disingenuous (the "best way of communicating" surely
involves some kind of technical skill), one cannot deny that the
power of Sircar's theater lies in the direct conveyance of its message.

When his actors confront the audience, look them in the eye, and tell them that in such-and-such village a man is dying because he has no means of subsistence and no one to help him, it is difficult to be indifferent to this fact. There is nothing to interfere with it—no spectacle, no obtrusive acting style, no melodrama. The spareness of Sircar's theater is what makes it so effective: it compels the audience to concentrate on what the actors are saying. In this respect, the plays of Satabdi are more instructive than the "revolutionary" spectacles of the People's Little Theater, where the message is generally overwhelmed by the proliferation of scenic effects, bursts of deafening music, and loud rhetorical passages.

Another crucial difference in the aesthetics of these two groups concerns the size of their audiences. It is very easy to lose oneself in the mass audiences of Dutt and react uncritically to the action of the play. While a production by the People's Little Theater is invariably exhilarating (rather like a soccer match), it does not sufficiently challenge an audience to rethink its assumptions about life and society. The basic problem with Dutt's theater is that it is too large to confront the spectators as individuals. The theater of Badal Sircar, on the other hand, can concentrate on the spectators as individuals because it is much smaller in scale. It takes place in one room where there are barely a hundred people. The eye contact between Sircar's audience and actors facilitates a most immediate form of communication. Questions are directly addressed to the audience, who are made to confront their indifference to particular issues.

Samik Bandyopadhyay, the most perceptive critic of the Bengali theater, believes that this proximity between audience and performer in Sircar's theater is what makes it so much more effective than Dutt's "epic" productions where "one just reacts with the crowd."[5] Countering Dutt's proud assertations that he has performed for twenty thousand spectators at a time, Bandyopadhyay asks: "What does that prove?" Is a political theater more effective because it addresses thousands of people rather than a hundred? Are the loud cheers of a crowd more reliable indications that a play is making them think than the attentive silence of a few people? What is more important—the size of an audience or the impact of a play on the lives of people?

Responding to Dutt's predilection for mass audiences, Bandyopadhyay makes an interesting parallel with the expansion of the

Marxist party in Bengal. "On the one hand, the Party is bigger than ever with a large following," he says, "but are those who are following the Party really thinking about Marxist precepts or are they just going along with the current?" This is an astute question that highlights the essential limitation of mass-scale movements. Just as the relation between an individual and the Party flounders with the expansion of the Party, so also the connection between a spectator and the spectacle on stage becomes increasingly nebulous with the participation of thousands of spectators.

Apart from emphasizing the sheer size of his audience, Dutt claims that his theater reaches the working class while Sircar's theater is "too intellectual for the people."[6] Such statements convey Dutt's assurance, even arrogance, that he knows what the people want. He needs to acknowledge, however, that there is more than one way of doing political theater and that the working class can respond to a more "intellectual" theater than *jatra* or the productions of the People's Little Theater.

Though Sircar's theater focuses on the lower middle class in Calcutta—their struggle for survival and indifference to the poverty in rural areas—Satabdi has performed many plays in the working-class districts of Bengal and the villages of Sundarbans (where Sircar has conducted workshops). The audience response in these impoverished areas where the people are predominantly illiterate has been most enthusiastic. Even Sircar is somewhat surprised that the villagers were not bewildered by the absence in his theater of traditional conventions such as plot, characters, farcical interludes, melodramatic gestures, and ornate diction. On the contrary, they responded positively to his innovative theatrical devices: a fragmented script, a chorus of voices, stylized movement, and non-verbal acting techniques. Recalling the enthusiastic reception to his somewhat abstract production of *Spartacus*, Sircar emphasizes that, "The people often understood the main points and spirit of the play more than the so called urban intelligentsia."[7]

The Politics of the Third Theater

There are no red flags in Badal Sircar's theater, no Marxist jargon, no propaganda for any party. This theater is not explicitly political. It avoids all the stereotypes associated with bourgeois theater

groups who propagate revolution with lectures on dialectical materialism, quotations from Mao, glorified accounts of the Communist movement, and exhortations for the good of the people. The
Third Theater asserts its political independence by resisting party
politics. Though its plays frequently deal with the false promises,
hypocrisies, and the corruption of politicians, there are no specific
references to the misdeeds of the Congress party or the CPI(M)
party. The Third Theater does not side with one party against
another. It is less interested in featuring controversial personalities
and topical events than in dramatizing the contradictions of politics and their effect on the lives of the people. It is the individual
caught in the network of politics who concerns Sircar.

Apart from maintaining a scrupulous distance from the exigencies of party politics, Sircar does not contend that the problems of
the people can be solved by the removal of "reactionary" elements
within a particular party or, more extravagantly, by the overthrow
of the "repressive forces" in the central government. His theater
does not pretend to be militant. It does not incite its audience to
think in terms of necessary violence. Instead of advocating strikes,
lockouts, and the destruction of government property, it is content
with merely disturbing the consciousness of its spectators.

One leaves a play by Satabdi acutely aware of the exploitation
and injustices that pervade life in Calcutta and rural Bengal. Sircar makes his audience confront their indifference to the chaos and
corruption that characterize urban life. He never fails to emphasize that his spectators are responsible for the world they live in.
Instead of exaggerating the threat of the exploiters and the callousness of the political leaders (as Dutt tends to do), Sircar focuses on
the callousness of the middle class and their capacity to watch the
suffering of the people without doing anything about it.

Despite his attack on the bourgeois values and innate selfishness
of his spectators, Sircar never fails to appeal to their humanity.
Instead of advocating revolution with platitudinous speeches, he
urges them to feel more compassion for the underprivileged, who
have been denied the basic necessities of life. In this respect, Sircar
represents a kind of radical humanism one associates with William
Blake, who believed that no revolution was possible in the social
and political structure until men were prepared to break "the
mind forged manacles" which governed their lives. If there is any-

thing Sircar preaches to his spectators—he is the least dogmatic of thinkers in the Bengali theater—it is the necessity of changing their own lives before endeavoring to change the world.

The Early Career of Badal Sircar

Sircar committed himself to the Third Theater in the early seventies. Prior to that, he was actively involved in a predominantly nonpolitical theater and widely recognized as a playwright. Though his early career lies outside the scope of this discussion, I will deal with certain aspects of his dramaturgy and thought that he later developed in his exploration of the Third Theater.

It is difficult to believe that Sircar began his career in the late fifties writing domestic comedies and science fiction fantasies based on the plots of popular Hollywood films like *Monkey Business*. As an employee in the Town Planning section of the Calcutta Corporation, he probably had little time for anything but a superficial involvement in the theater. He merely wrote plays to amuse his friends in a club called Chakra, which has been described by Samik Bandyophadhyay as "a serious group of people who did not take the theater too seriously."

In 1957, Sircar went abroad for the first time and saw a great deal of theater, including three productions by Joan Littlewood— *The Hostage, A Taste of Honey,* and *Oh! What a Lovely War!*— that inspired him to think in terms of the theater-in-the-round. His two-year stay in London, however, was significant for another reason. Away from home for the first time, Sircar maintained a diary containing poems and snatches of dialogue that were the beginnings of the most inspired Indian play written in the sixties, *Evam Indrajit* (And Indrajit). It is the *Waiting for Godot* of the Bengali theater.

Though Sircar believed that his play was "a private piece of writing" not meant to be staged, it was spontaneously received by the theatrical community in Bengal, who discovered in the protagonist Indrajit all their dreams and compromises and moments of futility. One could say that *Evam Indrajit* is about an enlightened middle-class youth in Bengal who passes through various stages in his life unable to fulfill his dreams, and yet unable to accept the triviality of the world around him epitomized by three representations of the bourgeoisie, Amal, Vimal, and Kamal. Their names rhyme to suggest their uniformity. In the final moments of the play, when Indrajit attempts to become a "Nirmal" by accepting the materialism and mundanity of everyday life, he is reminded of his destiny by the Writer, a commentatorlike character who has attempted to write a play about Indrajit through *Evam Indrajit.* The final section of the play is worth quoting at length.

WRITER: Indrajit . . .

INDRAJIT: You must be mistaken. I am Nirmal Kumar Ray.

WRITER: Don't you recognize me, Indrajit?

INDRAJIT: Who are you? . . . The Writer?

WRITER: I can't finish the play, Indrajit . . .

INDRAJIT: What's the point of finishing it? It will never be complete. Its end is its beginning . . .

WRITER: Yet one has to write.

INDRAJIT: It's your job to write. So write away. What have I to do with it? I am Nirmal.

WRITER: But you are not looking for a promotion—or building a house—or developing a business scheme. How can you be Nirmal?

INDRAJIT: But . . . I'm just an ordinary man.

WRITER: That does not make you Nirmal. I am ordinary too— common! Yet I am not Nirmal. You and I can't be Nirmals.

INDRAJIT: Then how shall we live?

WRITER: Walk! Be on the road! For us there is only the road . . . so walk on. We are the cursed spirits of Sisyphus. We have to push the rock to the top—even if it just rolls down.

INDRAJIT: Must we, even when we know?

WRITER: Yes, we must, even when we know. We have no hope because we know the future. Our past is with our future. We know what's behind us will also be ahead of us.

INDRAJIT: Must we still live?

WRITER: We must, we must, we must. We must live. We must walk. We know no sacred places. Yet we must go on with the pilgrimage. . . . There's no respite.[8]

This section, taken out of context, may mislead the Western reader unfamiliar with the play to believe that *Evam Indrajit* is a tendentious play that ends on a note of impossible determination and hope. However, there are moments of utter despair in the play which Sircar crystallizes with a laconic simplicity that is his forte as a playwright. Some examples of Indrajit's disillusionment:

My wife looks after the house. I work in the office. My wife goes to a film. I go with her. My wife goes to her parents' house. I eat in a restaurant. She comes back. I go marketing. (P. 54)

There is no world beyond our geography. At least not in this country. (P. 38)

I walk between the rails of the railway line. It's a straight line. I look back—the iron rails meet in a point far away. I look ahead—the same two iron rails meet in a point far away. The farther I move the more the points move too. What is behind is ahead. There is no distance between the past and the future. What's there in the past is in the future as well. . . . I used to hope for the arrival of the train. . . . But nothing happens. Because no train runs on those rails. (P. 55)

It is through such "abstractions of situations and attitudes" that Sircar explores "an area of middle-class consciousness."[9] Over the years, he has perfected this "abstract" mode of writing where the words resonate ideas rather than personal feelings.

Many of the rhetorical techniques of Sircar's recent plays can be traced back to passages in *Evam Indrajit*. For instance, there is the juxtaposition of disparate comments which the actors state mechanically without seeming to comprehend them.

KAMAL: Power corrupts . . .

AMAL: Politics is dirty . . .

VIMAL: Just concern yourself with your own work.

KAMAL: If I am well, all is well.

AMAL: There has been no promotion.

VIMAL: The living quarters are terrible.

KAMAL: Business is bad.

AMAL: My family is ill.

VIMAL: My son failed again.

KAMAL: My father has died.

AMAL: Bloody shame.

VIMAL: Damned nuisance.

KAMAL: Ugh!

AMAL: Vimal . . .

VIMAL: Kamal . . .

KAMAL: Amal . . .

(P. 47)

Then there is an accumulation of phrases and non sequiturs that Sircar generally uses with ironic effect:

WRITER: [*in the role of the boss*] Hello—hello—yes—yes—the
          Board of Directors—conference—budget—Annual Report—
          yes—yes—bye! . . . With reference to the above letter—I shall
          be obliged if—forward us at your earliest convenience—let this
          office know immediately—fifteenth ultimo—twenty-fifth in-
          stant—thanking you—assuring you of our best cooperation—
          yours sincerely, sincerely yours.

(P. 33)

There is also the repetition of words to create an effect of incanta-tion:

VOICES: [*whispering in the dark*]
          Amal, Vimal, Kamal, and Indrajit
          Vimal, Kamal, and Indrajit
          Kamal and Indrajit
          And Indrajit
          Indrajit
          Indrajit
          Indrajit

(P. 7)

Apart from rhetorical similarities, the depiction of middle-class lassitude and inertia continues to be a major theme in Satabdi's productions. However, Sircar's attitude to the middle class has changed significantly since *Evam Indrajit*. In this play, the Writer clearly represents Sircar's reticence to speak about the masses when he says, "I've written many plays. I want to write many more. But . . . I know nothing about the suffering masses. Nothing about the toiling peasants. Nothing about the sweating coalminers" (p. 6). This reticence has not entirely disappeared in Sircar's recent plays but, at least, there is an attempt on his part to address the poverty and exploitation of the masses with a candor that was not possible for him in his early career.

When Indrajit confronts poverty, he can react to it only with an incoherent, somewhat helpless rage. The following section from *Evam Indrajit* epitomizes the inability of a middle-class youth to surmount his guilt about poverty.

INDRAJIT: You know, one day at the bus-stop a boy of about seven started pestering me. Wanted to polish my shoes, he said. But he had a child on his waist and it was playing with the polishing rag. . . . I didn't get my shoes polished. I chased him away. If he had bothered me I would probably have beaten him.

MANASI: But why?

INDRAJIT: I don't know. I don't know who should be beaten. I know I shouldn't hit him—still I would have. I could not accept him. I can't accept the rule either—the rule by which a boy of eight with a child in his arms has to go polishing shoes.

(P. 22)

It seems unlikely that Sircar could write such a scene today. Or if he did, he would probably juxtapose it with another scene or attitude that would be more pragmatic in its response to poverty. Such juxtapositions will be examined later in the chapter, but for the moment, let us continue with our critical survey of Sircar's early career.

The Trilogy: *Baki Itihas, Tringsha Satabdi, Shesh Nei*

Evam Indrajit was not the only play written by Sircar when he was away from India. A particularly prolific period in his playwriting career occurred between 1966 and 1967 when he wrote six plays while working as a town planner in Nigeria. Three of his early plays—*Bagh* (Tiger), *Jadi Aar Ekbar* (If There Were Another Chance), and *Pralap* (Mad Speech)—were inspired by Murray Schisgal's *The Tiger*, J. M. Barrier's *Dear Brutus*, and James Saunders' *Next Time I'll Sing To You*, respectively. While these plays are not inconsequential, they are far from what Sircar believes is his central concern as a playwright—nothing less exacting than "the responsibility of mankind for the events of our times."[10] The horror of Hiroshima, in particular, obsesses Sircar in at least three plays which can be read as a trilogy—*Baki Itihas* (The Remainder of History), *Tringsha Satabdi* (The Thirtieth Century), and *Shesh Nei* (There's No End).

Baki Itihas is a particularly fascinating play in its juxtaposition of domestic comedy and bleak vision of history. Like *Evam Indrajit*, it focuses on the educated middle class in Calcutta but, unlike the earlier play, it goes beyond an exploration of middle-class responsibilities and traumas. In the final scene, Sircar presents his audience with a frenzied hallucination of oppression in world history.

The first two acts do not prepare an audience for the final statement of the play. They are deceptively self-contained and domestic. We see Basanti, a story writer, and her husband, Sharadindu, a lecturer of Bengali literature, arguing about unpaid electricity bills and discussing different plans on how to spend their Sunday. They eventually decide to improvise stories on a common subject —the suicide of an acquaintance which has been briefly reported in the newspaper. Their fictionalized versions of the suicide are enacted in the first two acts of *Baki Itihas*. (Sircar acknowledges that the idea of dramatizing a number of versions of the same story was inspired by Kurosawa's *Rashomon*). While one version of the suicide is interpreted in a sensational manner, the other is more derivative of Ibsen's psychological drama. Once the versions are performed, the husband and wife squabble over the relative merits of their interpretations. The audience does not expect the play to transcend its theatrical conceit.

Suddenly, in the third act, Sharadindu encounters a mysterious figure who introduces himself as the dead Seetanath. Sircar provides no rationale for the intrusion of this phantom of death into the domestic framework of the play. During the course of the confrontation between the two men, it becomes increasingly clear that Seetanath is the "private self" of Sharadindu that has been suppressed. The confrontation becomes traumatic for Sharadindu when Seetanath hands him an album of pictures depicting the history of oppression in the world from the building of the pyramids and the persecution of the Christians to more recent calamities of history like Auschwitz, Hiroshima, and Vietnam.

When Sharadindu claims that he cannot accept the history of mankind, his "private self" goads him to examine this history more rigorously and not to forget it in his preoccupation with academic and domestic concerns. Unable to face the burden of history, Sharadindu asks the obvious question: "What can I do about it?" Seetanath answers coldly:

> You can't do anything. I couldn't do anything. Nobody can do anything. Oppressions, killings, riots, wars—all these will continue. The man who is satisfied with two meals a day will pierce another man with a bayonet. The scientist who cannot bear the pain of an animal will create a weapon to kill a million people. They are all men. . . . Like you. They have all tried to live on some meaning or the other that they have given to life.[11]

Listening to the tradition of oppression and bestiality that he has inherited as a human being, Sharadindu laments the absurdity of his existence. Seetanath taunts him to commit suicide, whereupon Sharadindu yells, "Go away, Sharadindu." Seetanath has to remind him, "I'm Seetanath."

Sharadindu goes through the motions of preparing to commit suicide rather like the ficitonal characters he and his wife had created in the play's first two acts. The lights come on and a friend rushes into the room and jubilantly informs Sharadindu that he has received a promotion in his job. Sharadindu reacts to the news with his face buried in his hands, unable to reconcile his craving for security with his horrifying awareness of the oppression in history.

Baki Itihas is not one of Sircar's favorite plays. He says that if he had to rewrite it, he would intensify Sharadindu's guilt. In his next play, *Tringsha Satabdi* (The Thirtieth Century), he moved beyond

the question of guilt to that of responsibility. To what extent are we
—the peace-loving members of the middle class, secure in our little
worlds—responsible for a calamity like Hiroshima? This is the
enormous question that Sircar dares to confront in his play. Based
on a terrifyingly vivid account of the Hiroshima experience entitled *Formula for Death: E = mc²* and inspired by Sartre's *The
Condemned of Altona*, *Tringsha Satabdi* is Sircar's first attempt at
documentary drama.

One should qualify at this point that it is not an objective presentation of facts (insofar as a documentary can be objective), but
rather an orchestration of particular facts relating to Hiroshima
calculated to disturb the complacency of a middle-class Bengali
audience. When Sircar first wrote the play (which has been revised
considerably in the recent production by Satabdi), the documentation of Hiroshima was contained within a domestic framework.
Significantly, Basanti and Sharadindu reappear in the somewhat
artificially constructed prologue to this play. There is a knock on
the door and a friend who has been in France for a year walks into
the room. Basanti urges him to recall the night before he left for
France, when he discussed the impending disaster of war with
Sharadindu. According to Basanti, the conversation had affected
her husband so profoundly that he had suffered from some kind of
mental aberration ever since. More inexorably than the Sharadindu of *Baki Itihas*, the Sharadindu of *Tringsha Satabdi* is unable
to accept the violence of his century. Responding to Basanti's
request to recall the conversation, the friend begins to speak. The
prologue ends and the tragedy of Hiroshima is enacted.

Later, Sircar regretted the conventional theatricality of the
flashback sequence. In order to project the facts of Hiroshima
more directly, he removed all the excrescences of the script. The
play was revived, most significantly, when India exploded its first
nuclear missile. When most of the politicians and artists of India
(including many Marxists) applauded this "achievement," Sircar
was probably one of the very few people in India who protested
against the potential threat of nuclear power. Not surprisingly, the
play has an even greater significance today when India has become increasingly vocal about developing nuclear power as a pre-
ventive against foreign aggression. *Tringsha Satabdi* is frequently

performed by Satabdi for audiences who are gradually beginning to realize that the horror of Hiroshima is not so remote from their lives as they had imagined.[12]

Shesh Nei (There's No End) can be regarded as signalling the end of a phase in Sircar's playwriting career. It extends all the motifs of guilt and responsibility treated in his early plays but, instead of abstracting them, it concentrates them in the analysis of one character, Sumanta. The play is somewhat static as Sumanta, a successful writer, suddenly and quite inexplicably finds himself involved in a Kafkaesque trial. Figures from his life, past and present, accuse him of various crimes. His mother condemns his selfishness and cynicism, a former girlfriend accuses him of breach of faith, a former friend derides his betrayal of the Party for his pursuit of self-interests, a professor chides him for abandoning his quest for knowledge, a former employer accuses him of irresponsibility. Even Sumanta's wife, his strongest ally in the play, is somewhat disconcerted when he asserts that "nothing is more precious than the self within me."

The most unsettling section of the trial occurs when five anonymous figures emerge from Sumanta's troubled psyche and accuse him of his essential cowardice as a writer. They remind him of all the unpleasant realities he has so scrupulously avoided—the beggar in the street, the unemployed worker, the victim of a communal riot, the survivor of an atomic explosion. Tentatively, Sumanta accepts the accusations of the figures but is unable to fully accept his guilt.

SUMANTA: Milord, my reasoning is leaving me, the paths are getting lost, I can't see clearly. There—that person who sleeps on the pavement and dies of hunger, he is no one to me, he is outside my set of laws. Yet he can neither be forgotten nor accepted. There—that person whose father was killed in a riot and the bayoneted body of whose brother hangs limp on the barbed wire—he means nothing to me. And yet he comes back again and again in lawless nightmares. Those who are daily dying out of fear of the world blowing up, those who have become desperate out of fear of annihilation . . . they are nothing to me, they are outside the pale of my laws—and yet they exist. . . . Milord, by what set of laws then shall I write today?

> On one side is my own law and on the other, all these lawless
> nightmares. How do I reconcile them, milord? . . . I do not
> know if I am guilty or not guilty.[13]

Responding to his passionate statement, the twelve members of
the jury simultaneously point accusing fingers at Sumanta. But the
trial cannot be resolved because there is no judge. Sumanta assumes the role of the judge and accuses the counsel for the prosecution. He declaims that he, the jury, and the counsel are together
responsible for the crimes raised in the trial. "We are all the
accused," he says. This statement can be regarded as a leitmotif of
Sircar's oeuvre. Though he has diverted considerably from the
dramatic structure and characterization of *Shesh Nei*, Sircar continues to return to the same questions raised in that play: What is
the responsibility of the middle class to the pervasive terror and
injustices of this world? What is the role of the individual in collective action? How does one make another person confront his or her
guilt without in some way concealing one's own? These are difficult questions, which Sircar continues to grapple with in his exploration of the Third Theater.

Before examining his attempts to confront these questions, it is
necessary to provide more biographical information on how Sircar formed his group Satabdi. As mentioned earlier, its modes of
production and processes of work are blatant reactions to the
established conventions of the Bengali theater. Sircar's *form* of theater is directly related to what he has to say as an artist and human
being. Therefore, it is necessary to examine how his ideas of form
evolved in his early years as a socially committed artist.

SATABDI

When Badal Sircar returned from Nigeria in 1967, he found that
his plays were being performed by some of the leading theater
groups in Calcutta. Not content with being a successful playwright, he wanted to be actively involved in the theater. When he
inserted a small advertisement in a newspaper inviting actors to
form a theater group, he was suprised to receive as many as nine
hundred applications. (This detail gives the Western reader some

idea of the passion for the theater that prevails among Bengalis in Calcutta). Satabdi was formed as a predominantly amateur theater group that had no pretensions apart from wanting to entertain a middle-class audience. It performed the most inoffensive comedies in the most predictable manner possible using all the conventions of the commercial theater. Within a year, the group ran out of money and inspiration.

Sircar disowned the theater, though he continued to discuss its possibilities with a few friends. At this time, he was fortunate enough to tour the U.S.S.R., Poland, and Czechoslovakia on a cultural exchange program and see some of the most innovative theater in the world—Yuri Lyubimov's productions of *The Good Person of Setzuan, Galileo, Ten Days that Shook the World,* and a rehearsal of Gorki's *The Mother;* the productions of the Cinoherni Klub Theater and Jari's pantomime in Prague, and most important of all theater events, Grotowski's *Apocalypsis Cum Figuris* in Poland. It is not surprising that Sircar realized that he had to do something radically different in the theater when he reorganized Satabdi in 1969.

Satabdi was the first group in the Bengali theater that recognized the validity of a "poor theater." It gradually minimized its use of sets, costumes, background music, tape recorders, and projections. The body of the actor and its relation to the space on stage were Sircar's most immediate concerns as a director. Though his production of *Sagina Mahato* was initially performed in a proscenium theater, it emphasized the physical elements of acting—mime, dance, and rhythmic movement—more than the speech of the actors. Sircar also attempted to break down barriers in theatrical time and space by emphasizing the simultaneous action of his play and its nonsequential mode of narration.

The strength of his production, however, was not fully discovered until Satabdi performed the play in nonproscenium conditions at the All Bengal Teachers' Association hall on October 25, 1971. This performance convinced Sircar that the theater did not have to function within the confines of a stage; all it needed was a space. Ironically, he was only fully convinced about this fact when an accident took place during the performance: an electric fuse blew during one of the most dramatic moments in the play. The

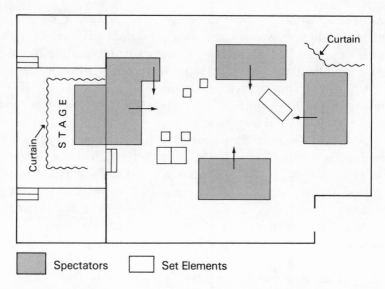

Spectators ▢ Set Elements

Figure 1

performance continued in total darkness for almost a minute and a half. Then the house lights came on, the harsh white glare of neon contrasting sharply with the warm glow of the spotlights. Sircar claims that his actors continued to perform in this light for five minutes during which time "there was not a comment, not a murmur, not even a sigh or a rustle of movement in the audience."[14] The concentration of the audience during this accident convinced Sircar that he could perform plays without using stage lights.

The mise en scène of *Sagina Mahato* in the A.B.T.A. hall was Sircar's first attempt to structure a theatrical experience in a room. Though the chairs in the hall were arranged in such a way that there was a central arena for the main action of the play, there were passages between and behind the rows of chairs that enabled the performers to move around, between, and in front of the audience. Figure 1 illuminates the structure of action in *Sagina Mahato*. Despite the freewheeling use of space, Sircar admits that the blocking of the play was rigorously determined by him. His actors did not have the freedom to explore the space according to their stimuli and perceptions. Sircar orchestrated the space for them.

He continued to dominate as a director in this manner in Satabdi's next production, Girish Chandra Ghosh's *Abu Hossain*, a nine-teenth-century musical based on a fantasy in the *Arabian Nights* that appealed to his sense of humor. Here again the production was carefully structured by Sircar during the rehearsal process. It was further limited by its constrained use of space within the pro-scenium despite its ingenious use of platforms as modules and can-vas sheets as backdrops. After *Sagina Mahato*, the members of Satabdi failed to find a space that was appropriate for its nonpro-scenium exploration of the theater. While the search for a suitable space continued, Sircar realized that it was time to train his actors as "a group of workers" rather than as individual "characters." He also realized that it was necessary for him as a playwright to aban-don a conventional "plot" in favor of a more physical and impro-vised treatment of a "theme."

By January 1972, Sircar found the appropriate material for his investigations of the theater—the legend of Spartacus. After writ-ing the first draft of his play *Spartacus* (based on the famous novel by Howard Fast), he did not proceed to designate the roles and rehearse the actors according to the physical demands and motiva-tions of their characters. Rather, he submitted his script to the entire group of actors who "confronted" it by improvising sections of the dialogue and finding visual equivalents for his words. The rehearsal became a workshop.

It was a fascinating experience for Sircar to watch his play being molded, edited, tested, and ultimately transformed by his actors, who discovered their own potentialities as performers in the process of discovering his play. For the first time in his career, Sircar realized the value of a workshop; not only did it engage all the members of his group in a collective creative process (includ-ing those who considered themselves "bad actors"), it also enabled his actors to confront and reject many of their inhibitions and psy-chological blocks.

The process of discovering *Spartacus* was greatly facilitated when Anthony Serchio, a director from the La Mama Theater in New York, conducted a number of workshops. He taught Sircar's actors important exercises devised by Grotowski including "the cat," a series of exercises that enables an actor to relax the ten-sions in his muscles and vertebral column. The workshops convinced Sircar that he needed more experience as a director to conduct the physical training of his actors.

In the summer of 1972, he accepted an invitation by Richard Schechner to observe the rehearsals and workshops of the Performance Group in New York. The influence of the American avant-garde theater on Sircar cannot be denied. His first exposure to Schechner's "environmental theater" greatly intensified his own awareness of the spectator's contribution to the shaping of a theatrical event. Commenting on the production of *Commune* performed by Schechner's group at the University of California at Berkeley, Sircar observed:

> Although there was a central performing area, the performers quite often used areas within, behind, and over the spectators. The "environment" encompassed the whole space . . . and the spectators constituted part of the environment. In other words, the experience of any spectator did not come only from the performance and the decor of the "stage" . . . but from other spectators as well. The spectators were never *manipulated*, but their participation was apparent by their presence in the *space* encompassed by the *environment* of that particular theater. Altogether it was a new *language* of communication. (Sircar's italics)[15]

Sircar attempted to project a similar "language" in his production of *Spartacus* (to be discussed in a later section). While watching Schechner conduct workshops and rehearse *The Tooth of Crime* with the Performance Group, Sircar learned a number of valuable techniques, exercises, and games that he later incorporated into the training process of his actors. What impressed him about Schechner's actors was their stamina (they often rehearsed from 10 A.M. to 6:30 P.M. with just two breaks which never exceeded an hour) and their ability to "confront" every line and situation of Shepard's script till it became "a play *felt* and *made* by the performers."

This inner process of developing the "score" of a text contrasted sharply with the more rational and analytical methods of the Living Theater, who were working on *The Legacy of Cain* when Sircar was in New York. This was the emergence of the political phase in the career of Julian Beck and Judith Malina. Sircar was impressed by their commitment and seriousness—qualities one does not readily associate with the Living Theater. He attended some of their discussions on the interrelations of money, war, and love which constituted the subject matter of *Cain*. He was also drawn to their idea of politics, which had less to do with the propagation of particular issues than with their exploration of "basic political philosophy" concerning "man's consciousness and responsibility."[16] While emphasizing that his theater and philosophy "differ considerably from those of the Living Theater," Sircar acknowledges that the "purpose" of his theater (which he never defines but which, one may assume, is the awakening of social consciousness in the spectators) corresponds "almost exactly" to that of the Becks. For both Satabdi and the Living Theater, theater is more than a profession or pastime or passion: it is a way of life.[17]

Sircar is defensive about the influence of the American avant-garde on his theater. While acknowledging that his experiences in New York were "very useful in formulating [his] ideas of the theater," Sircar emphasizes that they were useful "mostly in terms of reaction." Certainly, there is an overall restraint, even an austerity, about Sircar's theater that is fundamentally opposed to the innate narcissism and sexuality of the experimental theater in America. Even though there are some obvious borrowings from the work of Schechner, Chaikin, and the Becks in the plays of Satabdi—the fragmentation of the script, the coupling of the actors' bodies in the formation of "machines" and image-structures, certain contortions of movement, some nonverbal sounds and cadences—these borrowings are not, for the most part, intrusive or indulgent. They have been incorporated into the body and texture of Sircar's plays.

Occasionally, a particular element in Sircar's mise en scène calls attention to itself and seems somewhat alien to the mode of expression of his actors. For instance, in Satabdi's production of *Bashi Khabar* (Stale News), which was created by the entire group without the direct supervision of Sircar, there is a particularly jarring moment when the actors copy the famous "rite of birth" sequence from the Performance Group's *Dionysus in '69* in which Pentheus is dragged through the legs of four or five women. In *Bashi Khabar*, this sequence was repeated to portray the birth of man, with unconvincing groans and gyrations. I have observed (having seen all the productions of Satabdi at least two or three times) that Sircar's actors are least convincing when they assume postures of abandon and ecstasy that evoke the worst excesses of the American theater in the sixties. Fortunately, such moments of abandon are rare.

Despite its use of American theater techniques and conventions, Satabdi remains fundamentally Bengali in its mode of communication. Instead of distancing him from his own people, the foreign influence on Sircar has enabled him to create a physical language that reaches his audiences more directly than the conventional theater language of the commercial Bengali theater. One reason why Sircar has been able to control the foreign influence in his work is because he is in a position to question it. Like all great artists of the theater, notably Brecht, he "steals" whatever he believes is good for him and his theater and rejects what is of no use. Sircar is entirely pragmatic about what influences him in the theater.

AT THE ANGAMANCHA

Back in Calcutta toward the end of August 1972, Sircar was unable to continue his rehearsals of *Spartacus* as he had originally planned. At long last, Satabdi had found a suitable space for its theater—a room of 850 square feet on the second floor of the Academy of Fine Arts, one of the most active cultural centers in Calcutta. Despite its acoustical problems and limited capacity of sixty to seventy-five spectators, the room was an ideal space for workshops and nonproscenium performances. Significantly, it was named Angamancha, which can be translated as "Space Theater." Between September and the first week of November when Angamancha opened, Sircar and his group were busy conducting a membership drive in addition to constructing benches and fixing electric lights in their minuscule theater. They even drafted a manifesto that represented their ideas and form of organization.

> Angamancha run by SATABDI is an intimate theater in the flexible form where performers and spectators are much closer, sometimes intermingled, so that the barriers between them are minimized.

Angamancha is run not as a commercial theater house but as a theater established and developed by the efforts of a community of theater-lovers comprising of performers, organizers, and spectators. Hence, the usual ticket system is replaced as far as possible by a system of membership.

Although the terms of membership have been kept at a minimum (the subscription is Rs. 6/- annually) to enable all genuine theater lovers to participate, it is expected that a member joins the organization as a positive participant in this community effort of building a new theater, and not in the spirit of calculating "value for money."[18]

Satabdi received as many as 325 members in its first and last campaign for an audience. After *Spartacus*, the audiences came of their own accord. Sircar's theater needed no publicity for its survival.

Spartacus

As a production, *Spartacus* had no precedent in the contemporary Bengali theater. To describe it as an intimate experience is, perhaps, to understate the torrential immediacy of its impact. It is difficult to imagine a production so violent, and yet so rigorous in its orchestration of movement. In the very first moment of the play, one is simply thrust into a world of terror and brutality as the slaves rush out in a mass from a single entrance and swarm around the audience. Figure 2 shows the strategic placing of the spectators about the room, particularly of those in the central seating area.

The proximity of the spectators and the audience increases the physical intensity of the first ten minutes of *Spartacus*. There are no words but a steady crescendo of rhythmic pants that becomes deafening in the small room. The relentless movement of the actors as they raise their hands and thrash them down in unison conveys the sheer agony of the slaves' labor. Apart from watching them toil, we see the slaves being captured by a group of anonymous Roman soldiers who look like the military police in Calcutta —impassive, steely eyed, and ruthless. Once caught, the slaves are sold in the market where patricianlike figures clad in the spotless *kurtas* and pajamas of the Bengali aristocracy examine the teeth and limbs of the slaves with brutal gestures. The most savagely

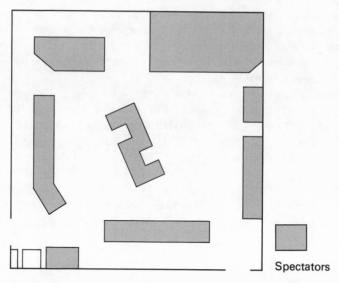

Spectators

Figure 2

choreographed scenes depict the fight of the slaves in the arena.
There are no gladiatorial movements, no virtuosic somersaults and
throws, no sadistic tortures of limbs. Sircar's actors fight with their
bare hands. They use few gestures which are violent in their starkness and momentum. After the fight, a slave is crucified for an act
of defiance. The raising of his body in the air, the outstretched
hands of the slaves in a semicircle, their faces turned upwards—all
are images that remain with the audience long after the production of *Spartacus* ends.

Sircar's production does not rely entirely on violent images for
its total effect. There is an ideological thrust, however naive, that
underlies the frenetic action of the play. The central idea of the
Spartacus legend that concerns Sircar is what Howard Fast describes as its "descent through common struggle." The war of the
oppressed continues in our century in Cambodia, Afghanistan,
and elsewhere in the world, while repressive regimes have survived the rising of the proletariat.

Sircar finds an immediate political significance in the great
slave revolt led by Spartacus in 71 B.C. and its eventual destruction
by representatives of the empire. He does not, however, elaborate

on this significance by inserting contemporary political parallels into the dramatic framework of the play. Nor does he concentrate on the historical details of ancient Roman history. He does something more subtle: he abstracts the essence of slavery and oppression in history by finding appropriate visual images and words for it. One could say that Sircar accentuates the predicament of Spartacus by universalizing it. This is one of the very few instances in the political theater of Bengal where a "universalizing" perspective of history does not prove to be a limitation.

Significantly, the Spartacus in Sircar's production is neither a Roman gladiator, nor is he an allusion to any particular political leader in Bengal. He is represented as a *group* of slaves. All of Sircar's actors playing slaves constitute the reality of Spartacus. The most arresting moments in the production occur when they lie in a circle with their faces buried in the ground and intone their freedom chant. In the following sequence, they speak of their oppressors with that peculiar terseness and impersonality that characterizes the dialogue of the play.

> We are slaves. The slaves are saying: they no longer want to hear the songs of the whip of Rome.
>
> In the beginning of creation all men were equal. Today by the courtesy of Rome, men are divided into two castes—Master and Slave.
>
> But we are more than you. We are much better than you . . .
>
> You have turned the earth into a dirty dungeon.
>
> You have turned man into a beast.
>
> You have taken killing for play.
>
> But no more of that, that's over . . .
>
> We'll break into your Senate.
>
> We'll clean your dungeon.
>
> And then we'll build a beautiful city.
>
> A beautiful country.
>
> Where there won't be any wall.
>
> No killing.
>
> No master.

No slave.

There'll only be peace and happiness.[19]

Contradicting this hopelessly optimistic vision of "peace and happiness," we see a line of slaves torturously moving around the space in the room. Their hands, arms, and legs are interlocked as they drag their bodies along. The heightened physicality of this image reveals as much about their state of oppression as the single refrain that is sung by the slaves at significant moments in the play. Sircar does not exaggerate when he says that this refrain—a haunting melody that uses barely six or seven notes—expresses the suffering and determination of the slaves more effectively than pages of dialogue.

The least convincing sections in the play, in my opinion, are the verbose episodes featuring the Roman patricians. The following confrontation between the *sutradhara* (stage manager) and Gracus (a Roman senator who craves Varinia, the wife of Spartacus) could be an excerpt from a conventional historical play about Spartacus.

SUTRADHARA: Senator Gracus. After buying and selling of votes, rowdyism, and political murders, today you rise to be the central figure of the Senate. . . . Do you know what Spartacus has but you don't?

GRACUS: I have my Rome.

SUTRADHARA: Rome is a whore!

GRACUS: [*calmly*] I know. That whore is my mother.

SUTRADHARA: Then why look for Varinia?

GRACUS: To know.

SUTRADHARA: To know what?

GRACUS: Whatever is good, whatever is precious, beautiful—everything we've discarded. We've thrown out civilization and acquired courtesy instead, abandoned joy for pleasure, and lust for love. We don't have appetite, we have food; we don't feel thirsty but we have drinks. I know all this. What I don't know is how the slave Spartacus has picked up all these good precious and beautiful things that we have dropped, and how he has distributed these things among the lowest class of men on earth.

[*pausing*] I want to know why Varinia is the wife of Spartacus
and why Rome my mother is a whore.[20]

Fortunately, such rhetorical passages do not dominate Sircar's
production of *Spartacus*.

In fact, the wordiness of the script was almost entirely elimi-
nated when Sircar edited sections of the dialogue for the first open-
air performance of *Spartacus* in Surendranath Park. Sircar recalls
this performance on March 17, 1973, with particular fondness. He
had been somewhat skeptical whether *Spartacus*, which had been
rehearsed in a room with a small audience in mind, could reach
hundreds of people in the casual atmosphere of the park. He was
also aware that *Spartacus* was more sophisticated in its mode
of narration and shaping of the mise en scène than the political
plays performed in the park (notably, by a group called Silhouette).

Sircar's fears were quite unfounded. The response to his play
was overwhelming: five hundred people watched it with "absolute
silence and concentration." Satabdi was compelled to perform
Spartacus in the park on a regular basis. With his characteristic simplicity that barely conceals his innate romanticism, Sircar
states that his actors discovered "a new kind of involvement" in
these open-air performances as they confronted not merely hundreds of people but the earth and the open sky.

Prastab

Despite the people's enthusiastic response to *Spartacus*, there were
dissensions among Sircar's actors, who were roughly divided into
two groups—those who wanted to continue exploring the Third
Theater with total commitment and those who wanted to compromise by doing a few proscenium productions. After the success of
Sagina Mahato and *Abu Hossain* on the proscenium stage, some of
Sircar's actors were not prepared to abandon their individual
careers in the theater by immersing their identities in the group
creations of works like *Spartacus*. Reflecting on these actors, Sircar says, somewhat sourly, "If a person in the theater is in search of
'success,' 'fame,' and a 'career' (and the matter of money lurking

behind all these)—then the switch-over to the Third Theater . . . is certainly disastrous to him."[21]

Sircar did not, however, indulge in a jeremiad against his recalcitrant actors. Demonstrating his matter-of-fact way of dealing with problems, Sircar claims, "We did not fight. We sat down and faced the problem squarely. And we came to the decision of going our separate ways by unanimous agreement." The only difficulty was that Satabdi had to rework all its old productions with new actors. In this period of transition, Sircar decided, in his words, "to take a step in the theater that I would probably never have dared in normal conditions. That step was a very significant one, not only in my theater, but in my life as well."[22]

Prastab (Proposition), a one-man show performed by Sircar, voices the essential credo of the Third Theater. In many ways, its denunciation of money is so violent, so absolute, that one is almost tempted to reject it as an appallingly simplistic statement. It is difficult to speak of *Prastab* as a theatrical event because it defies all notions and conventions of entertainment. One can speak of it more accurately as a *human act* that incorporates a deeply personal statement by Sircar.

Significantly, there is no admission fee for *Prastab* whether or not the spectators can afford to buy a ticket; it would contradict the raison d'être of Sircar's statement. The audience enters the room and sees Sircar spread-eagled on platforms that are shaped to form a T. It is impossible to ignore the ropes tied to Sircar's wrists and ankles. One notices that the ropes are stretched to the four corners of the room. The audience has no idea what to expect when the lights in the room are casually switched off. A strong light shines on the platforms. All attention is concentrated on the still, corpselike figure of Sircar behind which loom three silhouettes of "sentries" who hold a knife, a whip, and a gun, respectively.

Sircar begins by asking the audience to look at an "obscene" picture that is concealed behind a screen in the room. Somewhat embarrassed, the audience moves to one end of the room to peep at the picture—a collage of bank notes and coins. When the audience returns to their seats, Sircar makes his *"prastab"* to abolish the obscene picture and the materialism it represents. It all sounds

very trite. The sentries and three actors who have been planted in
the audience break into raucous laughter. Once it subsides, Sircar
begins to argue against the evil system of money in our society.
There is no script. But the gist of what Sircar improvises can be
conveyed in the following passage:

> It is my personal belief, and I am sure that I am not alone in my
> belief, that human beings have made a mess of their own affairs. I
> believe that the resources in the control of Man—the most intelligent
> man in this planet—are enough to provide everybody with the basic
> necessities of life, even much more than that; and the bogey of over-
> population is a myth deliberately built up by some people with
> vested interest. Apart from the starvation and killings resulting from
> the system established and supported by such people, we have been
> brought to the position where the total destruction of the planet is
> physically possible by using a minute fraction of the atomic weap-
> ons stocked already. The system has made *money* a monster which,
> instead of serving man as it was supposed to do, has made slaves of
> human beings.[23]

Sircar's reasoning is very simple, very uncompromising, but his
speech in *Prastab* is expressed so clearly and, above all, so sincere-
ly, that one is compelled to listen to it. Sircar does not have a mesmeric presence as an actor. He is a slight man, balding, with sharp
features (rather like the Wizard of Oz), but his eyes can blaze with
indignation and anger. Despite his bursts of ferocity against the
indifference and inhumanity of men, he remains the kind of person
one is likely to meet in a bus or outside a government office. Sircar's strength as an actor is his honesty. He says what he has to say
with a belief that is sometimes intimidating. It might be argued
that honesty is not necessarily a theatrical virtue (a sincere actor is
often less convincing than a technically equipped one), but Sircar
is an exception. One does not mind if he totally lacks virtuosity as
an actor. His integrity is what makes his theater so significant.

After Sircar finishes improvising a diatribe on the enslavement
of human beings to money, a bell rings in the room. The sentries
exhibit the picture to the audience, whereupon the three actors
who have been planted among the spectators rush toward the picture with exaggerated zeal. They resemble animals as they career

and genuflect before the picture with their tongues hanging out. They eventually disperse and there is silence in the room. In this indeterminate moment when the audience is not sure whether or not to leave, Sircar asks the audience to "release" him. Some of the spectators invariably untie the ropes on his wrists and ankles. Sircar sits up and walks around the room looking into the eyes of each of the spectators. Then he leaves and the "play" is over.[24]

What are we to make of this event? How does one react to it? Is it theater? Sircar believes that it is "genuine theater—a theater of feelings, a theater of direct communication" but he also acknowledges "how hopeless it is to describe it in writing." There can be no doubt that *Prastab* is a deeply personal statement by Sircar about his position as an actor and human being. It was made at a time when he had deliberately isolated himself from the practice and economics of the existing theater in Bengal. *Prastab* demonstrates this isolation most blatantly in its total absence of conventional norms one associates with the commercial theater.

Instead of making any attempt to entertain the audience (in the traditional sense of the word), *Prastab* asks the spectators to change their lives by specifically changing their attitude to money. It is less a message than a plea. Sircar makes it without using any of the gimmicks and strategies one associates with the political playwrights in Bengal. It might be argued that the politics of *Prastab* is too personal to be taken seriously. One must emphasize, however, that it is not egotistic. Sircar does not exhibit his martyrdom as an artist. Nor does he at any point indulge in the kind of self-congratulatory righteousness to which representatives of the "poor theater" succumb in their most rapturous moments. Sircar cares as much for the lives of his spectators as he cares for his own life. It is not surprising, therefore, that the most affecting moment in *Prastab* occurs when Sircar asks the spectators to release him. At that moment, Sircar does not stand apart from them like an enlightened guru. He is one with them.

Michil

After *Prastab* and a few hectic performances of *Mukta Mela* (Open Fair) which relied on improvised conversations with the specta-

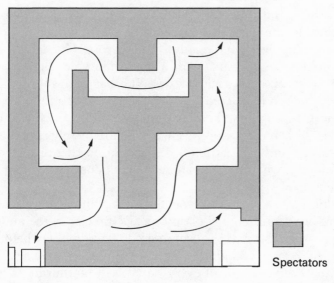

Figure 3

tors, Satabdi staged a full-length play called *Michil*. *Michil* is one of Sircar's most intricately structured plays, with innumerable transitions and juxtapositions. The relentless flow of events in the text is most skilfully concretized in the swirling movement of the mise en scène. The actors are constantly on the move—walking, running, dancing, and jogging through the room's L-shaped passages. Figure 3 illustrates the acting areas in relation to the seats of the spectators.

The benches in the room are placed in such a way that the spectators feel that they are part of a maze. A number of benches are placed against one another so that some spectators sit with their backs to one another. Sircar creates a most bewildering environment with the bodies, backs, faces, and profiles of the spectators. When the actors begin to move between and around the environment created by the spectators, the effect is startling: one can almost see a procession winding its way around the streets of Calcutta.

The play begins abruptly with a confusion of voices in a blackout. At first it seems that there is "load-shedding"—a familiar occurrence in Calcutta, which has power cuts daily lasting eight to twelve hours. But it is more serious than that. Someone has been murdered. In the darkened space of the room, we see a group of actors bending over what seems to be a corpse. The lights snap on and a policeman appears. With a stentorian voice, he orders the people to return home. His lines—"Who has been murdered? . . . No one has been murdered . . . Lies! Go home"—are repeated like a leitmotif throughout the play along with the enactment of the "murder." When the people onstage (who are members of a chorus distinguished only by number) disperse in obedience to the constable's order, we anticipate another play about police repression in Calcutta.

Michil, however, is not a conventional political play. The Boy who has been murdered rises and speaks directly to the audience: "I was murdered today. I was murdered yesterday. Day before yesterday. And the day before that. . . . I am murdered every day. Murdered every day, dead every day. I will be murdered tomorrow."[25] As the play progresses, the Boy continues to be "murdered" by the daily pressures, the political hypocrisies, and the everyday calamities of life in Calcutta. The dreadful irony, of course, is that he continues to survive being murdered.

His predicament is examined in *Michil* in juxtaposition with the dilemma of another character, the Old Man (played by Sircar himself). If the Boy is constantly murdered, the Old Man is hopelessly lost till the end of the play. He makes his entrance reminiscing about a particular day in his childhood when he got lost. With infectious charm, Sircar plays the curiosity of a child discovering streets for the first time. He runs through the passages in the audience marvelling that the corner of one passage leads to another which ends in a corner that leads to yet another passage. When Sircar runs offstage, the chorus takes over the search for the lost child, announcing various SOS messages (over the radio, through the Customs stations) and chanting promises of presents and gifts to lure the child home. After this marvellously evocative scene, the Old Man returns, maintaining that he is still lost. He continues to roam the streets but they are a maze to him. Looking tentatively at the audience, he asks: "Which procession will be able to show me the way?"

Life in Calcutta interrupts the Old Man's search for the "true' procession as the members of the chorus enter the room. They jog around the performing area shouting headlines from various newspapers that highlight the rise of prices, the deterioration of public transport, the postponement of examinations, and the black marketeering of essential products. These problems are intensely familiar to Sircar's audience.

The "newspaper" sequence is juxtaposed with a most effective evocation of sounds in a railway station. Vendors, salesmen, and beggars vie with one another to attract the attention of the spectators. Just when the cacophony becomes unbearable, Sircar presents yet another vignette of life in Calcutta—passengers hanging out of the entrance to a bus. The actors simulate this familiar sight by clustering together in a mass with their hands stretched upward and clasped in a tight knot. When they begin to shuffle around the room in this state, fighting, arguing, shouting, one has a most vivid image of the people of Calcutta getting to work every morning. It is through such images that Sircar conveys how life in Calcutta continues from day to day.

The Old Man and the Boy reappear briefly, both of them lost in their search for the "true procession." The Policeman makes a sudden appearance, repeating his familiar lines: "No one is murdered. No one is lost. Everything is all right. Continue working." Almost in reaction to this reassurance that life in Calcutta is normal, the members of the chorus march around the room playing various musical instruments off-key. The musical interlude leads to a riotous sequence where the chorus enacts the frenzied "devotion" of young Bengalis who take clay deities to the river Hooghly where they are immersed during the Pujas. The goddess Kali is represented by an actor who sticks out his tongue irreverently. The enthusiasm of the religious activities (which reveals an enormous waste of the energy of Bengali youth) is the counterpoint for a medley of patriotic cries and slogans—"Quit India," "Hindu Muslim Ek Ho," "God Save the King," "Death to the British Dogs."

Most strategically, Sircar alternates the nationalist slogan of India, *"Bande Mataram,"* with the religious cry of the Muslims, *"Allah O Akbar."* Instantly, this alternation precipitates a communal riot. The actors fight and eventually collapse on the floor. They recover slowly and begin to walk around the room, going up to

individual spectators and begging for some aid. Just when the audience is beginning to feel the total helplessness of these refugees,
the chorus gathers together at one end of the room and sings "*Sare
Jehan se Accha*"—one of the most popular songs of the Freedom
movement in India. There could not be a more ironic juxtaposition
even though the rendition of the song is appropriately fervent.

Sircar begins to expose the essential hollowness of Indian patriotism more explicitly in the next sequence. A caricature of the ruling class dressed in an immaculate *punjabi* and a Nehru cap
minces his way into the room. The members of the chorus dutifully crouch on the floor while he sits on their backs and mouths
pious platitudes.

> You will keep in mind our national tradition. You will keep in
> mind the innumerable martyrs of the freedom struggle. . . . Also
> remember the invincible power of non-violence. India has the re-
> sponsibility of preaching spiritualism to the world. Keep in mind the
> supremacy of Indian democracy. Do not forget the fundamental
> rights of the Constitution. Remember—the Green Revolution, Bank
> Nationalization, Family Planning, Help the Dollar, Atomic Welfare,
> and Arrest by M.I.S.A. (P. 23)

The preposterous juxtapositions of "Help the Dollar" (an imaginary scheme), "M.I.S.A." (a repressive law passed by Indira Gandhi during the Emergency), and Indian "democracy" never fail to
amuse Sircar's audience.

The political satire continues in the next sequence where preparations for an election campaign are depicted. The very name of
Kaloram Bajaria, the candidate for election, conjures up an image
of an obese black marketeer with hoards of money and grain. The
actors go around the room simulating fat, clumsy movements
chanting all the material objects one associates with Bajaria like
rice, *dal* (lentils), oil, sugar, flour, and coal. In distinct contrast to
the sense of well-being and plenitude conveyed by this sequence, a
member of the chorus, the only woman in the play, drifts around
the audience begging for money. At this moment, the Boy reap-
pears and tells the chorus members to keep quiet. He is tossed from
one chorus member to another, each laughing at his anguish.

It becomes increasingly clear in the course of *Michil* that the chorus represents that mass of people in Calcutta who continue passively to accept the corruption that pervades their lives. Ironically, they rely on the ruling class for their sustenance. Sircar shows the members of the chorus begging for enlightenment and relief from the grotesque caricature of the ruling class who appeared earlier in the play. They touch his feet while he reassures them with false hopes. Despite his hypocritical blessings, nothing changes in the life of the chorus. They continue to suffer from unemployment, factory lockouts, and the most abject poverty that prevents them from getting married or paying doctors' bills. In desperation, they turn to their mentor, beseeching him to provide them with some direction to their lives. He offers them a bottle of wine, whereupon they promptly get drunk.

The Old Man stumbles into the room and refers to the bottle of wine as an instance of "comic relief." He promptly gets drunk himself. As he tries to find his way in the maze of streets, there is a blackout and the opening sequence of the play is repeated. The Policeman appears and orders the people to go home. The Old Man encounters the Boy who informs him that he has been killed. Unperturbed, the Old Man reassures him that he has simply lost his way. He advises the Boy to go home and even offers to show him the way. The irony, of course, is that he himself has lost his way and has no sense of direction. The two characters walk around the room in circles. A group of devotees pass by chanting religious songs. Without paying attention to the Old Man, who clamors to know where the sun rises, they lift the boy up on their shoulders like a corpse and leave intoning a funeral chant—*"Bolo-bori Horibol."* Left alone, it seems as if the Old Man confronts the imminence of death. The Policeman enters and orders him to go home. It is through such juxtapositions that Sircar crystallizes the dilemmas of his characters.

In accordance with the nonsequential movement of the entire play, the next sequence is radically different in tone and perspective as the chorus voices a litany of middle-class prejudices, complaints, and demands. It is Sircar's most direct condemnation of the values and assumptions shared by his bourgeois spectators. Instead of attacking their ennui and selfishness directly, he lets his chorus reveal their shortcomings in a matter-of-fact manner.

CHORUS: This country needs military dictatorship. All kinds of
unruly elements should be mercilessly suppressed.

I saw boys and girls sitting closely together in the park nestling
against one another. What is this country coming to?

Only strikes and *gheraos!* No wonder the price of commodities
is rising. . . .

Will we always remain weak? Everybody has started to make
an atom bomb!

How the lower classes are beginning to pride themselves! Even
the *rickshawallah* speaks angrily with you.

(Pp. 36–37)

Sircar implies that such middle-class views strengthen the power
of reactionary governments. Significantly, the Boy enters the room
exhorting the audience not to listen to the chorus while the Policeman pursues him with threatening movements. It is at such moments that Sircar, very subtly, interweaves political and social
commentary.

A more farcical episode with the Policeman occurs when the
representative of the ruling class, raised on the shoulders of the
chorus members, expounds on peace using hilarious non sequiturs.
The Policeman follows in front like an obedient dog. Periodically,
he emits piteous howls punctuating the platitudes of the ruling
class:

In the power of tradition—in devotion to god—in peace and non-
violence—out of social responsibility—in the context of the constitution—in legal procedures—on the basis of class unity. (P. 40)

The juxtaposition of the howls and these platitudes (which are spoken by the actor with a ridiculous simper) is one of the most outrageous instances of Sircar's political satire.

As the play draws to an end, there is a frenetic sequence where
the members of the chorus chant slogans from a multitude of processions. The Boy enters screaming that he does not believe in their
processions, their slogans, their rhetoric, their lies. Confronting the
audience, he shouts out his despair: "You have seen murders—
murders. Sitting quietly, you watch these murders. I, you,—we are
all murderers. We all commit murders and are murdered. . . . Stop

it!" The Polceman enters the room and seizes the Boy. He is assisted
by members of the chorus who become accomplices of the law. In
a series of vivid tableaux, they murder the Boy in different ways by
beheading him, hanging him, firing a machine gun at him, and
gassing him to death. Hearing the cries of the Boy, the Old Man
enters the room. The final encounter between him and the Boy
reveals a meeting of minds that is at once perfunctory and profoundly moving.

The play acquires a more abstract quality as the two characters
refuse to yield to their sense of loss. The past and the present, youth
and age coalesce as the Old Man and the Boy discover that they
are part of the same continuum and share a similar dilemma. In
one breathtaking sequence that becomes increasingly spirited and
hectic, the two characters stride around the stage chanting, "Was.
Is. Was. Is . . . ," two seemingly innocuous and colorless words that
bind them together in their final search. Their voices get louder,
their faces more flushed as the momentum of the scene increases.
Suddenly, when they are out of breath and somewhat awed at their
own newly found stamina, the Old Man hears the sound of "the
true procession—the procession that will show the way. The way
home. . . . The procession of men."

As he speaks, the members of the chorus enter the room holding
hands. They sing a most haunting song which suggests that the
procession could be a dream. Nonetheless, they fill the space of the
room with their expansive gestures and resonant voices. Gradually, they move closer to the spectators, who are compelled to
become part of the procession. The spectators and actors inter-
mingle and the entire space of the room becomes a swirling mass
of humanity. It is one of those moments in the theater when one
becomes acutely aware of the possibilities of life and the essential
brotherhood of men. Transcending the immediate issues of the
play, it lingers long after the play ceases, compelling the spectators
to reexamine their affinities and responsibilities as members of a
society.

Tringsha Satabdi

The last production in the Angamancha at the Academy of Fine
Arts (after *Prastab*, *Evam Indrajit*, and *Michil*) was Sircar's revi-

val of *Tringsha Satabdi* (The Thirtieth Century). As mentioned earlier, this play was edited by Sircar when he realized that its domestic framework was somewhat tepid and irrelevant for the exposure of facts relating to nuclear power and its devastating impact on the lives of men. The immediacy of the play (in its most recent draft) is conveyed in the very first moments when Sircar steps forward and addresses the audience informally. "Our play," he says, "is not beautiful. We do not know how to make such a play [on Hiroshima and nuclear power] beautiful. We do not want to know." Instead of dealing with the obvious contradictions an artist faces when he aestheticizes calamities like Hiroshima, Sircar is content with the more simple task of disseminating certain facts and attitudes relating to Hiroshima and its effect on our lives today. *Tringsha Satabdi* can be described as the most pragmatic and down-to-earth of Sircar's plays.

What saves the play from becoming pedestrian is the dramatic structure of the trial. Significantly, the only piece of furniture in the room is a witness-box. Before the trial begins, however, Sircar raises a few pertinent questions in the role of a character ridden with guilt about Hiroshima. This character, who is almost indistinguishable from Sircar himself, refuses to believe that the American government is solely responsible for the devastation caused by the atom bomb. Turning to his friend, another character so nondescript that he could be a spectator in the audience, he poses a most unsettling question: "How do you know that you would not have dropped the bomb?" This is a typical instance of Sircar's seemingly naive, yet fearsome, mode of reasoning. Unlike most political playwrights who concentrate on particular villains (the U.S. government or the Soviet Union), Sircar is more concerned with the villains that exist within us. Though he never fails to remind us of anonymous systems of bureaucratic power that monitor calamities like Hiroshima, Sircar also emphasizes the innate destructiveness of man and his indifference to other men. "The system alone is not responsible for the calamities in the world," Sircar seems to say, "we have to admit our guilt for allowing such calamities to happen."

A number of difficult questions are raised in the opening sequence of *Tringsha Satabdi*, often through inference rather than direct statement: Are we frightened of confronting Hiroshima?

Can we examine its facts without destroying our equilibrium and belief in humanity? Can we survive our knowledge of Hiroshima with any confidence that such a calamity will not be repeated in our lives? These are complex questions and Sircar does not appear to have sufficient power and skill as an artist to fully confront their intricacies. But at least he has the intelligence and strength of character to raise them.

As a means of providing background information on Hiroshima, Sircar reveals a number of statistics and facts to an inoffensive "interviewer" who sits cross-legged on the floor. We learn about the site of the bombing, the names of the pilots who volunteered to drop the bomb, and the clandestine organization of the entire event. The drama begins with the sound of American bombers; a hum resonates around the room. It stops abruptly and the cross-examination of the American pilots begins with Sircar assuming the role of a counsel for the prosecution.

Significantly, all the pilots are played by the same actor, who makes little attempt to highlight individual differences in character. Sircar makes it clear that these pilots are mere pawns in a system and that they share a similar anonymity. Instead of highlighting their callousness as human beings, he stresses their self-righteousness and sense of duty. It is very disturbing to hear these officers defend their actions with appallingly pedestrian justifications: one stresses that "orders are orders" while another emphasizes the advantage of receiving a "promotion." When the third officer is asked if he had visited Hiroshima after the war, he replies that his visit had convinced him that the bombing was "a job well done."

The most emotionally charged cross-examination involves a wife whose pilot husband has not been able to accept his participation in the bombing as blandly as his colleagues. The wife informs us (as spectators in the trial) that her husband had never recovered from the shock of Hiroshima and that he was subject to frequent fits of paranoia. In a tempestuous reversal of action, Sircar assumes the role of the tormented husband while the wife leaves the witness box and assumes her role in everyday life. Together they enact a somewhat melodramatic scene where the husband hysterically admits that the pension he receives from the U.S. government is nothing less ignominious than "a premium for murder." Despite the emotional excess of the scene (which unfortunately reveals Sircar's limitations as an actor), the audience is made to feel the horrifying impact of Hiroshima on an individual.

The strength of *Tringsha Satabdi* lies in its juxtaposition of individuals and the larger, unalterable fact of Hiroshima itself. Though not initially perceptible, these juxtapositions become clearer as the play progresses. After the cross-examination of the American pilots, a quaint schoolmaster from Hiroshima is called to the witness box. He reads out a number of essays written by children who experienced and survived the explosion. While he speaks, the chorus members quietly sit in a circle with their heads placed between their knees. At a critical point in the schoolmaster's reading, they rise with a deafening cry that gradually becomes a prolonged wail and writhe their bodies and hands in all directions. It is a simple yet effective way of conveying the effect of an explosion—certainly more effective than any use of projections or strobe lights.

As the actors writhe on the floor, their bodies occasionally twitching in pain, the schoolmaster stops reading the essay, which continues to be narrated by one of the chorus members. The narrative is horrifying in its vivid use of detail: a child watches her mother die and sees the skin peeling from her brother's face. For once in Sircar's theater, the words are more effective than the movements of the actors. To hear a voice speak of the rain and blood, the blackened faces, and total destitution of the survivors is more convincing than to watch actors contorting their bodies and gasping for breath in the most theatrical manner possible. It never fails to strike me that Sircar's actors are least effective when they attempt to be "expressive."

In the following sequence, a doctor treating the victims in Hiroshima enters the scene of action. The members of the chorus lie down on the floor as "patients," their bodies spaced at regular intervals. The doctor is extremely loquacious. He cannot stop talking as he moves from one patient to another detailing their particular ailments and complaining about his lack of adequate medicines and facilities. After talking nonstop for two to three minutes, the doctor comes to the last patient only to discover that she is dead. There is total silence in the room. The actor playing the doctor leaves without saying a word. The audience can feel the futility of his situation.

Set against this sequence, where the individuality of the doctor is not fully developed, is a more personal experience of Hiroshima enacted by another survivor (played by Sircar). This man confides most pathetically to the audience that he never imagined that the Americans would bomb Hiroshima. On the day of the explosion he heard the familiar sounds of the planes followed by an all clear siren. He rushed out into the street along with many other people when the bomb exploded. Sircar conveys the absolute terror and panic of this man by frantically running around the room describing the scenes of horror encircling him. The simultaneity of the movement and the narrative, the objective description of facts, and the agonized first-person perspective make the scene very startling and cinematic.

The initial panic of the man ceases and he becomes increasingly exhausted. He then joins a straggling line of people (who remain invisible) and eventually follows them into a relief train (also invisible). As this narrative unfolds, Sircar's movements get slower and more lethargic. He crouches on the floor and moves ever so slightly from side to side. In this mesmeric movement we can almost see the bodies of hundreds of destitute people swaying with the motion of the train. It is a strangely tender image. The man looks out of the window and sees a green field, some trees, and hears the sounds of birds. The horror of Hiroshima seems very distant, almost unreal. This moment of respite, however, is shattered when the train stops at another town. The passengers get out and then, most absurdly and tragically, there is another explosion. Nagasaki— another town, yet another annihilation.

This universal tragedy, seen through the eyes of an individual, is followed by more generalized statements about atomic pollution and radioactivity. Here again the perfunctory writhings of the actors (victims of air pollution) do not particularly convince the spectators. Another somewhat arbitrary sequence involves Einstein reading out a cautionary letter to Roosevelt that apparently never reached the president. The play seems to lose its momentum and focus till the very last moments when the "interviewer" who appeared at the beginning of the play advises Sircar to forget about Hiroshima and to think of something else. Responding to the interviewer's claim that it is not "our" responsibility to confront calamities like Hiroshima, Sircar answers back, using his most simple and devastating mode of reasoning:

> You and I are passengers in a bus, backseat customers. The driver drives on recklessly at a speed of eighty miles per hour. We don't have the right to tell him: Watch out, keep your eyes open. There's a child crossing! Be careful! We don't have the right to ask him whether he has a license, whether he is sane. No, we have to look out of the window all the time, keep our eyes away and say, "How beautiful!"[26]

It might be argued that the image of the rash bus driver is too pedestrian to sustain the larger issues of the play. But this is precisely Sircar's strength as a writer. He makes his audience confront some of the most problematic issues in life by using images that are familiar to them. As Samik Bandhopadhyay observes so accurately about *Tringsha Satabdi*, "Sircar manages to suggest the sheer size of the crisis and its aftermath and yet keep it within human dimensions, within individualized modes of suffering."[27]

The coda of the play is emphatic. Sircar returns to his fundamental belief that we—the spectators, the actors, and the people around us—cannot be indifferent to seemingly distant calamities like Hiroshima. As he harangues his audience in one of his most hectoring moments as a director and actor, his actors line up against a wall and silently face him. They do not respond to his outburst and remain immobile for the rest of the play, resembling the audience. As Sircar addresses them, he acquires an almost patriarchal role. (In fact, this is one of the rare moments in Sircar's theater when one realizes how old he is compared to them.) Turning away from his actors, who continue to stare at him without seeming to comprehend his anger, Sircar succumbs to despair for a few brief moments and laments that "the light has left the earth." Suddenly, in an upsurge of affirmation and desperate hope, he enters the witness-box and declares that he will confront the impending disasters of our life. Pointing to particular spectators in the audience, he questions: "Will you? And you? You?"

This climax, which ends the play, receives no applause. The audience leaves the room silently. They are left with many questions, thoughts, and indecisions. Sircar does not attempt to "show them the light." Despite his fervor, there is nothing evangelical about his role in *Tringsha Satabdi*. However, there can be no doubt that he wants his audience to confront the calamities in this world with greater rigor and compassion.

A New Angamancha

After *Tringsha Satabdi*, Sircar's group had to search for another peformance space. Their first term of tenancy at the Angamancha in the Academy of Fine Arts had expired and the management wanted to raise the rent of the hall by 60 percent. Refusing to yield to such pressures, Satabdi embarked on a period of free theater in Surendranath Park and in various villages. Eventually, it found a most suitable space for its theater in the library of the Theosophical Society of Bengal, conveniently located near Calcutta University, Presidency College, and the legendary Coffee Shop on College Street, that haunt of intellectuals, students, politicians, and artists from all over Calcutta.

Shukhpathe Bharater Itihas

One of the first plays staged at the new Angamancha in the Theosophical Society library was *Shukhpathe Bharater Itihas* (Indian History Made Easy), a play that analyzes the colonial history of India in the form of a history lesson. The title of the play is reminiscent of those innumberable "mug books" sold on College Street that advertise "short cuts" and "guarantees for success" in examinations. The mug book, which most students in Calcutta rely on to pass examinations, is the most glaring instance of what is wrong with education in Calcutta. With a hundred thousand students in Calcutta University, it is a widely accepted fact that most students view a university education as the only alternative to unemployment. Apart from this frustration and the fact that results may not be published for six to eight months after an examination (among other administrative problems), the structure, teaching methods,

and curriculum of Calcutta University remain intrinsically colonial. This is the most disheartening aspect of education in Calcutta: its adherence to models prescribed by the British.

It is significant that Sircar chooses to dramatize some central
aspects of the history of British India by conducting a history lesson for his spectators. The lesson is a microcosm of the colonial
rule in India. The play opens with three teachers, ridiculously
authoritative figures, conducting the roll call—an interminable ritual in Calcutta University, where there are close to a hundred students in each class. The students, who are seated in the audience,
answer mechanically. The banality of the teaching process is skilfully parodied in the repetition of words and the prescribed modes
of interrogation and response—"Good. . . . Very good. . . . Clear?
. . . Yes sir." The students are denied the freedom to question the
rhetoric and absurdities of their lesson. They repeat all the words
of their professors with an appalling subservience. The effect, of
course, is quite hilarious because the progression of the words—
"Ram . . . Shyam . . . Raj . . . Rajo . . . Ramrajo . . . Shyamrajo
. . . Gramshomaj"—epitomizes the ludicrous thinking process of
the teachers. When the students occasionally moan in unison in
Bengali, "What does this mean, sir?" the teachers yell in English,
"Silence, no noise please, stand up on the bench!"[28]

As the class continues, a woman carrying a Union Jack saunters
onto a platform at the end of the hall. Demonstrating their colonial affinities, the teachers shout, "Three cheers for Britannia! Rule
Britannia! Three cheers for the Battle of Plassey!" Their cheers
ring hollow and only serve to highlight their subservience to a
dead past. A particularly obsequious character (called the Anglophile for the purpose of this discussion) runs on tiptoe toward the
Woman with the Union Jack and addresses her as "Ma, Ma Britannia!" The Anglophile behaves like a dutiful son before his "ma."
Like a child waiting for a treat, he tells her about all the money
that is accumulating in the East India Company. Responding like a
distraught and possessive mother, the Woman with the Union Jack
asks him, "How much will I get?" She gloats when she hears the
sum of forty lakhs and is positively ecstatic when the three teachers genuflect in front of her and chant, "We will lay everything at
your feet, Ma."

The Woman ceases to be a mother figure and acquires the sanctity of a deity. In response to her metamorphosis and the choked emotions of the teachers, the members of the chorus, including the students, form a make-believe palanquin using a few props, such as a brightly colored umbrella, and march around the room singing "God Save Our Gracious Queen." The Woman with the Union Jack listens in rapture while the Anglophile nestles on her arm like a baby. The teachers continue to genuflect, begging for more favors like electricity and other industrial amenities. The Woman responds to their obsequiousness most graciously. "What do I have to worry," she simpers, "you are giving me gold, silver . . . oooh, I will get so much more." While voicing her acquisitive desires, she caresses the baby on her arm and murmurs the most inane endearments to him.

After this farcical satire, we return to the history lesson, where the students are gradually becoming restless. Suddenly, with the introduction of a new term in their lesson—*shilpo biplob* (industrial revolution)—the class breaks up and the actors form a gigantic "machine" with their bodies. While their legs and hands move rhythmically like pistons, an actress playing a destitute woman rushes into the room with a prolonged scream. The machine disintegrates; the actors writhe on the floor. The three teachers stalk around the room like petty officers of the British Raj, chanting, "We want more! more! more!" Simultaneously, an actor in the background voices a commentary on the economic exploitation of the British. As the statistics of the British "loot" become increasingly alarming, the actors on the floor gradually become inert. The three teachers transform themselves into vultures—ugly, heavy creatures with sharp talons—and move from one corpselike body to another with clumsy movements and grotesque hops. These transitional movements within the history lesson are the most inventive instances of Sircar's mise en scène.

Back in the lesson and the reign of Cornwallis during the British Raj, we learn that "marketing capital has been replaced by industrial capital" in India. Juxtaposing this academic maxim spouted by the teachers, a commentator informs us that the British are suppressing the "native" industries of India by forcing the people to buy goods manufactured in Britain with Indian resources. Though an atmosphere is created to rouse the materialistic instincts of the people, it soon becomes clear to the British that they cannot sell as many goods as they want to. Somewhat apprehensively, the Anglophile goes over to his ma, who reprimands him with sharp words for his remisses, *"Ei cholbe na!"* ("This won't do!"). However, when she hears that Warren Hastings has been impeached for corruption, she informs her son with the cloying attitude of an overprotective mother, "We have sent all the wicked children away. Now go and play."

We learn there is a growing demand for foreign goods in India and a subsequent impoverishment among the people. The chorus calls attention to this state of affairs by singing a song about mother's love, that most sacrosanct theme of Bengali literature and art. As the Anglophile tiptoes into his mother's arms in an absurd demonstration of filial love, the destitute woman reenters the room with a scream. As she informs the audience of her son's death, the Woman with the Union Jack tells her "son" to be more careful. "Take care of yourself," she murmurs protectively. It is through such juxtapositions that *Shukhpathe Bharater Itihas* transcends a mere documentation of facts relating to British colonialism in India.

Throughout the play, we are made to feel the continuing ethos of colonialism in India. The most jarring reminders occur when the students demonstrate their use of the English language—"Yes sir no sir very good sir I am sir your most obedient servant." This example epitomizes the fundamental subservience of *"babu* English," the most pervasive legacy of the British Raj. It is the kind of language most Indians use when they apply for jobs. Though alienated from it, they have to use it if they want to "rise in life." Apart from these bursts of *babu* English, the actors sing a parodic song about the *zemindari* system (landlord rule) that was deviously strengthened and abetted by the British at various stages during the Raj. The sequence is likely to make a Westerner wince because the actors do the twist while singing the song. Their movements seem unnatural, their bonhomie false. In no sequence of Sircar's theater does the Western influence on his actors' movements seem more jarring.

As India's history becomes increasingly turbulent, the class be-

comes more riotous and disorganized. By the time they reach the
outbreak of the First World War, the students can no longer tolerate their history lesson. The class is disbanded. With the emergence
of the Quit India movement, even the teachers abandon their former roles as sycophants of the Raj. Most ironically, they become
prominent national leaders. Their hypocrisies are engagingly revealed when the Anglophile, who continues to support the Raj,
goes up to them and asks them in the sweetest of tones, "What
would you like?" They demand whatever is of immediate appeal to
the contemporary middle class in Bengal. They want cars, private
tuition facilities for their children, admission for their children
into English-medium schools, even tickets for the "Test Match" (an
amusing topical reference for most Bengalis, who are passionate
about cricket matches between India and the West Indies and
other major international teams.)

After some of these demands are satisfied, the leaders are momentarily placated. But in the second phase of the Quit India
movement, their demands become more aggressive and difficult to
meet. While the negotiations for freedom are discussed by the
national leaders, the destitute woman rouses the patriotism of the
chorus, who represent the Indian masses. They march around the
room chanting slogans against the supremacy of the British Raj.
With a sudden and violent movement, the Anglophile grabs the
woman and throws her on the floor. He then stamps on her body.
After this savage display of loyalty to the Raj, the Anglophile
leaves the room followed by the other actors. The audience is compelled to concentrate on the condition of the woman lying on the
floor.

The woman rises and tells the spectators in a quiet and matter-
of-fact manner to prepare themselves for more deaths. The members of the chorus reenter the room, participating energetically in
a freedom chant. Gradually, it gets slower and slower, merging
into cries of despair, pleas for food, and hoarse lamentations. The
words *rakta ar khudha* (blood and hunger) are repeated intermina-
bly. They evoke a world of destitution and famine. As the dispersed
cries continue to sound in various parts of the room, the teachers
make a sudden reappearance reading the roll call, their strident,
clipped voices contrasting sharply with the cries of the people. In a

carefully orchestrated eruption of violence that rises in a swift crescendo, the actors converge on the teachers who almost disappear
in the mass of bodies that surrounds them. It seems as if the last
upholders of colonialism in India have been finally annihilated.

But the spirit of colonialism still exists in India. We are reminded of this by the actress playing the destitute woman. Abandoning any pretense of "acting," she steps outside her role and
speaks to us directly, reminding us that the exploitation and misery
of the masses continue. A brief epilogue follows her statement. We
see the Anglophile and the Woman with the Union Jack waltzing
at one end of the room to the tune of "Around the World in Eighty
Days." The Woman, however, no longer carries the Union Jack.
Instead, a huge dollar sign is pinned on the back of her sari. It is an
insidious reminder of the omnipresence and power of capitalism.

Bhoma

More powerfully than any other play written by Sircar, *Bhoma*
confronts the dichotomy between urban and rural life in India.
The title of the play refers to a destitute villager called Bhoma who
lived in the Sundarbans—a wasteland of a district, marshy and
desolate, where nothing grows and the people are lucky to eat a
meal a day. When Sircar came in contact with the villagers of the
Sundarbans, he was shocked by the dehumanized conditions of
their life. But more than shocked he was enraged by the fact that
the urban community of West Bengal (despite its own problems
of transportation, generation of electricity, distribution of food)
could be so totally indifferent to the impoverishment of the villagers in the Sundarbans.

Anger is the driving force of *Bhoma*—a relentless, though rigorously controlled anger directed against the well-fed, easy-going
bourgeoisie of Calcutta. It is this anger that makes the play more
than a lament for Bhoma himself as an individual or for the thousands of Bhomas who continue to survive from day to day in
Bengal, scavenging for food in garbage heaps and sleeping on
dusty pavements. *Bhoma* is Sircar's most vigorous indictment of
West Bengal's urban bourgeoisie.

There have been many productions about characters like Bhoma in the Bengali theater. In fact, the "oppressed peasant" pro-

vides as many stereotypes for a Bengali audience as a maharaja or a politician. He is generally played by actors who desperately attempt to identify with his problems and state of oppression. This process of identification creates dilemmas for the spectators. My own experience as a spectator of this "identification process" has been somewhat disturbing. It seems to me that the more an actor from the city attempts to give an authentic performance of a villager, the more distant he seems from the realities of rural life. The more accomplished his mastery of rural dialects, the more destitute his appearance, the more tattered his costume, the more remote he seems from the life of the oppressed peasant. The distance between a *bhadrolok* actor and the oppression of the villagers he attempts to depict is often an embarrassment.

Though Sircar's actors, it might be argued, are as middle class as most of the actors in the Bengali theater, they are more successful in their dramatization of the life of the oppressed peasant precisely because they do not attempt to identify with him. On the contrary, they present his conditions of life and everyday problems without abandoning their perspectives as performers. Not only does Sircar's impersonal mode of acting—spare, matter-of-fact, unpretentious—enable his actors to comment on the situation of the oppressed peasant with astonishing accuracy, it prevents them from expressing his suffering with a surfeit of melodramatic gestures and sensational movements.

The simplicity of *Bhoma* is its strength. Sircar concentrates on his subject without calling attention to the talent or virtuosity of his actors. Watching the production a number of times has made me understand Sircar's aversion to technique. On a certain level, no one can deny that Sircar's actors require a great deal of skill in order to project the suffering of an oppressed people with such intensity. But the skill is not displayed; the technique of the actors remains invisible. What matters is the direct communication of the subject between the spectators and the actors—a communication so immediate and simple in its mode of transmission that it almost makes one question its reliance on any form of technique.

The first moments of *Bhoma* are so unobtrusive that it takes time to realize that the play has started. Six actors dressed in black shorts and loose black shirts sit around the acting area and do some preliminary exercises and warm-ups to relax their muscles.

After lying on their backs, they begin to pant with varying rhythms and pitches that increase in volume and suddenly stop. The actors rise, join hands, and look intently at one another. Then they walk around the room, occasionally stopping to stare at a particular spectator in the audience. Their movements are stealthy, somewhat tentative. A chorus chants in the background, and the actors on stage crouch on the floor, responding ever so minutely to the mournful cadences of the song. The crouching of the actors, as they cave their bodies inward and bury their faces in their hands, evokes the suffering of the people in an uncanny way. It is by no means overdone or melodramatic.

The action of the play begins with an evocation of rural life. Despite the sounds of the birds and the actors posing as trees, there is nothing particularly idyllic about this pastoral scene. Two actors playing laborers cut down the trees with savage motions. "Farmers" sow seeds and cut wheat while a machine hums in the background suggesting the proximity of urban development. When the actors begin to speak, they cut into each other's line. We hear fragments of messages relating to the predicament of Bhoma—"Now I know what I have always known. . . . People don't know. . . . I want to tell people who don't know. . . ." When the name of Bhoma is first sounded, it is instantly repeated by the actors with one harmonious wail. Then follows what can be described as the "Bhoma litany," flat funereal statements that are repeated throughout the play with a restrained lyricism.

> *Macher rakta thanda* [The blood of fish is cold]
>
> *Age manusher rakta chilo garam* [At one time the blood of men was warm]
>
> *Akhon manusher rakta thanda* [Now it is cold]
>
> *Thanda*
>
> *Thanda*
>
> *Thanda*[29]

The word *thanda* has an eerie resonance as it is repeated by the actors in the refrain. It is through such repetitions of words that Sircar reinforces his views concerning the indifference of man to other men.

Having evoked the suffering of Bhoma, the actors play typical middle-class characters who resemble Amal, Vimal, and Kamal in *Evam Indrajit*, except that they are more disillusioned and jaded. One character (who will here be called the Stenographer) separates himself from the other actors and paces the room stating his name, his job at Samson and Blackbird Company, his salary, and the number of children he has. While he rattles off his speech, another character tries to tell the actors around him that he once loved a girl. He continues to repeat that line somewhat desperately while the actors laugh raucously. Yet another actor interrupts this jumble of sounds by saying that a man was found dead in Sealdah Station. Someone adds: "At another section of Sealdah Station, a child was born."

These contradictory statements merge into a proliferation of jingles as the actors parody the advertising campaign of the West Bengal Tourist Board. The very sound of the jingles—"*Sundar* Calcutta," (Beautiful Calcutta), "See India"—are unpleasant reminders of an industry (one among many in Calcutta) that makes profits at the expense of attending to the needs of the people. While the jingles continue with a jarring effect, an actor goes up to Sircar (who is one of six actors in the play) and asks him what Bhoma means. There is no need for Sircar to provide an explanation; the faint cries of destitute people begin to sound in the room evoking the reality of Bhoma.

"*Jol chai, jol dao*" ("We want water, give us water"): these words are repeated over and over till they seem to echo without being voiced. Disrupting this aura of destitution, Sircar rises from the floor and informs the audience in a loud, urgent voice that the people have "no water, no fertilizer, no seeds, no land, no work, no water." His outburst is followed by the most haunting statement in the play, which has been intoned earlier: "*Manusher rakta thanda, thanda, thanda*" ("The blood of man is cold, cold, cold"). Sircar emphasizes this statement by making another actor disbelieve it. While this actor protests that men are not inhuman, the refrain of the statement "*thanda . . . thanda . . . thanda*" continues to sound. This technique of accentuating the significance of a statement by opposing it in some way or another is constantly used by Sircar in *Bhoma*.

In a later sequence, while four of the actors participate in a

lusty rendition of a popular Hindi film song with whistles and improvised sounds, Sircar attempts to tell them that there is no electricity in the villages. The opposition to his statement provided by
the incessant background of the Hindi film music only serves to
highlight it. After the song builds to a climax, the actors lie on the
floor and continue to chant *"Jol chai, jol dao"*—words that resonate the predicament of thousands of villagers suffering from
drought.

Like all of Sircar's plays, *Bhoma* relies on juxtapositions to illuminate the contradictions and disparities of the socio-economic situations examined in the play. The following sequence of action
should be carefully studied for its strategic use of transitions. The
actor playing the Stenographer (of Samson and Blackbird Company) rattles off his speech at breakneck speed. Another actor playing a representative of a small engineering company (blantantly
exploited by Samson and Blackbird) interrupts this speech by
requesting a loan from a bank manager. The actor playing the
Manager struts around the room with a pipe in his mouth occasionally emitting garbled sounds like a computer with technical
problems. Abruptly, he turns to the company representative and
peremptorily demands ten thousand rupees as a security loan. The
telephone rings and we hear the Manager speak like an accomplished diplomat to a representative of Samson and Blackbird who
also requests a loan. No security is needed for this business transaction.

The injustice of this situation is objectified in the narrative that
follows. Two actors stand on either side of the room facing the audience and speak of the predicament of a farmer who needs a loan
from the bank to buy a pump. Unfortunately, the bank demands
too much security and the pump cannot be obtained. The Manager continues to speak to the representative of Samson and Blackbird urging him to take a larger loan. This is followed by the Stenographer's speech and sporadic cries of "blood" and "water." The
chant of Bhoma continues in the background: *"Manusher rakta
thanda, thanda, thanda."*

At this point in the play it is still not clear who Bhoma is. Only
the actor played by Sircar persists in believing in his existence. "I
haven't seen Bhoma," he admits, "but unless he's alive, unless he
sustains us, I can't live, nobody lives." The other actors reject this

belief and claim that they alone exist. In a frantic scene, they begin to chant, *"Aami! Aami! Aami!"* ("I! I! I!"). The repetitions of the first person singular are used, quite obviously, to emphasize the selfishness of the bourgeoisie. Sircar has his actors run a number of stylized races that evoke all the greed and ruthless competition that control the lives of people in cities.

The movements of the actors get increasingly frenetic. Then the Stenographer breaks the action with his speech (fragments of which have been constantly repeated in the play). The Stenographer now completes it. Apart from telling the audience where he works and how many children he has, he adds that if he had gone to an English-medium school he could have earned a higher salary. He confides that he is now sending his son to such a school so that he can be admitted to the Indian Institute of Technology and, perhaps, pursue his studies in America. These comments are intensely familiar to Sircar's middle-class audience, who share similar views. The Stenographer's reference to America triggers a number of snide comments on dollars. The audience is reminded of the power of dollars—"Dollars can build roads." "Everyone wants dollars."—and the practice of the rich who accumulate their unrevealed incomes in Swiss banks. An anguished cry—"Bhoma!"—overpowers all this talk about dollars and money. It is followed by the refrain, *"Manusher rakta thanda, thanda, thanda."*

In a subsequent sequence calculated to unsettle the audience, Sircar plays a physically handicapped vagrant who is one among two million victims of radioactivity in our world. With a fixed smile, he says, "We are all at peace." While he goes around begging for alms, one of the actors asks somewhat ingenuously, "What is to be done? To make our blood warm again?" He is told by another voice in the group to remember Bhoma. "We drink the blood of Bhoma and live in the city"; the statement is meant to assault the complacency of Sircar's middle-class audience. As they confront their lack of concern for Bhoma, they hear the muffled tones of an actor speaking in the voice of Bhoma. It is a strangely disembodied voice even though the actor lies on the floor in full view of the audience, his face pressed against the ground. It seems to come from nowhere. As it continues to sound, the actors run around in circles trying to find Bhoma.

In their search, they transport the audience to the port of Gosa-

ba in the Sundarbans, miming a boat with astonishing verismili-
tude. The physical dexterity of the actors in this sequence (which
stimulates the audience to relax and admire the sheer invention of
Sircar's stagecraft) is neutralized by a narrative that is shocking in
its suddenness. Without any preparation, the audience is told that
Bhoma is dead, his parents are also dead, his mother a victim of
snake bite, his father killed by a crocodile; his older brother continues to live, earning three rupees (thirty-eight cents) a day for
three months out of the year.

In an abrasive switch of tone, the actors forget about Bhoma
and behave like a typical group of middle-class friends who are
planning to go to the Sundarbans for a picnic. The preparations
for the picnic, which are banal, giddy, and infuriatingly inane, are
interrupted by Sircar, who informs the spectators that there are no
doctors, no jeeps, no adequate security measures in the Sundarbans. If there is a crime on one of these islands, he says, the police
arrive three days later. The appalling facts of the daily existence in
the Sundarbans are heightened by the eruption of a cyclone on one
of the islands, which is physicalized by the actors with flailing
hands, wild movements, and piercing screams. It is a magnificent
piece of group acting, which evokes the horror and tragedy of the
event without sensationalizing it. People drowning, people left destitute, the land swept away: these realities are visualized without
the aid of sensational gestures or picturesque tableaux.

Once the cyclone ebbs, the actors pick themselves up and life
continues. While five of them walk around the room in a stupor,
they are individually asked by the remaining actor if they know
Bhoma. It appears that Bhoma still lives. He can be found, one
among thousands of beggars, vagrants, and refugees who live per-
manently in Sealdah Station and on the pavements of Calcutta.
Sircar urges his audience not to ignore these human beings who
have been left on the streets to die.

Most powerfully, he makes his audience confront its indifference
to Bhoma by staging two disparate scenes at once. In a corner of
the room, an actor representing Bhoma dies slowly and despair-
ingly while Sircar attempts to speak to him. In the center of the
room, a group of four actors sit cross-legged on the floor and
avidly watch a Hindi film. When the cries of "Bhoma" become

increasingly anguished, the audience watching the film starts shouting, "Stop interrupting the film." A moment later, a matinee idol appears on the screen and they begin to whistle. Bhoma continues to die at the other end of the stage.

After this grotesque juxtaposition of events, Sircar's statement—*Manusher rakta thanda*—which has been repeated relentlessly throughout the entire play, acquires a terrifying significance. More immediately than any play I am aware of in the Bengali theater, *Bhoma* makes an audience confront its indifference to poverty. Sights like Bhoma are everyday presences in Calcutta. One cannot avoid them. They are to be found everywhere, like the garbage in the streets. One walks past them without feeling a twinge of guilt. They are part of Calcutta's landscape. Occasionally, when their clamor becomes obtrusive, one drops a few coins beside them on the pavement. But more often than not, one is more anxious to keep an appointment or reach the bus stop on time. It is precisely this absorption in the minutiae of everyday life that Sircar attacks in *Bhoma*. Without lecturing us, he urges us, even demands from us a recognition of our callousness. I can think of no other play in the Bengali theater that makes an audience question its relation to the oppressed people with such emotional power and clarity.

Toward a Theater of the Oppressed

Even though *Bhoma* is specifically addressed to a middle-class urban community in Bengal, it was first performed for a predominantly rural audience on an open-air platform in Rangabaylia, a village in the Sundarbans. This performance had a special significance for Sircar because Bhoma had once lived in Rangabaylia. His younger brother was among the six thousand spectators who witnessed it. Though no documentation of this performance exists, Sircar informed me in an interview that the villagers were not bewildered by the presentational form and methods of his theater, so remote from the conventions of the *jatra*. On the contrary, they responded to their predicament enacted and addressed on stage with a concentration one does not readily associate with rural audiences.

The rapport between the inhabitants of the Sundarbans and

Sircar's theater was even more perceptible in a workshop conducted by Sircar in Rangabaylia. Of course, the workshop could
not function with thousands of people; there were just twenty-five
to thirty participants. Half of them were totally illiterate, unable
to write their own names. The other half had studied through
grade three or four until their poverty had made it impossible for
them to continue. Only two or three of the participants had matri-
culated. Initially, with his characteristic humility, Sircar believed
that he would not be able to communicate with these people. But
within two days he had established a relationship with them based
on trust and mutual respect.

Quite understandably, Sircar was not interested in teaching the
villagers of the Sundarbans "how to act." What concerned him
was something more fundamental. He described it to me as "the
training of the person" that involved the removal of psychological
blocks and inhibitions. In order to make his participants realize
the strength of their interrelations as people, Sircar improvised situations and games that compelled them to respond instinctively
and as members of a community. Like all significant workshops,
the one in Rangabaylia was generated by the participants themselves. Sircar functioned less as a leader and more as a catalyst
who enabled the participants to discover themselves as people by
confronting their inner resources, tensions, and moments of communion.

The most illuminating section of the workshop involved playwriting. There was only one restriction imposed on the participants: they had to write the play within ten minutes. Sircar was
quite astonished by the "writings" (enactments) of the villagers.
Instead of using the cliches and rhetoric of local *jatra* productions
(which Sircar had imagined would be the most powerful influence
on the villagers), the participants of the workshop "wrote" about
their lives in a colloquial, often nonverbal idiom. Instead of dealing with fictitious themes and characters, they concentrated on
their everyday activities with a telling use of detail.

There were plays about their experiences in the forest involving
the proximity of man-eating tigers or the constant threat of dacoits
and poachers. There were plays dealing with the interference of
the police and the exploitation of the moneylenders. Most poig-

nantly, there were plays that dramatized the loss of lives. One play concentrated on a man dying of overwork. It was so powerful that it needed neither criticism nor commentary. Other plays dealt with more commonplace activities like cutting wood in the forest or collecting honey—everyday activities that indirectly illuminated the economic exploitation of the villagers.

Collecting honey, for instance, is one of the major sources of employment for villagers in the Sundarbans, who are employed by local manufacturers of honey, including various government organizations. It is a well-known fact, however, that the villagers are miserably paid. Their labor is so cheap that it enables their employers to amass huge profits at their expense. By merely enacting the collecting of honey, a villager might come to understand the value of his work. He could realize how much he is worth in terms of his labor and he could contrast this with how much he is paid by his employers. His exploitation would be even clearer to him if his colleagues could play his employers, thereby allowing him to voice his grievances. By enacting the role he plays in life, the villager might be able to articulate his problems with greater precision and confidence. He could learn to face his real-life employers with a more concrete awareness of his rights as a human being.

Sircar's playwriting workshop with the villagers might have been more useful had each individual's play been altered by all the participants. There is a great deal to be learned from discussing a play as a community and altering its perspectives in such a way that it opens up possibilities of change in the lives of the people. In such an experiment, the play ceases to be an expression of an individual: it becomes the forum of a group of people.

Sircar would, in all probability, be drawn to Augusto Boal's model of "forum theater" where a specific problem dramatized by an individual is tested by a group of people. In *Theater of the Oppressed*, Boal describes how one of the participants in his workshop presented his predicament to the forum. The participant claimed that he worked in a fish factory from eight in the morning to eight at night, there were fewer than ten employees in the factory, and his boss was a ruthless exploiter. What could he do about his situation? After presenting his problem, he enacted it and even offered a solution—working so fast and filling the machine with so much fish that it broke down, enabling him to rest for a couple of hours while the machine was repaired. After this solution was enacted, the participants in Boal's workshop disagreed violently about its viability. They protested that the worker would have to return to the factory after the machine was repaired: nothing would change in his life.

The actor who suggested the first solution was then replaced by another, who wanted to destroy the factory. The only problem with his solution was that he did not know how to manufacture a bomb or even how to throw it. A third participant entered the scene and proposed a strike. But the actors playing his employers presented an obstacle to his solution: they coolly ignored him and recruited unemployed workers to replace the strikers. And so the various solutions were tried out. . . .

The purpose of forum theater, Boal reminds us, is not to provide the best solution but to offer the means by which all the possible solutions can be examined. The formation of a union would probably be the best solution to the problem of the worker discussed above. But, for Boal, the process of realization by which the spectators/participants understand the power and limitation of each solution is more important. Boal believes that when a worker "*rehearses* throwing a bomb, he is concretely rehearsing the way a bomb is thrown; acting out his attempt to organize a strike, he is concretely organizing a strike." Although the activity of theater may not be revolutionary in itself, it is potentially a "rehearsal of revolution."[30]

The forum theater is just one among many structures provided by Boal to raise the social and political consciousness of the people. It seems to me that Sircar can use these structures most profitably and improvise on them in his workshops with villagers. It should be stressed that Boal's models of theater are not merely theoretical fabrications; they have been tested, questioned, and fully explored by people in Peru, Argentina, and Brazil, whose impoverishment and oppression can compare with the appalling conditions of life in the rural areas of India. If Boal's models of political theater were adopted by Sircar, they would not, I think, be foreign to him. On the contrary, they would simply extend his own exploration of theater as a "rural-urban link."

There is a temperamental affinity between the work of these two men in their resistance to Marxist dogma, political rhetoric, and party politics. Besides, both Boal and Sircar share a fundamental attitude toward the political theater that is, to my mind, exemplary. Neither of them is interested in teaching the people what they don't know. Neither of them assumes an evangelical role. Boal begins his work with the assumption that "when an educator comes to the villages with the mission of eradicating illiteracy (which presupposes a coercive, forceful action)," his presence inevitably works as "an alienating factor between the agent and the local people." Consequently, what Boal provides is neither a script nor an ideology but a situation in which the people can confront their own problems and question their possibilities for development.

This is precisely what Sircar offered the villagers of Rangabaylia with his workshop. He did not attempt to write or think for them. They thought and wrote for themselves, about themselves. Ultimately, Sircar shares Boal's faith that the people can create a theater for themselves that will enable them to understand and shape the conditions of their life.

THE FUTURE OF THE THIRD THEATER

There can be no doubt, to my mind, that the future of the Third Theater lies in the direction of Boal's "theater of the oppressed." Instead of merely performing plays for the people, it is time for Satabdi to work actively with the people. If Sircar claims that the Third Theater is a "theater of synthesis" that attempts to confront the dichotomy between urban and rural life, he needs to open his theater to the people so that they can actively participate in it and change its structure and modes of communication. As admirable as his efforts have been in depicting the oppression of the people, they have been somewhat limited by the middle-class milieu of his theater. Satabdi needs to move beyond the confines of the Angamancha and interact more dynamically with the people in fields and open spaces. Only then will it be able to confront the problems of the people with a perspective that synthesizes rural and urban attitudes.

There is yet another reason why Satabdi needs to move in the direction of the theater of the oppressed. While continuing to challenge the norms, conventions, and economic structure of the commercial theater, it has established its own norms, conventions, and economic structure. Like many alternative theater movements that succeed, the Third Theater seems to have institutionalized itself. It tends to repeat the same ideas using the same techniques. What was once daring has now become familiar. What was once unobtrusive now calls attention to itself. In fact, one can now begin to speak of a "Satabdi aesthetic," objectionable as it may seem to Sircar and his actors.

Perhaps, the major problem has to do with the fact that Sircar has recently been producing adaptations of foreign plays rather than his own plays. While *Gondi* (Circle), an adaptation of *The Caucasian Chalk Circle*, was a refreshing contrast to the overproduced and melodramatic version of the same play produced by the Bengali theater group Nandikar, it was not a particularly illuminating production.[31] Although I admired the spareness of Sircar's script and the skilful transformation of Brecht's songs into choral recitatives, I found myself missing the subtle dialectics and interplay of contradictions that pervade this extraordinary play in its original text.

Sircar's adaptation had the simplicity and lyricism of a Bengali folk tale, with many of Brecht's characters deftly transformed into recognizable Bengali types. The production was undeniably intimate, but it failed to raise questions, however tentative or subtle, that had some bearing on the lives of a Bengali middle-class audience. *Gondi* was curiously removed from the turbulence of life in Calcutta. After seeing the production, I could not understand why Satabdi had produced the play? What was its specific purpose? How did it relate to the process of Satabdi's development? How did it serve as a nucleus for Sircar's investigations of theater as a "rural-urban link"? These questions concerned me long after I had seen the play.

I was even more bewildered by Sircar's recent adaptation of Weiss's *Marat/Sade*, which revealed many limitations of the Third Theater. It is a curious paradox that Sircar's actors are least convincing when they are compelled to "act." Marat, Sade, and Charlotte Corday are demanding roles that require particular vocal and technical skills associated with rigorous schools of acting. When Satabdi's actors (including Sircar) attempt to play these roles in that matter-of-fact, impersonal style they have cultivated in recent years, they are particularly unconvincing. On the other hand, when they attempt to project hysteria with Artaudian gestures and screams, they are appallingly amateurish. It is strange that Sircar should choose to work on such a sophisticated play that demands what he so supremely disdains to acknowledge in his theater—technique.

It is not easy to determine why Sircar has been working on these adaptations of Brecht and Weiss. Perhaps they are part of a transitional phase in his career. Certainly they do not represent his strength as an artist. A more interesting experiment than these adaptations was his production of *Bashi Khabar* (Stale News), which was collectively researched and shaped by all the actors in Satabdi. Sircar wrote the text of the play only after it was fully investigated by the group.

Focusing on the Sanyasi rebellion against the British in the mid-nineteenth century, the play attempts to expose the collaborationist role of the Bengali middle class during the British Raj. It also tries to relate this historical phenomenon to contemporary bourgeois attitudes prevalent in Bengal, particularly in relation to everyday calamities and dilemmas.

Part of the problem with this production was its overly abstract treatment of historical material. Featuring prominently in the mise en scène was a corpselike figure swathed entirely in white cloth who periodically raised his hand. Though surely arresting as an image, it was unclear what this figure was meant to symbolize or, more important, how he related to the rest of the action in the play.

Apart from obfuscating history, the production was also indiscriminately physicalized. There was no coherence in the transitions of the mise en scène. Many of the sections, which seemed to be deliberately tacked onto the production, were sensational in effect. Earlier I mentioned the lurid evocation of the birth of man in *Bashi Khabar*, which blatantly imitated the "rite of birth" sequence in Richard Schechner's production of *Dionysus in '69*.

Needless to say, its relationship to the Sanyasi rebellion was nebulous.

In no production by Satabdi was one more aware of a lack of direction in the shaping of the material and the utterance of the message. There were too many conflicting perspectives on the subject matter, which itself was never clarified in the course of the production. After a point, it seemed as if the Sanyasi rebellion was incidental to the diverse action of the play. Perhaps Sircar and his actors need to acknowledge that "collective creation" does not necessarily result in a rigorous or particularly intelligent production.

Since *Bashi Khabar*, Sircar has produced one new play based on his own script. Entitled *Hattamalar Oparey*, it depicts the confusion of two runaway thieves incongruously placed in a utopia where money and property do not exist. According to Samik Bandyopadhyay, a primitive communism underlies the existence of this imaginary world, which is governed on the principle of absolute equality—"each according to his capacity and to each according to his need." The play seems to be in part a resurfacing of Sircar's penchant for fantasy, a genre he explored in his early production of *Abu Hossain*.

While acknowledging Sircar's right to experiment in different theatrical modes, one can only hope that he will continue to write plays in which the suffering of the people is concretely confronted and questioned as in *Bhoma*. It would be useful for him to reassess his own investigation of theater (prior to the adaptations of Brecht and Weiss), which he had pursued so rigorously till the creation of *Bhoma* and the workshop at Rangabaylia. I regret that, to the best of my knowledge, he has not conducted similar workshops in the rural areas of Bengal. If there is any director in the contemporary Bengali theater who is capable of creating a genuine people's theater—a theater supported and created by the people and not merely performed for the people—it is Badal Sircar.

4
Varieties of Political Theater in Bengal

The theaters of Utpal Dutt and Badal Sircar represent two of the most striking and contradictory approaches to the political theater in Bengal. Differing significantly in their scale, purpose, and modes of productions, these two theaters nonetheless share a fundamental affinity in their level of energy and their relationship to the life in the streets of Calcutta. After watching a play by Dutt or Sircar and walking out into the street, with its familiar sights of children scavenging for food in garbage heaps and people hanging out of buses and trams, one feels relieved that the play one has just seen is not removed from this turbulent reality.

The theaters of Dutt and Sircar are strong enough to convey the pressures of life in Calcutta: they belong to Calcutta. Each relates in its own radically different way to this tortured city with its eight-and-a-half-million people and innumerable problems, but ultimately both are committed to Calcutta and its people with an intensity that transcends their differences. In their individual ways and with varying degrees of success, both Dutt and Sircar confront the problems of the people in Calcutta and rural Bengal with the fervent belief that these problems can be surmounted. Their solutions to these problems vary significantly—Dutt advocates his brand of Marxism while Sircar appeals to the humanity of his spectators. While their commitment to changing the conditions of life in Calcutta is sometimes inconspicuous (in the case of Sircar) and blatantly egotistic (in the case of Dutt), it is perceptible in most of the plays performed by Satabdi and the People's Little Theater.

At this point, it seems appropriate to analyze a number of productions in the Bengali theater that exemplify different forms of commitment in the political theater. It is not necessary to represent all the theater groups in Bengal, since I am interested only in those groups that have consciously attempted to confront the socio-economic conditions of life in Calcutta and the rural areas of Bengal.[1] This confrontation does not necessarily mean that the only valid political theater in Bengal is agitprop. Local issues and topical events are not the only means by which the socio-economic problems and oppression of a people can be illuminated. As we have examined in the theaters of Dutt and Sircar, it is possible to relate seemingly distant historical events like Vietnam and Hiroshima to the immediate exigencies of life in Bengal.

Foreign subject matter of a political nature should be confronted by theater groups in Bengal. But what about foreign models of theater such as Brecht's "epic theater"? Does the phenomenon of Brecht in Bengal have validity in relation to the urban political theater of Calcutta? How effectively can bourgeois actors from the city address the problems of the people? What are the inherent contradictions of producing a "people's theater" in the city? These questions are examined in relation to the daring and innovative work of the Living Theater of Khardah, one of the most committed theater groups in Bengal today.

Before reflecting on that immensely popular, if idiosyncratic, phenomenon of Brecht in Bengal, it is necessary to point out that what distinguishes the efficacy of a political theater group in Calcutta is not its adherence to an ideology but its connection with the life in the streets. This connection does not necessarily involve a representation of Calcutta's familiar sights and everyday occurrences—fights at bus stops and cinema houses, stampedes at soccer matches, processions, policemen chasing street vendors and pavement dwellers—it has more to do with capturing the frenetic energy that pervades the city. This energy can be conveyed in a number of ways—one cannot specify its mode of expression—but its absence is most conspicuous in the Bengali theater, particularly among those groups with political pretensions.

What is so specific about the energy conveyed in the plays of Dutt and Sircar is its undercurrent of anger—an anger that is directly related to the resentment and sense of deprivation shared by thousands of people in Calcutta who do not have the basic necessities of life. While this anger is more explicit in Dutt than in Sircar, it is integral to both their theaters insofar as it directs the pervasive energy of their plays. Without it, their depiction of the energy in the city would be a mere indulgence, a form of abandon.

BRECHT IN BENGAL

Nandikar's Brecht: *Tin Poyshar Pala* and *Kharir Gondhi*

There are many socio-political plays in Bengal that project an energy that seems to correspond to the life in the streets. More often than not it is not motivated by anger; rather it is a tour de force, a display of virtuosity and stamina on the part of the actors. *Tin Poyshar Pala*, an adaptation of *The Threepenny Opera* produced by Nandikar in 1969, epitomizes this kind of Bengali production.[2]

In this spirited production, where Macheath was played as a romantic bandit by Ajitesh Banerjee, the star of the company, there were many laughs, countless burlesque situations, hilarious songs with innuendos, and a consistently festive atmosphere. But, as Samik Bandyopadhyay impatiently points out, there was no connection between this production and the political situation in Bengal. Speaking to A. J. Gunawardana, who interviewed him for *The Drama Review*, Bandyopadhyay says:

> When we [in the Bengali theater] have a production of *The Threepenny Opera* which simply goes in for wild fun, we regard it as a compromise, a betrayal. This production has no point when there is serious political violence in Calcutta. When Macheath says, "This is your bourgeois society," people laugh. They take it as a joke for that is the spirit of the entire production. And when I come out of the theater, the life I live, the connections and associations to which I respond are very different from what I get in *Tin Poyshar Pala*. This is status quo theater, which means nothing to a generation that thinks in political terms. This production makes us very angry, not merely unhappy.[3]

Bandyopadhyay's anger is justified. There is no reason to stage *The Threepenny Opera* as a farce, particularly since Brecht's examination of the bourgeois view of the world in the play is relevant to the materialistic mentality of the bourgeoisie in Bengal. I do not believe that all of Brecht's plays can be successfully adapted for the Bengali theater. But unlike a play like *Arturo Ui* (discussed later), *The Threepenny Opera* can be strategically adapted to highlight the corruption of traders and profiteers in Bengal. This adaptation is only possible if the Bengali actors are in a position to examine the attitudes toward money and property of Brecht's characters which determine their functions in the play.

Unfortunately, Nandikar's actors romanticize Brecht's characters and transform their bourgeois vices into endearing characteristics. Macheath is played like a matinee idol whose manner is so engaging that one cannot believe he is capable of opportunism and exploitation. Likewise, the Bengali Peachum does not seem to regard human misery as a commodity, unlike his German counterpart: he is simply a patriarchal figure with a caustic sense of humor. His wife is a shrew, his daughter an ingenue, his employees a wretched lot of buffoons and innocuous villains. At no point in the production do the actors seem to criticize the attitudes and choices of their characters. They are too busy empathizing with them and enjoying themselves in their roles.

In a recent seminar on Brecht organized by the Max Müller Bhavan in Calcutta, Ajitesh Banerjee defended his production of *Tin Poyshar Pala* as an attempt to situate Brecht in a "Bengali experience." "Adaptation," he said, "is possible only when one knows one's own country. I would like to know Brecht through my own tradition. I am not interested in a German presentation of Brecht."[4] This is a legitimate point of view, but what does the Indianization of Brecht really signify? Does it simply imply an alteration of certain facts and a transformation of German characters into corresponding Bengali types? Or does it involve something more integral—an interpretation of the socio-political conditions in India in accordance with (or in contradiction to) the view of the world offered in Brecht's play? At the moment, the Indianization of Brecht does not seem to go beyond an indiscriminate alteration of details and characters. It has yet to extend to that process of analysis by which Brecht can be reinterpreted according to the contradictions of the political situation in India.

Certainly, the Indianization of *Tin Poyshar Pala* is not particularly analytical because it concentrates on details rather than on attitudes, principles, and views of the world. For instance, the Mounted Messenger who appears on a horse toward the end of *The Threepenny Opera* is transformed into two absurd Indian caricatures–the god Shiva, who appears in his tigerskin, and a policeman dressed in baggy shorts, who seems to be a remnant of the British Raj. While these transformations are most amusing (they are among the most inventive directorial choices in the production), they indicate the level of complexity on which Ajitesh Banerjee operates when he Indianizes Brecht.

Tin Poyshar Pala is symptomatic of what happens to Brecht in the Bengali theater when his plays are viewed primarily in terms of their entertainment value, unrelated to the contradictions that permeate the socio-economic situation in Bengal. Of course, this tendency to abstract the plays of Brecht from their social context is not confined to Bengal. The American theater, in particular, has succeeded in converting the parables of Brecht into musical entertainments which are invariably nostalgic in tone and politically reactionary in content.

In the "Brechtian production," that particularly synthetic species of the contemporary theater, the spectacle dominates the commentary, the narrative overpowers the *gestus*, the coordination of the entire production resists the idea of interruption, and the music proves to be more appealing than the argument. This blatant commercialization of Brecht is, perhaps, inevitable in a capitalist society, but in Bengal, where the poverty of the people in the street and the dissensions among the bourgeoisie are so conspicuous, it is somewhat shocking that Brecht can be played for laughs. Instead of unsettling the bourgeois assumptions shared by a middle-class Bengali audience, Nandikar's Brecht caters to these assumptions by providing a reassuring view of the world.

Another problem with the Brecht productions of Nandikar is their pretentious imitation of the formal aspects of the "epic theater"—posters, placards, projections, addresses to the audience, and abstract set elements—without any sustained comprehension of their significance to the unfolding of action in the play. *Bhalo-manush* and *Kharir Gondhi* (Nandikar's adaptations of *The Good Person of Setzuan* and *The Caucasian Chalk Circle*, respectively) epitomize the commercialization of Brecht in the Bengali theater.

While both productions are directed with considerable verve and theatricality, they are hopelessly cluttered with a surfeit of emotional effects. Like the conventions in any commercial Bengali melodrama, these effects encourage the spectators to lose themselves in the action rather than criticize the choices of the characters. There are very few choices and attitudes in Nandikar's productions that demand a critical response; there are simply effects of a particularly sensational nature. Perhaps it is only fair to describe some effects of one of their productions, *Kharir Gondhi*, which exemplify the limitations of Indianized Brecht.

A particularly revealing choice that illuminates the vacuity of this production occurs when Grusha is being chased by soldiers. There is an extended strobe light sequence where we see the shadows of Grusha and her pursuers flicker at lightning speed. On the two occasions that I saw the play, this sequence was enthusiastically received with loud cheers and prolonged applause. Strobe lights are a novelty in the Bengali theater; they are invariably used by directors when they have nothing significant to say. Rudraprasad Sengupta, who directed *Kharir Gondhi*, does not seem aware that Brecht demands to be played with the barest minimum of effects. He uses tasteless background music to create suspense (rather like a commercial Hindi film) and employs a lot of mood lighting with distracting colors and shadows.

The most innovative directorial moment in the first half of the play occurs when Grusha steals toward an exit in a darkened stage and suddenly screams when she sees the head of her former *nawab* (lord) dangling in front of her face. It is nineteenth-century Grand Guignol with a vengeance. There are also a number of crowd scenes reminiscent of the Victorian theater, where the actors genuflect en masse and indulge in a great deal of stylized cowering and raising of hands in unison. This demonstration of ensemble acting makes one realize the validity of Brecht's maxim—"One good actor is worth a whole battalion of extras, i.e. he is more."[5]

I concentrate on these effects because they are highlighted at the expense of any illumination of the choices and issues in the play. Brecht's oppositions, particularly those that make Grusha's life so painfully contradictory, are evened out by the emotional excess of the production. It is for this reason that the end of the first act of *Kharir Gondhi* fails to stun the audience as it should. When the actress playing Grusha vacillates between accepting the child as her son (in order to protect him from the soldiers) and denying any relationship to him (in order to placate her sweetheart), there is little tension in her acting because the maternal instincts of her character are so obviously overstated that they dominate her more pragmatic aspects, notably the urge to survive. A most cloying demonstration of Grusha's maternal love occurs in the final scene of the play: the actress playing Grusha speaks of her anguish with a spotlight focused on her while Azdak and the child join her to form a tableau reminiscent of Bengali family dramas.

Melodrama is one of the severest limitations of the contemporary Bengali theater. It is particularly offensive in the adaptations of Brecht, where the tendency of certain actors to wallow in the crudest of emotions for their own sake never fails to jar. Strangely enough, a Bengali actor is more likely to give an intelligent performance when he endeavors to be funny. When he attempts to psychologize a role, however, he is frequently tempted to indulge in his innate emotionalism.

One of the most satisfying performances in *Kharir Gondhi* was given by an old actress who played Grusha's wily mother-in-law. In the scene where she is scheming to marry her dying son to Grusha, she wails without interruption, periodically peeking out of the corner of her eye to see if her weeping is having any effect. She repeats this sly glance at least three times with a clarity that illuminates her attitude as a character. Though it is unlikely that the actress had even the crudest notion of "epic acting," she was at least aware that she was acting and more in control of her performance than the principal characters onstage. Nor did her winks and darting glances distract the spectators from what she had to do as a character, her stage business was directly related to her function as a character.

In distinct contrast, Rudraprasad Sengupta, who played Azdak, indulged in so much meaningless shtick that he totally negated

Brecht's important statement that, "Azdak is utterly genuine, a disappointed revolutionary posing as a human wreck, like Shakespeare's wise men who act the fool. Without this the judgement of the chalk circle would lose all its authority."[6] Sengupta succeeded in destroying all authority as the purveyor of justice in the play by swaggering and behaving like an unqualified boor. For instance, in the scene where Azdak condemns Ludovika, the girl who sways her hips, for provoking a man to "rape" her, Sengupta ends the scene leering at the girl. Just as he follows her out of the courtroom, he turns to the audience questioningly as if to imply, You want to come as well? He then leers at the audience in a tasteless improvisation. This is an instance of Sengupta's attempt to make Brecht more familiar to audiences in Bengal.

Reflecting on such details makes one wonder why Nandikar attempts to do Brecht. Not only do its productions fail to confront the essential contradictions of his plays, they flagrantly distort the theoretical premises of the epic theater implicit in any play by Brecht. Certainly, it is not easy to demonstrate the principles of the "alienation effect" and "gestus" in a Bengali production of Brecht: the audiences in Bengal are used to a more emotional and operatic mode of dramaturgy which relies on climaxes and suspense rather than on interruptions and critical inquiry.[7] If a Bengali group decides to do a play by Brecht, however, it would seem that it has some responsibility to confront the text in relation to the mode of dramaturgy and method of acting outlined by Brecht.

At this point, I should qualify that I am not advocating perfect copies of the Berliner Ensemble in the Bengali theater (such copies are neither relevant to the Bengali theater nor sufficiently responsive to the conditions of life and contradictions of politics in Bengal). I also acknowledge that Brecht has to be adapted if he is to be produced in Bengal but adapted in such a way that the central issues and oppositions of his plays are valid in an Indian context. If a Bengali director feels that there are no equivalents for these oppositions and issues, then he should not do Brecht.

Nandikar's attempt to stage Brecht with all the stereotypes and paraphernalia of the Bengali commercial theater (with some imitation of the formal aspects of the epic theater) is utterly irresponsible. Not only are its productions blatant distortions of Brecht, they depoliticize the thought of his plays by failing to confront it on even the most rudimentary level. If Nandikar distorted Brecht in order to illuminate the political and social conditions of India, one would want to examine its theater with greater respect. Unfortunately, its productions fail to engage in any dialectic with the political turmoil of Bengal and the life in the streets of Calcutta.

Brecht and the Theater Unit

Though one can criticize the Brecht productions of the Theater Unit for failing to confront the politics of India, one must also emphasize that they are much more rigorous and faithful to Brecht than the productions of Nandikar. The Theater Unit is led by Shekhar Chatterjee, whose exposure to the contemporary theater in West Germany has influenced the direction of his plays in Bengal. If the productions of Nandikar suffer from a surfeit of crudities, the productions of the Theater Unit are, perhaps, too sophisticated for the audiences of the Bengali theater.

Chatterjee's productions of *Puntila* and *Arturo Ui* have been unanimously praised by critics in Calcutta as the most authentic productions of Brecht in the Bengali theater. Unlike the Nandikar productions which wallow in melodrama and sprawl with no seeming design, the productions of the Theater Unit are remarkably restrained in tone (for the Bengali theater) and carefully orchestrated in structure. Their mise en scène is invariably unsettling for a Bengali audience in its angles of vision, irregular groupings of actors, and nonillusionistic mode of dramaturgy. Its avoidance of stereotypes contradicts the expectations of the Bengali audience, who are accustomed to somewhat traditional blocking and stage conventions reminiscent of the nineteenth-century theater. The self-assured quality of Chatterjee's direction, its poise and concentration on detail, its avoidance of melodrama, seem somewhat foreign to most practitioners and spectators of the Bengali theater.

This distancing quality of Chatterjee's direction is even more conspicuous in his refusal to Indianize Brecht if he feels that the play does not lend itself to local color. While he felt that the ironies of *Puntila* could be sustained in a Bengali adaptation (with a pre-

dominantly Bengali milieu and ambience), he was less sure that
the study of fascism in *Arturo Ui* could be presented without the
allegorical framework created by Brecht. His decision to retain the
milieu of Chicago in his production was attacked by Utpal Dutt in
a violently polemical article "Kabarkhana" ("Cemetery") where
Japenda, Dutt's alter ego and spokesman for the political theater
in Bengal, criticizes the Theater Unit production in no uncertain
terms.

> Some dense, illiterate intellectuals say that they are doing Brecht
> to introduce him to the local people. Such posturings do not con-
> vince anybody. . . . *Arturo Ui's* symbolism will not be understood by
> the Bengali audience. To show Indian fascism, why not choose an
> Indian background? Like Indira Gandhi as a Chambal dacoit? . . .
> Actually, your main interest is not to communicate the message of
> the play but to pose as intellectuals. You want to stick the label "cul-
> tured" on your backsides. Brecht used to term such status-seekers as
> "kopflos hund." You want to be the dogs of the élite class but the
> truly educated people are not even prepared to accept you as dogs.[8]

Responding to these accusations in an acerbic rejoinder, the
members of the Theater Unit pointed out that Dutt himself had
used a German political background for his play *Barricade*. Countering Japenda's absurdly dogmatic assertion that "the only *raison
d'être* for doing Brecht is to spread the revolutionary message in
Bengal," the members of the Theater Unit tactfully assumed a
moderate stance:

> Who has informed you that we have done *Arturo Ui* to spread the
> message of revolution? No, we do not suffer from such hypocrisy. We
> have learned from all our years in the theater that one cannot start a
> revolution through theater. We can only hope to raise the conscious-
> ness of the people a little.[9]

While appreciating the modesty of this stance, I should point
out that it is precisely this absence of revolutionary fervor in the
Theater Unit that makes their productions so essentially remote
from the exigencies of Bengali life. I find it particularly difficult to
accept Shekhar Chatterjee's assertion that, "The value of Brecht

lies in his concern for the exploited. . . . He is relevant in a situation of hunger and starvation. He must be taken to the villages, to
the masses."[10] This statement rings very hollow when one considers the sophistication of Chatterjee's recent productions, which
have never, to my knowledge, been performed for a rural audience. Villagers would not be able to grasp the significance of the
westernized techniques used in his productions. The visual imagery of his production of *Arturo Ui* (closely modelled on the production of the Berliner Ensemble) may have satisfied the critics and
the intelligentsia but I cannot believe that it would be understood
by the people.

The imagery of any production of a political play has to emerge
from the lives of the people. It has to incorporate familiar gestures,
expressions, and attitudes which illuminate their conditions of life
and their relation to the political situation in the country. An
image in a political play should reflect a class attitude or a political position in relation to a particular situation. If the image is to
have any effect on an audience, it has to be rooted in the world of
the audience with its particular problems, resistances, and modes
of survival.

Why should a Bengali production imitate the minutiae of gestures and movements of the actors in a Berliner Ensemble production of *Arturo Ui* when those gestures relate so intrinsically to the
conditions of life in Germany? One could say that this imitation
could result in an intelligent production of *Arturo Ui*, perhaps the
most "perfect" production possible in the Bengali theater. Brecht
himself advised his followers to copy models of his productions
before proceeding to create their own. He once remarked in an
interview with E. A. Winds that, "We must realize that copying is
not so despicable as people think. It isn't the easy way out. It is no
disgrace, but an art."[11] On a certain level, Shekhar Chatterjee is to
be praised for "copying" Brecht with such artistry. But, at the
same time, he needs to question whether the Bengali theater needs
such perfect replicas of the Berliner Ensemble, particularly at a
time when the political situation in Bengal demands a more specific concentration on its own dissensions and areas of corruption.
Perhaps Chatterjee needs to acknowledge that "authentic" Brecht
is something of a luxury in the Bengali theater.

As much as I dislike Dutt's indiscriminate attack on the Theater Unit, I believe there is something to be learned from Japenda's pragmatic views on the political theater in Bengal and his criticism of productions like *Arturo Ui.*

> Suppose an Indian playwright depicts two groups of *mastans* (gangsters) who try to divide a city into two sections so that they can indulge in rampant rowdyism, and a half-naked Sanyasi (mendicant) stands in their way. Eventually, one of the *mastans* shoots the Sanyasi who dies uttering "Hai Ram." This is quite intelligible to the Indian audience because the underlying political event is well known. Everyone will understand that the Sanyasi is Gandhi, and the two groups of *mastans* are the Congress and the Muslim League respectively, and the city which they want to divide stands for India. But if this play is translated into the German language and is staged in Berlin, will the German audiences understand it? No, they will simply view it as a fantasy. Hence, they will never stage this play in Berlin because they respect their audience. But in this unfortunate country everything is possible! Here we have projected German symbols to show the fascism in India! In order to understand the motives of Indira, the Bengali audience will have to deal with the most complex and obscure details of German history! . . . What is the point of turning to Chicago, my friend, when you see everything at home? If you want to produce a Hitler-story for the Bengali audience, it must be easier, more "footnotes-marked," and more intelligible than the story in *Arturo Ui.*[12]

Even though Chatterjee attempted to clarify the symbolism of *Arturo Ui* by providing the necessary historical information on slides, the intricacies of Brecht's narrative proved to be a hindrance. I tend to agree with Japenda that the historical parallels to the Chicago framework of *Arturo Ui* are much too obscure for a Bengali audience. If the point of the production was to confront the similarities to fascism in contemporary India, then Chatterjee should have chosen a play with more immediate parallels to the events and personalities that dominate the political scene in India. If he could not find such a play, he should have written one himself.

Perhaps it is unreasonable to expect directors to be playwrights, particularly in the Western theater where direction and playwriting are intensely specialized activities. But the situation is very different in Bengal, where the most significant theater is almost inevitably produced by men who write, direct, and act in their own plays. Bijon Bhattacharya, Utpal Dutt, and Badal Sircar exemplify this unique phenomenon. While it is unfair to expect Chatterjee to write plays when he prefers to concentrate on direction, it seems to me that his reliance on the plays of contemporary German playwrights is seriously restricting his growth and efficacy as an artist.[13]

In recent years, however, Chatterjee has attempted to establish a closer rapport with the Bengali audience by working in the commercial theater. His enormously successful farce *Judge Sahib* has played to packed houses. While one would not want Chatterjee to continue producing entertainments of this nature, I believe that his work in the commercial theater is a necessary transitional phase for his development as an artist. One hopes that Chatterjee will find a way of producing plays in the Bengali theater without resorting to the crudities and compromises of Nandikar. His knowledge of Brecht and the epic theater is too rich to be abandoned. Chatterjee needs to adapt this knowledge to the existing conditions of theater and life in Bengal. Only then will the productions of the Theater Unit cease to be exclusive.

Brecht continues to be the most popular playwright in Bengal. Certainly his plays are more frequently produced than the symbolic dramas of Tagore. In fact, it seems that whenever a group fails to find a new play worth producing (and there has been a dearth of good plays in the last few years), the solution is to adapt yet another play by Brecht. Apart from the productions examined above, there have been new Bengali adaptations of *Schweyk*, *The Measures Taken*, and *Galileo* (with Sombhu Mitra playing the title role). According to Dharani Ghosh, the drama critic of Calcutta's prominent newspaper the *Statesman*, these adaptations may be disagreeable to students of Brecht but they "satisfy the aspirations of the Bengali middle-class."[14] Perhaps the ultimate problem with most Bengali adaptations of Brecht is their seeming acceptance of conventions and values that are ineluctably bourgeois.

THE URBAN POLITICAL THEATER

Theater Workshop: *Rajrakta* and *Chakbhanga Modhu*

For over two decades, there have been a number of political plays that have been specifically written for urban audiences in Calcutta. Theater Workshop was, perhaps, one of the first groups with a Marxist orientation to explore sophisticated modes of addressing political issues which contrasted sharply with the agitprop techniques of Utpal Dutt. Its production of Mohit Chattopadhyay's *Rajrakta* (Guinea Pig), a symbolic play about institutionalized power, attracted much attention for its hectic, often disjointed, language and sense of the surreal.

Written in a variety of styles, at once parodic and expressionist, the play moves with a jolting rhythm from one charadelike situation to the next. We see two figures of authority, the Raja Sahib and his accomplice, confront, bully, and seduce a Boy and a Girl with the repressive ideology of the ruling class. While the Raja Sahib himself is anonymous, his tyranny becomes increasingly obvious in the course of the play when he assumes various roles, including that of a professor who pontificates about conformity and order, and a salesman who offers the Boy a promising future on condition that he surrenders to the system.

Just as the character of the Raja Sahib becomes increasingly complex in the course of his various impersonations, the character of the Boy ceases to be nondescript the more he resists the manifestations of authority in the play. *Rajrakta* builds to a truly virtuosic climax when the Raja Sahib becomes enraged that the Boy, so seemingly vulnerable to the lure and power of authority, continues to resist his tactics of intimidation and persuasion. In a violent action reminiscent of scenes in the mad scientist's laboratory in science fiction films, the Raja Sahib extracts the Boy's blood for clinical examination so that he can eliminate the virus of revolt that animates it. A grotesque complication develops: the Boy's blood corpuscles enlarge and begin to attack the Raja Sahib.

While a Western audience would, in all probability, associate this bizarre coup de theatre with the grotesquerie of cult films like *The Exorcist*, the Bengali audience viewed the scene without any cynicism. The virtuosity of the acting and the ingenuity of the staging were excessively praised. In a sense, this was to be expected because *Rajrakta* was one of the first productions in the Bengali theater that explored an absurdist dramaturgy. On seeing the play in its most recent revival, I realized that the surreal aura of the production conceals the essentially simplistic ideas at the core of the play. Though the manifestations of authority in *Rajrakta* are varied, they are neither adequately analyzed nor juxtaposed to socio-political realities.

Rajrakta has dated in a way similar to certain plays by Ionesco which seem to be burdened with obtrusive symbols and contrived devices. Chattopadhyay's drama has lost whatever political or social significance it might once have resonated. The figures of authority in the contemporary political scene of India are more deadly in their dispassionate misuse of power than the figure of the Raja Sahib suggests in the play. *Rajrakta* indicates that a play with socio-political resonances has to constantly reinvent its form in order to maintain the immediacy of its content.

A more complex drama staged by the Theater Workshop, Manoj Mitra's *Chakbhanga Modhu* (Fresh Honey Taken From The Hive), is one of the finest examples of urban political drama in Bengal. Written in refined verse, occasionally precious in its subtleties of phrase, the play deals with a subject that seems to contradict its style: the oppression of Bengali peasants.

The action of the play focuses on a group of viliagers, snake charmers by profession, who are exploited by a *jotedar*, a figure representing feudal power who controls the lives of the villagers. The conflict of the play intensifies when the *jotedar* is poisoned by a snake and comes to the villagers to be cured. The village "medicine man," who has inherited his knowledge of snakes and the secrets of snake charming from his forefathers, debates whether he should let the *jotedar* die and thereby spare the villagers further persecution, or save the *jotedar*'s life and thereby retain his professional pride. Ultimately, he values his profession more than he fears for his exploitation and saves the *jotedar*'s life.

The consequences are disastrous for the *jotedar* does not change his attitude to the villagers when he recovers. On the contrary, he demands his rent. This leads to more resentment on the part of the villagers, who realize that the *jotedar* cannot respond to acts of

compassion. In a startling climax, the daughter of one of the villagers pretends to offer the *jotedar* some honey and strategically
arranges for a snake to kill him.

Ostensibly based on a legend from the Sundarbans, *Chakbhanga Modhu* reaches a contemporary Bengali audience with the
immediacy of a myth. What is so admirable about the play is that
it dramatizes the oppression of the people without using naturalistic stereotypes and colloquial banalities. On the contrary, it succeeds in creating a poetic language that crystallizes the issues of
the play without etherealizing them. The language serves to distance the audience from the choices and impulses of the characters. At the same time, it does not intrude on the lives of the characters. Therein lies the particular quality of *Chakbhanga Modhu*:
it dramatizes the lives of the people using refined conventions that
do not, however, detract from its concern for the people.

This use of a sophisticated dramaturgy to reveal a concern for
the people is a rarity in the Bengali theater. Manoj Mitra himself
has not been able to write another play like *Chakbhanga Modhu*.
He has succumbed to abstractions and rhetorical excesses rather
like Mohit Chattopadhyay, whose play *Mahakalir Baccha* (The
Children of Kali) is yet another surreal drama that capitalizes on
appallingly sensational theatrical effects and gimmicks. The Theater Workshop itself has ceased to function as a significant group
despite commercial successes like *Schweyk Galo Juddhey* (the Bengali adaptation of Brecht's play).

A considerable amount of the group's energy is now spent in
criticizing other theater groups, notably those committed to the
Third Theater initiated by Sircar. In an issue of *Theatre Bulletin*, a
journal edited by Ashok Mukherjee of Theatre Workshop, there
was a totally unqualified attack on the political confusion, reactionary ideology, and lack of originality demonstrated by Sircar
and his followers. Reporting on this attack, Ella Datta of the *Business Standard* raised some appropriate questions: "Why this over-
reaction, I wonder? Is it a form of insecurity? Do the established
groups feel so threatened by the emergence of this alternative form
(of theater)?"[15]

It seems to me that the established groups like Theater Workshop are clearly threatened by the Third Theater movement be-

cause it is they who lack originality, commitment, and coherence. Not only are they failing to reach the mass audiences in Calcutta, who prefer Hindi films to their abstract plays, they are also failing to attract young people to their groups. When questioned about this problem, Manoj Mitra, the current playwright and director of Sundaram, acknowledges that, "It is true, we cannot offer the younger people money. Nor can we offer them regular work. Most of the groups are producing only one play a year. So we cannot hold them with a variety of theater experience."[16]

Mitra also adds that the young generation in Calcutta is becoming increasingly attracted to the possibilities of working in film and radio. While this attraction cannot be denied, I strongly believe that the youth in Bengal would commit themselves to the theater if they believed in its validity. Despite its supposed allegiance to social and political issues, the Theater Workshop (among other established groups in Calcutta) reveals its insularity only too conspicuously in its productions. Rarely does it engage in any kind of dialogue with the audience that focuses on the tensions and problems of life in Calcutta. It is no wonder that young people are beginning to search for new forms of theater where the confrontation with life is more immediate and tense. We shall examine one of the youngest (and most committed) theater groups in Bengal, the Living Theater of Khardah, later in the chapter. Now let us concentrate on another urban political theater group in Calcutta —Chetana.

Chetana: *Marich Sangbad* and *Jagganath*

One of the more imaginative groups in Calcutta to succeed in doing political plays for a predominantly urban audience is Chetana. Directed by Arun Mukherjee, a most versatile man of the theater who sings, dances, acts, directs, writes, and mimes with exceptional skill, this group has attracted considerable attention for its original productions of *Marich Sangbad* and *Jagganath*. Like most outstanding productions, they are articulate and richly textured with sharply defined directorial choices and modes of discourse. While their coordination is meticulous, they do not not function metronomically like machines; they have an interesting range of rhythms and dynamics. Leisurely cinematic sections can be interrupted by short, sporadic bursts of songs followed by longer discursive sections which tend to meander and stop abruptly. Just as the formal aspects of Chetana's productions vary with nuances and surprises, the ideological content of their plays is by no means rigorously argued. There are areas of ambiguity underlying the seemingly categorical statements of the plays.

Marich Sangbad operates on many levels—mythological, social, and political. Mukherjee uses the ingenious device of first presenting three narratives, disparate in tone, texture, and content, and then dovetailing these narratives to create a semblance of unity in the play. While the narratives basically deal with the same theme—the capitulation of good people to the pressures of the ruling class—they have specifically different manifestations. The first narrative deals with the mythological character Marich (from the *Ramayana*) who fails to resist the pressures of the demon-king Ravana, who orders him to lure Ram away from Sita. The second narrative concentrates on a peasant's resistance to his *zemindar* (landowner), who urges him to disrupt a peasant revolt. The third narrative, set in the U.S. during the sixties, focuses on an earnest American, disillusioned about his country's aggression in Vietnam, who eventually commits suicide when the authorities (ostensibly the C.I.A.) force him to accept the "democracy" of his country.

These are the three discrete stories contained in *Marich Sangbad*. The intellectual play of the production occurs when a character from one story begins to speak like a character from another story thereby establishing the similarity in their points of view. For instance, Ravana interrupts his mythological discourse by speaking like a *zemindar*, while a U.S. senator, quite inexplicably, begins to speak like Ravana. These incongruities help the spectators to establish connections between the various stories.

Apart from the interruptions between the narratives, which tend to disappear toward the end of the play, there are two major sources of interruption in *Marich Sangbad*. In the first place, the narratives are enclosed in the larger structure of a street play. A flamboyant character called Ustad, the master of ceremonies who directs the action of the play, opens *Marich Sangbad* with exuberant verses inviting the audience to participate in the spectacle. In the course of the play, which he witnesses in the presence of the audience, the Ustad passes critical comments and expresses his bewilderment whenever the identities of the various characters tend to merge into one another. In true Brechtian spirit, he objectifies the narratives by not allowing them to run into one another.

The other source of interruption in *Marich Sangbad* is a troupe of singers led by the *mool-gayen* (central singer), played by Mukherjee himself, who sings satiric songs about the ruling class and the C.I.A. with an astonishing display of mime and histrionics. His facial expressions are like a series of masks; they embody particular attitudes ranging from puppetlike submission to militaristic regimentation to artful connivance. The political direction of *Marich Sangbad* is conveyed primarily through these songs. While they avoid specific references to Indian politics or the states of the various parties in Bengal, they are clearly anti-U.S. and anti-imperialist in focus.

The message that is conveyed in each of the three narratives is reminiscent of Brecht's *The Good Woman of Setzuan:* it is difficult to be good in this world without being exploited. Goodness is particularly vulnerable in a capitalist society. This idea is most clearly expressed by the American humanist in the play, who even mentions that his father, a supporter of American democracy, had started to doubt whether true democracy could survive the pressures of capitalism. Significantly, his father (always a figure of authority for a Bengali audience) had started to question the democracy in his country after visiting Eastern Europe—an area of the world one does not readily associate with individual freedom and the acceptance of human rights.

In his review of *Marich Sangbad*, Ranan Banerji emphasizes this fact and speculates on the omission of any references to the state of oppression in Russia and other socialist countries. This omission along with the anti-U.S. sentiment of the play makes him wonder whether there is an "innuendo" in *Marich Sangbad* that "once the state bureaucrats commandeer all means of production, all power struggles cease, justice becomes natural and the lion lies down with the lamb."[17] It is unclear to me whether the play is advocating such a government. And yet, as eloquent as the play is about oppressors on a universal scale (Ravana, *zemindars*, the U.S.

Senate, the C.I.A.), it is strangely noncommital when it comes to advocating (even through inference) an alternative form of government to the capitalist one it denounces.

The politics of *Jagganath* is even more elusive. Inspired by the masterpiece of Chinese proletarian literature *The True Story of Ah-Q*, written by Lu Hsün (once described by Mao as "the chief commander of China's cultural revolution"), the Bengali play is a particularly subtle study of a man who could have been a revolutionary. Jagganath, a gentle, somewhat obtuse laborer, belongs to the meekest of the meek, the most downtrodden of the underprivileged class. It is ironic that he is named after one of the most illustrious deities in the Hindu pantheon, Jagganath, the Lord of the World, whose idol, it is said, so excited his devotees in ancient times that when it was dragged along on a car during a festival they threw themselves under the wheels of the car and were crushed. In Arun Mukherjee's play, it is Jagganath who is crushed, partly because he is surrounded by exploiters and partly because he cannot distinguish between fact and fiction.

Jagganath is constantly duped in the course of the play even though he does not seem to be aware of it. His predicament is that he constantly feels that he is one step ahead of the others when actually he is a couple of paces behind. The other problem with Jagganath is his innate tendency to fantasize about his situation. This gives him periodic moments of strength, even superiority, when he is immersed in a particularly fervent fantasy. But once it exhausts itself, Jagganath returns to his world, hungry, exploited, and homeless, with no increased awareness of his exploitation. Like Ah-Q, Lu Hsün's most enigmatic character, Jagganath "never learns from experience because he has no *continuous* interior life of his own."[18] As played by Arun Mukherjee in an astonishingly mercurial performance, Jagganath moves from one thing to another without changing his life or developing a more rigorous awareness of his situation. The only fact that stabilizes him and, in a sense, gives him an identity is his state of exploitation.

Jagganath is exploited from every direction and on many levels. Apart from his employer, a landowner who whips him at the slightest provocation, he is exploited by people who are themselves exploited. His colleagues take advantage of his naivete and ridicule his ignorance. They cheat him of the little money he has almost assuming that he deserves to be cheated. When Jagganath attempts to be cocky, the muscleman of the village deflates his ego. When he attempts to be discreet, no one pays any attention to him. Even the maid servant of the landowner's house favors another servant over Jagganath: in Jagganath's presence she is almost possessive of her favorite, passing tidbits to him. This is the greatest humiliation for Jagganath—to see his archenemy, another servant, receiving favors from yet another servant. In fact, this humiliation is so intense that when his rival ridicules his diminutive appearance using words like *"thuto"* and *"tuktuki,"* Jagganath's anger assumes epic proportions. Yet it does not build to anything because he feels instinctively superior to his rival. Besides, he has his fantasies, which enable him to forget his most painful humiliations.

After we see Jagganath being whipped by his employer, we expect him to convey some kind of resentment. But he accepts his humiliation in order to fantasize about it. In a heightened moment of his fantasy, he enters the living room of his employer and proceeds to terrorize the landowner and his bourgeois friends with a gun. Jagganath has them raise their hands in unison while he luxuriates in his sense of power. After this hilarious display of make-believe aggression, we see Jagganath sitting in his hut, hungry and frightened. Another juxtaposition of sequences that reveals his inability to act on his impulses occurs when he expresses his love to the landowner's daughter (Jagganath's only potential human contact in the play) using all the romantic gestures and expressions one associates with a hopelessly impassioned lover. This dream sequence is juxtaposed with a mute sequence where Jagganath stands in a shadowy area of the stage and gazes at the landowner's daughter not daring to reveal his presence to her.

The stepping in and out of fantasy proves to be fatal to Jagganath. Toward the end of the play, he confronts two revolutionaries who seek refuge in his hut while escaping from the police. It is clear that they represent the freedom fighters of India. Jagganath is awed by their presence and particularly impressed by their revolvers. He would like to join them but the revolution is less a reality than a source of hallucination for him. When the freedom fighters leave his hut, they leave a gun behind. In a most illuminating action that functions like a *gestus* in the Brechtian sense, Jagganath holds the revolver as if it were an alien object. He seems unable to decide whether it is real.

While lost in his delusions about whether or not he has transformed himself into a revolutionary, Jagganath is arrested by the police for being implicated in the freedom movement. When he pleads his innocence, the court laughs at his bewilderment and peremptorily sentences him to death. Ironically, instead of devastating Jagganath and making him aware of his oppression, his death sentence fills him with a sense of ultimate triumph. Jagganath believes that he has the last word. On hearing that his colleague, the rival servant whom he despises more than anyone in the world, has joined the revolutionaries, Jagganath dismisses his action as somewhat pedestrian. Joining the revolutionaries, he believes, is a poor substitute for dying for the revolution. As he ascends the gallows, he increasingly indulges in his bravado without any awareness that it will cease momentarily. At his greatest moment of glory, Jagganath is most ignominiously deluded.

The theatrical tour de force of his death is, of course, a brutal irony. Jagganath is not a conventional proletarian hero who dies for a cause. He dies hallucinating about a cause that vaguely exists but which he can comprehend only within the logic of his fantasies. Does this reduce his complexity as a character in an ostensibly political play? Is Jagganath merely a victim of the world and, more crucially, a victim of his fantasies of the world? Certain Marxist critics like Sakti Biswas believe so. Biswas, a member of the People's Little Theater, is one of the few critics in the Bengali theater to dismiss *Jagganath* as a reactionary play. In an impassioned interview, he told me that he believes Jagganath "dies like a fool." Unable to act consciously, he goes through his life without grasping the implications of his actions and with no transformation in his attitudes to the landowner and his environment. Biswas questions the playwright's decision to present Jagganath hallucinating about the revolution. Since the play is set during the freedom struggle of India, Biswas argues, and performed at a time when the working class in India is increasingly militant about its oppression, why should Jagganath not be presented as a fighter? Quite clearly, Biswas wants Jagganath to represent the "revolutionary struggle of the people" which is precisely what he contradicts by his very nature.

But does this mean that there is no statement about the struggle of the people in the play? There may not be a spokesman for the revolution in *Jagganath* as in a conventional political play, but why is it necessary for the protagonist of a political play to *represent* the revolution unequivocally? This tendency to view the meaning of a play through the character of the protagonist, once described by Richard Gilman as the "protagonistic fallacy," is most limiting; it applies as much to the classics *(Oedipus, Hamlet, The Master Builder)* as to more contemporary plays. I believe it is possible for the protagonist of a political play to be apolitical and yet contribute, as a constituent in the larger structure and dynamic of the play, to the political statement of the play. This is precisely what Arun Mukherjee achieves in his play, which transmits its message *around* Jagganath rather than *through* him.

If Mukherjee wanted to write a conventional political play, he could have shown Jagganath metamorphosing from a simpleton to a rabble-rouser or a conscientious member of the Party. This would have been somewhat perfunctory. Instead, he attempts to do something more subtle although he does not quite succeed. By juxtaposing Jagganath's fantasies against the concrete depiction of his oppression and impoverishment, Mukherjee highlights the extremity of his predicament. By involving him in the nationalist activity of the play, Mukherjee demystifies the romantic associations that surround the freedom movement in India.

There is a dangerous tendency, particularly in Bengal where patriotic feelings are somewhat rampant and unquestioned, to remember only the memorable events and victories of the freedom movement and to forget about the loss of lives and disillusionment of those countless, anonymous figures who were entrapped in a political situation that they did not understand. *Jagganath* is less interested in evoking an image of those brave peasant-heroes who died nobly for their country than in memorializing those nameless little men whose incomprehension of the nationalist movement further intensified their exploitation in life.

It might be argued, however, that the character of Jagganath is much too personalized to represent a particular mentality or attitude shared by a class of people to the freedom struggle. He does not seem to represent anything beyond himself. Perhaps there is also an excessive coloration of his character, too many nuances that distract the spectator from comprehending what Jagganath *represents*. In addition, Mukherjee's concentration on the psychology of his character, masterful and deeply affecting as it is, prevents him from exploring the possibilities of revolution in Jagganath's character.

In contrast to the presentation of Ah-Q's character in *The True Story of Ah-Q*, the presentation of Jagganath seems excessively sentimental, even simplistic.[19] In the first place, though Ah-Q is most ignominiously exploited, he is less passive than Jagganath. Something of an opportunist, he tries to improve his lot in life even though his self-deceptions prevent him from doing so. Nonetheless, he is entirely pragmatic about the revolution, which he responds to with contradictory attitudes. At first, he maintains a respectful distance from the revolutionaries.

> Ah-Q had long since known about revolutionaries and this year with his own eyes had seen revolutionaries decapitated. But since it had occurred to him that the revolutionaries were rebels and that a rebellion would make things difficult for him, he had always detested and kept away from them. (P. 43)

Later, when he notices with glee that the revolutionaries have instilled a psychosis in the minds of those very people who have exploited him, Ah-Q has second thoughts about the revolution.

> "Revolution is not a bad thing," thought Ah-Q. "Finish off the whole lot of them . . . curse them! . . . I'd like to go over to the revolutionaries myself. (P. 43)

Like Jagganath, Ah-Q does not take very long before he imagines himself to be a revolutionary.

> A troop of revolutionaries would come, all in white helmets and white armour, with swords, steel maces, bombs, foreign guns, sharppointed double-edged knives, and spears with hooks. When they

passed the temple they would call out, "Ah-Q come along with us!" And then I would go with them. . . . (P. 45)

Unable to keep his fantasies to himself, Ah-Q gains the instant respect of all the villagers when he shouts, "Rebellion! Rebellion!" in the street at the top of his voice. In contrast, it should be pointed out that Jagganath keeps his fantasies to himself: they have no effect on other people and the world around him. They merely serve to further interiorize his character. Ah-Q's fantasies, on the other hand, stimulate him to act. After wondering why the revolutionaries have not contacted him, Ah-Q reflects:

Simply to say that you had gone over was not enough to make anyone a revolutionary; . . . the most important thing was to get in touch with the revolutionary party. (P. 49)

Unfortunately, his meeting with the Fake Foreign Devil, who is ostensibly the leader of the revolution (which, incidentally, never materializes), is disastrous. Ah-Q is "debarred from the revolution." He is dismayed to see that almost everyone in the village has become a revolutionary, notably his former employer who had evicted him from his household. Terribly piqued, Ah-Q decides to turn informer against the Fake Foreign Devil.

In a sudden reversal of action, where he is accused of theft, Ah-Q is arrested and sentenced to death. Significantly, the imminence of his death does not make Ah-Q further fantasize about his situation. He does not fabricate a story defending his innocence as Jagganath probably would have done. When Ah-Q is questioned about his actions, he responds with total honesty: "Ah-Q thought, and decided there was nothing to be said, so he answered, 'Nothing.' " When he is being taken to be executed, he does not lose himself in an apotheosis of glory like Jagganth. In fact, he is a most disappointing specimen for a criminal: he neither swears nor sings. Before his body is "scattered like so much light dust," Ah-Q has a moment to reflect on his predicament: *"It seemed to him that in this world probably it was the fate of everybody at some time to have his head cut off."*

There is nothing in *Jagganath*, not a gesture, not a line, that con-

veys the laconic truth of this statement. Ultimately, the play succumbs to precisely those limitations that restrict the growth of
the theater in Bengal: emotionalism, melodrama, and virtuosity.
Though Mukherjee's performance as Jagganath is eloquent and
moving in its varied use of nuances and expressions, it is self-
absorbed and, perhaps, too subtly virtuosic for the dynamics of the
entire production. His Jagganath stands out as the star of the play.
Though his mime and movement are most accomplished, particularly in the section where Jagganath is shown walking through the
forest and responding to the feel of the trees and the call of the
birds, they call attention to themselves as technical skills and seem
a trifle decorative.

Perhaps the most offensive scene in the entire play occurs when
the landowner's daughter offers herself to Jagganath. Mukherjee
responds dramatically: he stares at the actress with an anguished
gaze and then falls down on his feet before her uttering "Ma" with
a heavy voice, choked with emotion. It is a moment in the play
that epitomizes Mukherjee's penchant for overplaying the emotion
of a scene without assuming any kind of critical attitude to it. It
might be argued, of course, that such an attitude is not possible in
the melodramatic scene with the landowner's daughter. But there
are many other, less perfervid, scenes in the play where a more
critical stance could have enhanced the choices and contradictions
of Jagganath. Despite the overt emotionalism of certain scenes,
however, and the tendency to emphasize the formal aspects of a
scene rather than its content, *Jagganath* deserves its recognition as
one of the most original productions in the contemporary Bengali
theater.

Prostuti: Social Melodrama

The artistic quality of a production like *Jagganath* becomes all the
more conspicuous when one compares it to less illustrious productions in the Bengali theater. It is not possible for me to list all these
productions or summarize their plots, but it is necessary to describe at least one production that exemplifies one of the most popular genres in the Bengali theater—social melodrama. I single out
Prostuti for criticism because it is symptomatic of many produc-

tions in the Bengali theater which are unable to view a social or political situation without a melodramatic perspective.

Before analyzing the production, however, it is necessary to indicate that social melodrama is most rampant in the commercial theater of Calcutta that flourishes in establishments like the legendary Star Theater. Most of the productions in the commercial theater are elaborate spectacles with songs, dances, melodramatic scenes, and stunning visual effects in the tradition of the nineteenth-century Bengali theater. Apart from titillating cabaret items (which are becoming increasingly lurid), these commercial plays lure their audiences with highly romanticized depictions of prostitution and poverty.

One of the most popular commercial productions in recent years was *Baarbadhu*, which has played for more than 1,700 performances. Capitalizing on bedroom intimacies and the melodrama resulting from unrequited love, the play deals with the relationship between a profligate and a prostitute who poses as his wife only to be abandoned at the end of the play. A more subtle use of social melodrama was evident in another commercial venture called *Namjiban* with the famous Bengali actor Soumitra Chatterjee playing the lead. Its attempt to portray the seamier aspects of life in Calcutta with some realism was hailed by the critics, who imagined that the production would lead to a more responsible and socially committed form of commercial theater. Unfortunately, cabaret and bawdy humor continue to be infinitely more alluring than social commentary, however simplistic, in the commercial Bengali theater.

Some directors of the commercial theater, however, are quite honest about their priorities. When Sunit Das, the director and star of *Laaj Rakho* (Cast Aside Your Modesty) was asked whether his play was a social drama (it deals with the degradation of a young girl who is forced to live a life of sin) he denied any social commitment on his part. "People flock to see my plays," he said, "because they need a momentary respite and escape from the complexities of life. The plays provide entertainment."[20] The candor of this statement, in a sense, justifies the blatantly commercial use of melodrama in the play. But when a more "artistic" director in the noncommercial theater uses melodrama for ostensibly "serious" reasons, his exploitation of commercial lures and stereotypes is more offensive. *Prostuti* is one such production that assumes a seriousness which is innately melodramatic.

First, the facts of the play: the father drinks and beats the mother, the mother accepts her situation, and the son is a worker on strike who goes to union meetings and fights with his father. This family lives in a one-room shack in a *bustee* (slum). Perhaps the only effective scene in *Prostuti* occurs at the start of the play before the first lines are uttered. The lights come on gradually as the sounds of the *bustee* infilitrate the stage, evoking the reality of working-class life in Calcutta. We hear angry voices, the clanking of buckets, snatches of Hindi film music, the incessant cries of beggars, shouts, whispers, a child crying. It is all very suggestive and real. Then the play begins and melodrama takes over.

It is not immediately perceptible because the father, who is the source of the melodrama in the play, is also something of a joker. He comes home drunk with an old school friend who is dressed in a red T-shirt and black jacket, signs of prosperity in a working-class milieu. The friend, who speaks mostly in English, claims to have travelled around the world in a "jumbo jet." Though his real name is Jaikishen, he now responds only to the name Jackson. He smokes expensive cigarettes and uses Americanized expressions like "a guy has a gal in every port." The father, who first appears as an illiterate, impoverished *bustee* dweller, suddenly begins to speak in English and is quite witty. He introduces his old classmate to his wife before ordering her out of the room and proceeds to reminisce about old times. It appears that the two men had attended the same nursery school as children. The audience is not given any information as to how their paths in life had diverged so radically that Jaikishen could afford to fly in a jumbo jet while the father had no alternative but to live in a *bustee*. The men do not seem to be embarrassed by the obvious disparity in their economic situations. To the bewilderment of the audience, they laugh and slap each other on the back and, at one point, recite "Little Miss Muffet" in unison.

On the last line of the nursery rhyme, when the spider frightens little Miss Muffet away, the son of the house enters the room glowering. It is a most dramatic entrance. The father commands him to touch the feet of Jackson as a sign of respect. After ordering his son out of the room, the father changes his attitude and begins to grovel in front of Jackson, informing him that he earns barely a hundred and ten rupees a month (approximately thirteen dollars) and often goes without food. He pleads for some financial assistance. Jackson interprets this as begging and regards his old friend with contempt. He walks out of the house ordering the father not to follow him. The old man remains in the room staring at the cigarette lighter that Jackson has left behind. In the background, we see the silhouettes of the wife and the son holding onto each other. For some mysterious reason, a red light shines on them. It gradually fades as the first act comes to an end.

How do we interpret this sequence? Initially, it seems that Jackson is a satiric portrayal of the foreign-returned traveller, a representative of the nouveau riche. In India there is presently a craze for what is known as "phoren travel" and "phoren goods." Anything "phoren" is irresistible, ranging from whiskey to deodorants. But Jackson is not a butt of ridicule in this sense. His "phoren" air is not ludicrous. It is the father who has most of the laugh lines. Is Jackson then a representative of capitalism or the evils of westernization? Unsubtle as these choices may be, Jackson does not represent either of them. In fact, he is presented rather blandly without the stereotypes one associates with villains in social melodramas. He is less a villain than a catalyst who facilitates the progression of the play.

By leaving his cigarette lighter behind, Jackson enables the father to sell it and use the money to buy provisions for the house. In fact, the father is so enthusiastic about his purchases that his wife believes that he has reformed himself. The son is more skeptical; he knows that his father's sudden concern for the family is a pretense. His mother reprimands him but he is too disillusioned to reason with her.

Throughout the play, the son has been in a dilemma whether or not he should return to work on the terms of the management. The *goondas* (toughs) employed by the management resolve this indecision by beating him up. In the final sequence of *Prostuti*, the son is lying in bed with his mother anxiously attending to his wounds when the father returns home drunk. In his alcoholic haze, he fails to realize the gravity of the situation. The son slowly turns to his mother, his voice heavy with emotion and pain, and says "Ma, didn't you say that *baba* would never drink again?" The actors freeze, the music builds, the lights change dramatically for the final tableau while the curtain slowly closes.

It is, perhaps, unnecessary to detail the limitations of the script. The plot lacks credibility, the characterization is either ludicrous or incomplete, and the melodrama (even on the level of melodrama) is unconvincing. It is unclear to me what the characters of *Prostuti* represent. Though the son is a worker on strike and is beaten up by agents of the ruling class, he does not seem to have strong proletarian feelings. As for the father, the actor who plays the role (Nilkantha Sengupta, who is also the author of the play) succeeds in parodying his state of impoverishment so that one is tempted to laugh at the depiction of poverty in the play. This is, perhaps, the worst offense of the production.

One would not mind a melodrama on *Prostuti*'s level if it did not have social pretensions. But when a play deals with the working class, it has a responsibility to confront the problems of this class with some commitment and seriousness. *Prostuti* epitomizes the inability of bourgeois actors to represent the attitudes and behavior of the working class: their imitation of low-class dialects and the rough gestures of the proletariat are painfully contrived.

There is a self-consciousness that most bourgeois actors bring to working-class roles which emphasizes their urban insularity. After seeing a production like *Prostuti*, one can understand why a great artist like Bijon Bhattacharya (whose work has been examined in chapter 1) could say toward the end of his life: "I feel sick when I have to use petit bourgeois actors in my productions: they merely ape the peasants."[21] There could be no greater insult to the working class than to present it on stage with an intrinsically bourgeois perspective and mode of presentation.

We have examined varieties of productions in the Bengali theater that seem to evade a rigorous confrontation with the social and political problems in India. They exemplify the attitudes of prominent theater groups in Calcutta that share some fundamental similarities in their organization and aesthetic priorities. Apart from these similarities, these groups also share some fundamental limitations. I would like to emphasize two of them: one is their insularity resulting from their excessively urban orientation, the other is their inability or reluctance to explore theatrical spaces and conventions unrelated to the proscenium stage.

Let us look at the first. The theater groups I have examined so far in this chapter perform almost exclusively in Calcutta, without touring the major cities of India or, more important, the villages of Bengal. In a sense, one can understand their inability to tour the cities since the cost of transportation is very high and most of the groups have barely enough money to meet their production expenses. Moreover, most of their actors work in government offices, which do not readily provide leave to their employees. But touring the villages of Bengal is not so expensive and can be arranged on the weekends when the actors are free to perform. It seems to me that these groups would shed much of their insularity and fake sophistication by performing for the people in villages. Producing a play in a village square or field would necessitate a more economical and direct method of staging. It would also compel the actors to clarify the choices and attitudes of their characters and make them realize the redundancy of their technical gimmicks and lighting effects.

It is true that certain groups have performed in small towns in the industrial regions of West Bengal. But the sponsors of these performances are invariably businessmen and industrialists who are obviously not interested in a theater that questions their power and corruption. Clearly, alternative modes of sponsorship are necessary for performances in rural areas. Arun Mukherjee of Chetana is quite right in advocating support from the trade unions and *kisan sabhas* in the villages of Bengal. Now that the Left Front government of West Bengal is actively supporting theater groups in Calcutta, it is time for both the government and the groups to work out ways in which productions from the city can tour the villages and towns of Bengal on a regular basis. Only by engaging in dialogues with rural audiences can the political theater groups of Calcutta confront their growing insularity.

The second limitation of most Bengali theater groups in Calcutta arises from their adherence to the proscenium stage. While the proscenium might be necessary for many plays and should not be categorically dismissed as "limiting" or "bourgeois," there is a great deal to be learned from performing plays in less circumscribed spaces which facilitate a more immediate relationship between the actors and the spectators.

There is a particular validity in performing a political play on a street, where its activity is absorbed in the life of the street and open to inspection by the masses. There are no economic or social barriers in this theater. Certainly, one cannot expect all political theater to be produced on streets or in fields. During particularly repressive governmental regimes such performances may not be safe. But, as Utpal Dutt knows so well, the *pathnatika* (streetcorner play) is more effective than almost any other form of revolutionary theater.[22]

The theater in the streets is capable of transforming the rampant feelings of a mass audience into concrete actions. It is in a position to question the assumptions of an audience more directly than a play performed within the confines of a proscenium. Its dissemination of facts is not hindered by the technical intricacies of a production. Perhaps it is on the streets that the political theater in Bengal can truly realize its raison d'être. The street is the very source of its energy. It is, to borrow a famous aphorism by André Breton, the only valid field of experience for the political theater in Bengal.

THE LIVING THEATER OF KHARDAH

There is one Bengali theater group that avoids the two limitations noted above. It is a nonprofit regional theater company called the Living Theater situated in Khardah, a small town in the vicinity of Calcutta. What distinguishes this group from Badal Sircar's Satabdi (which it closely resembles in its artistic direction) is that it is situated in Khardah: the members of the Living Theater deliberately avoid performing in Calcutta. They associate the city with commercialism and economic pressures. They resist these threats to their integrity by performing exclusively in Khardah and touring villages in West Bengal, Bihar, and Madhya Pradesh.

The commitment of the Living Theater to the people is intense but not doctrinaire. The members of the group consider it unethical to support a particular political organization. On speaking to the actors who are, for the most part, residents of Khardah, I was struck by their resistance to political dogmas and party restrictions. Their seemingly apolitical stance seems to be a reaction to the political violence of the sixties in Bengal. It also indicates their fundamental skepticism that political parties (Congress or Communist) are capable of changing the lives of the people. Like Satabdi, the Living Theater emphasizes that individuals have to change their lives through an act of will. Only then is it possible for them to change the structure of their society.

The actors of the Living Theater believe that it is somewhat dishonest to advocate solutions to the problems of the people when they themselves are searching for "the correct path." Whether or not this path will be found, the actors emphasize that it is necessary to search for it with the cooperation of the audience. Even more than Satabdi, the Living Theater affirms that the audience should share the responsibility of the actors to confront the chaos of life and, hopefully, provide some alternatives to it. While one cannot dismiss these undoctrinaire views, one almost wishes that the Living Theater could be more dogmatic about its attitudes to politics, the bourgeoisie, and the people. The point of view in their plays is nebulous, often concealed by the overt romanticism of their mise en scène and their universalized perspectives of oppression and freedom. Nonetheless, there is an energy and emotional intensity conveyed by the actors of the Living Theater that cannot, in my opinion, be compared with the theater of any Bengali group functioning in Calcutta.

Perhaps this energy is all the more conspicuous because it contradicts the rural milieu of the Living Theater. Away from the cacophony and bustle of Calcutta, the group performs in a small, rather dingy room, with poor ventilation and resounding acoustics. The room is used as a classroom during the day. Outside there is a small patch of ground, flooded and overgrown with thick grass, which could be described as the "foyer" of the Living Theater. A man sits in front of a table and sells tickets costing one rupee (approximately eleven cents) to the audience, which consists primarily of lower-middle-class and working-class residents of

Khardah and the neighborhood. Outside the "theater" runs the main street of Khardah, a narrow lane where pedestrians and laborers amble along as if they had all the time in the world while cycle rickshaws zip past with that whirring and jingling sound one associates with rural areas. Here, at last, is a theater which is situated away from the city. No cars, no buses, no trams, no crowds, no processions; their absence becomes increasingly conspicuous the more one is absorbed in a play by the Living Theater, which is invariably violent in its momentum and impassioned in its utterance.

What is particularly fascinating about the Living Theater is the way it gradually directs the attention of the audience away from the milieu of Khardah to the reality of its plays. The beginning of a play by the Living Theater is very subtle, very unobtrusive. A member of the group, who is not an actor, enters the room and talks to the audience about the group and the play they are about to see. Then the actors enter very casually, stand in a line and hold hands, and begin to sing two or three familiar Bengali songs that are almost too mellifluous for the environment of the "theater."

In *Akhon Majhrat* (It is Midnight), which is described at length in the following pages, the singing of the group is particularly soulful. While singing a patriotic song by D. L. Roy familiar to everyone in the room, the actors surprise the audience by moving toward them. The proximity of the actors in the small space is compelling and intimate. Continuing to sing, the actors lie on the floor forming a circular pattern with their bodies. The strains of the patriotic song fade away, and we hear the dispersed cries of a beggar, played by one of the few actresses in the group. This very skilful tonal counterpoint is reminiscent of Sircar's theater. So are many of the elements in the mise en scène of *Akhon Majhrat*.

In the first sequence of the play, three actors read the headlines of various newspapers in a matter-of-fact manner while waiting for a train to arrive. National and international calamities, bizarre occurrences and familiar problems are juxtaposed so that their innate absurdities are revealed. The train arrives, formed by the bodies of the actors who break away and assume the identities of various commuters in the train—loud passengers playing cards, vendors selling lozenges which are also advertised as purgatives, beggars pleading for alms, urchins singing songs. Like the vig-

nettes of everyday life dramatized in Sircar's plays, this sequence
in the train is evocative in its close observation of lower-middle-
class people, their attitudes and habits. Nothing develops during
this sequence, which simply merges into a depiction of office life in
Calcutta.

An actor representing the boss sways with stylized movements
from side to side signing various cash registers and files. While he
signs, employees grovel in front of him, clutching his legs while
begging for promotions and loans. The boss listens to their requests
with total indifference. In an ironic change of circumstance, he is
informed by his boss on the telephone that he has been transferred.
Instantly he becomes as obsequious as his employees. The sequence
reveals the levels of hierarchy to be found in the bureaucracy of
Calcutta and the extent to which a member of the middle class is
prepared to humiliate himself in order to satisfy his material
needs.

The more telling sequences of *Akhon Majhrat* occur when they
are juxtaposed with other disparate sequences. The following
chain of sequences indicates the value of juxtapositions in deepen-
ing the thought of a play. For instance, at one point in the play, the
chorus of actors simulates the rowing of a boat, their movements
capturing the very motion of the river, while another actor sings a
fisherman's song about the trials of life that seems to emerge from
the very heart of rural Bengal. The serenity of this scene is disrupted by the sudden intrusion of the rhythms of Calcutta. The
members of the chorus jog frantically around the room. Through
repetitions of phrases and slogans, they capture the "cricket fever"
that seizes the residents of Calcutta whenever there is a major
"Test Match" between India and an international team. This obses-
sive attraction for cricket, which diverts the young people of Calcutta away from more immediate realities, is almost as harmful as
Hindi films, another major source of escapism in India.

The members of the chorus convey the uncontrolled energy of
cricket fans, and then they parody the sensationalism and seductive lure of the Hindi film world. With drugged movements and
exhibitionist postures, the actors sing "Dum Maro Dum," a popular Hindi film song, and chant the names of famous Hindi film
stars with catchy rhythms. The very names of the stars convey the
synthetic, yet mesmeric, impact of the Hindi film world, particu-

larly on the masses, who crave any escape from the oppression of their lives. It is a widely accepted truism that the commercial Hindi film does not in any significant way change the consciousness of the masses concerning their oppression: it merely serves to highlight the fantasies of the Indian working class. And yet, it may be argued that such fantasies enable people to survive their degradation and squalor.

After evoking the lure of the Hindi film world, the actors of the Living Theater depict the rowdy, almost delirious behavior of the film fans lining up to buy tickets. Very often the enthusiasm to see a popular Hindi film can lead to violence. This enthusiasm also enables unemployed youths to earn a living by selling tickets at black-market prices. The black marketeering of cinema tickets has become a major source of income for many *goondas*, who often pay the police a percentage of their profits in order to stay out of jail. Without commenting on these facts, the Living Theater calls attention to them by dramatizing their contradictions in vivid detail.

Contradictions are the very substance of any serious theater. There is no need for the Living Theater to create the contradictions in its plays because they already exist in the everyday life of Bengal. A particularly incisive sequence that contains a disturbing, yet familiar, contradiction (for a Bengali audience) involves the activities of a funeral party: the pallbearers intersperse their funeral chant with witticisms and ironic remarks. Merriment at a funeral would shock many Westerners, but in Bengal the grotesque sight depicted by the actors of the Living Theater is quite common. Very often, when a person dies in a *bustee* and has no close relatives, his body is disposed of in a most casual and irreverent manner. The street boys have to be paid to take the body to the burning ghats. After the trials of life for most underprivileged people in Calcutta, the trivialization of death seems almost legitimate. The merriment of a funeral party can be viewed as an ironic commentary on the destitution of life.

Another contradiction that the Living Theater examines in *Akhon Majhrat* concerns the essential distance of the bourgeoisie from the problems of the villagers. Here again the treatment is deft and ironic. A group of friends from the city decide to take a holiday in Darjeeling. Once the idyllic summer resort of the British, exclusive and somewhat ethereal, Darjeeling has now become a tourist haunt for families and teenagers from all over India, particularly Bengal. The sahibs from the city are played as superficial, acquisitive, and fundamentally insular people. In an illuminating sequence, they talk to a local laborer from Darjeeling and listen with unconvincing concern to his problems. While pretending to understand the conditions of his life and work, the sahibs convey that their concern for the working class is at best a dutiful pretense. They offer advice to the laborer, voicing the platitudes of government officials. This sequence indicates the Living Theater's keen awareness of the contradictions involved in enlightening rural people. While the group has performed plays for the people in various villages, it never fails to remember that the people do not need to be taught anything: they have to be made to act upon what they already know about their conditions of life and state of oppression.

The contradictions examined in *Akhon Majhrat* extend to its depiction of politics. The Living Theater emphasizes its nonpartisan attitude to politics by juxtaposing two political murders: one where the victim is a member of the CPI(M) party (reputedly murdered by a member of the Congress party) and another where the victim is a member of the Congress party (reputedly murdered by a supporter of the Communist party). The actors convey their distaste for such indiscriminate violence in a strident sequence where they chant political slogans with a ferocity that I have never encountered in any political theater. There is a profound anger underlying the chanting, a bitter disillusionment with the false promises of the politicians.

The sequence is so violent, so deafeningly loud, that it seems to exhaust itself. While the actors gradually begin to hum the patriotic song first heard at the start of the play, a woman lies on the floor in a state of exhaustion. The juxtaposition of the song (celebrating India as a motherland) and the still form of the woman is profoundly disturbing. The song is repeated in yet another ironic sequence toward the end of the play when we see a group of actors taking a corpse to the burning ghats. This time there is no merriment. Instead, the pallbearers sing a song every Indian connects with the freedom struggle. The juxtaposition of patriotism and death prompts a question: In the face of death and daily oppressions, traumas, and sheer neglect, what does it mean for those hundreds of Indian people deprived of the necessities of life to love their country? Patriotism seems almost unreasonable in the context of pain and oppression.

After the second funeral sequence, more brutally ironic than the first, the actors go up to individual spectators and speak in metaphorical terms about their mutual dilemma. "There is no light. . . . Why aren't you showing us the way?" they ask. "After midnight passes, the path will be clear. How are we to accept this?" While it is somehow moving to hear the actors express their vulnerability so ingenuously, one cannot help resisting the romanticized rhetoric of their statements. The Living Theater has explored the physical language of the theater with daring immediacy, but it continues to use words in a manner reminiscent of second-rate lyrical poetry.

The most powerful moments in *Akhon Majhrat* occur when the actors are silent and concentrate all their energy in physical images and ensemble movement. For instance, in the final moments of the play, the actors stand in a circle and entwine their arms while chanting a song. The circle of bodies evokes an image of a tired community of people, exhausted yet determined to stay together. This image of the community is juxtaposed with the still figure of a woman who sits on the floor with her head bowed and her hand outstretched. In a spontaneous movement, the other actors turn to her and include her in their circle. It is a very naive gesture at a certain level but it is also strangely moving. In the last image of the play, we see the actors with their arms entwined around one another retreating to the far end of the room. They continue to sing after they leave the room, their voices muffled in the distance.

I have described *Akhon Majhrat* at length because it offers an experience that lingers long after one takes the train from Khardah back to Calcutta. What remains are memories, not so much of the play itself but of the group, the actors of the Living Theater, whose communion as human beings is so deep and profoundly generous that one ceases to think of their theater in purely aesthetic terms.

Even more convincingly than the actors of Satabdi, the company of the Living Theater expresses, without ever making an issue of it, that theater is for them a way of life.

Many of the actors come from very poor families, others work in offices in Calcutta. Almost all of them had no theater experience before Probir Guha, one of the initiators of the group, conducted workshops in Khardah modelled on the exercises he had observed in Sircar's theater. The technical proficiency of the group is quite astounding. The vocal range of the actors, the intensity of their cries, nonverbal sounds, and pants, the control and extension of their bodies are emphasized without seeming virtuosic. The Living Theater in Khardah demonstrates a physical awareness of the theater that cannot be compared with any group in Calcutta, including Satabdi. Reflecting on "the overpowering impact of a direct, innocent, unsophisticated communication" between the actor and the spectator in the theater, Probir Guha has stressed that "an actor must reach a certain height of experience so that the audience can respect him genuinely." An actor can attain this experience only if he "performs in close proximity with the audience and exerts his body."[23]

The Living Theater is also the first group in the Bengali theater which successfully demonstrates that it is possible to create theater on a collective basis. While Satabdi also functions as a collective, the presence of Sircar is too dominant to be ignored. As modest and undogmatic as he is as a director, he is still the unquestioned leader and playwright of the group. Guha also plays a central role in conducting the workshops of the Living Theater and in preparing the scripts for the productions, but for the most part, all the actors collectively participate in the shaping of the artistic policies of the group and the creation of their plays.

While I admire the solidarity of the group and the rigorous training of the actors, I should add that the Living Theater has not yet fully developed its potential. The group needs to confront the problems of the people with a more historical perspective. It is not enough to present images of the suffering of the people and abstractions of tyranny and oppression. This form of dramaturgy, so conspicuous in *Aami Tumi Aamra* (I You Us), a recent production of the Living Theater, indicates that the actors in Khardah seem to evade the rigors of analysis and do not sufficiently articulate their point of view in a production.[24] Their political naivete is the major limitation of their theater: it encourages them to romanticize the suffering of the people. Perhaps the Living Theater needs to perform more frequently for villagers in rural areas so that they can confront this limitation.

A spokesman for the group told me about a particularly rich experience shared by his colleagues when they visited a secluded village near the Bangladesh border. The actors were quite overwhelmed by the hospitality of the villagers, who shared whatever food and drink they could provide. After living with the villagers and discussing their problems, the actors staged *Gramer Panchali* (A Village Saga), one of the very few productions in their repertoire which assumes a definite position regarding the struggle of the people.

Set entirely in a rural area, the play dramatizes the oppression of an impoverished farmer by prominent members of the village. Enraged that the farmer refuses to sell a goat to him, the village butcher plots with a moneylender and some *goondas* to murder the farmer. They kill him after robbing him of whatever money he has. When the villagers discover the farmer's corpse, they suspect foul play and go to the *mahajan* who vainly attempts to pacify them. The *mahajan* contacts yet another hypocritical figure of the village, the quack doctor, who examines the corpse and blandly claims that the farmer has died of acute colic pain. The people are not taken in by this fake diagnosis. They resolve to be united and to kill the oppressors in their village.

Their revolt assumes a massive scale as the butcher, moneylender, and the *mahajan* assume the personae of various oppressors including the cooperative director, the leader of the *panchayat* (village court), and the village politician. All these figures of power ridicule the anger of the people. "The Establishment is in our hands," they claim. Initially, the people are intimidated by the power of their oppressors, but eventually they decide to revolt. "Help us," they entreat the members of the audience, "to eradicate these people."

According to the spokesman for the Living Theater, the impact of *Gramer Panchali* on the villagers was phenomenal. They participated energetically as spectators by shouting loud protests against the oppressors in the play. The immediacy of the narrative (based on Manik Bandyophadhyay's famous novel) and the archetypal nature of the characters (the farmer, the moneylender, the *mahajan*) combined to form a compelling drama that engaged the emotions and frustrations of the villagers on a most instinctive level.

The Living Theater should continue to produce plays on this model, where the motivations and attitudes of the characters are directly related to their position in the class struggle. Though the play may seem old-fashioned in its linear mode of narration, it has more political and social significance than the other abstract, fragmented, and allegorical dramas staged by the Living Theater.

Gramer Panchali exemplifies how necessary it is for the political theater in Bengal to *tell a story*: it is the surest way to involve the spectators in the issues of a play and raise their consciousness about the oppression of the people. Telling a story, however, is not the only way of doing political theater. The actors in Khardah could well adopt the techniques of Augusto Boal, notably the "forum theater," which I recommended for Badal Sircar. By involving the villagers in workshops, they would be able to establish an even closer rapport with them. Perhaps working *with* the villagers rather than performing plays *for* them may not be immediately possible for the actors of the Living Theater, but they should keep it in mind as their strongest, most challenging possibility of change and artistic growth. I have no doubt that they are eminently capable of extending their research in the theater by incorporating the active participation of the people.

Toward a People's Theater

I have constantly reiterated in this study how necessary it is for the practitioners of political theater in Bengal to work actively with the people. It is disheartening to realize that in a state where the vast majority of the people live in rural areas there is no theater that enables the people to speak for themselves. Certainly, there have been many plays in the Bengali theater, notably those by Utpal Dutt, where the struggle of the people has been represented

on stage in a revolutionary perspective. There have been plays
which have revealed considerable compassion for the predicament
of the people with or without melodramatic excesses. There have
been plays where the people have been symbolized, deified, defended, evoked, cheered, and warmly supported. But despite this
allegiance to the people, expressed in so many ways, some more
convincing than others, there have been very few plays in the
Bengali theater where the people can be said to have represented
themselves.

More often than not, the personality and ideology of the director or the playwright dominate the seemingly authentic depiction
of the people's suffering and oppression. While this domination is,
perhaps, to be expected in the urban theater and may not be necessarily obtrusive, I have seen more Bengali plays than I would care
to remember where the people have seemed incidental to the mechanics of the stage business and the virtuosity of the acting. In a
particularly superficial production, the people almost seem to be
exploited by the director and the actors in their pursuit of art and
theatrical subtleties. Perhaps this inability to represent the people
with any integrity can be solved, or at least confronted, if the theater groups in Calcutta could interact more dynamically with the
people—first by performing plays for them on a more regular basis
and then, at a later stage, by involving them in the creation of
workshop productions and plays.

This is by no means an easy enterprise, but it should not be dismissed as an overly idealistic form of political theater. Directors
and actors in the Bengali theater need to examine the recent work
of a theater group in Bangladesh called Aranyak that has actively
collaborated with villagers on plays that illuminate their oppression. The actors begin their work by listening to the villagers'
problems and discussing them from various perspectives. "True
incidents" relating to feudal corruption, hierarchical tensions
within the family, the exploitation of women, and the expropria-
tion of land are enacted by the villagers themselves. Then, after
witnessing these enactments, the actors (of Aranyak) collaborate
with the villagers on creating a story that integrates the various
incidents revealing the villagers' problems. Gradually, "characters" are created and a "narrative" is sketched wherein the individ-

ual problems óf the villagers are juxtaposed in relation to each other. In this way, many "plays" have been improvised in at least a hundred villages in Bangladesh involving five hundred performers with no theatrical experience whatsoever. Aranyak is committed to this form of theater—a "liberated theater" that actively involves the masses, and thereby prepares them to change the conditions of their life.[25]

Without the active participation of the people, the political theater in Bengal cannot fully develop its potential. No one stressed this fact more vehemently than Bijon Bhattacharya, the patriarch of the political theater movement in Bengal. Toward the end of his life, he attended a seminar on political theater (which he described as "somewhat unreal") where he expressed his despair about the "urban theater" in Calcutta, so essentially remote from the lives of the people. In a particularly moving statement, he questioned the significance of his own theater.

> I feel frustrated and insecure when I realize that I have not been able to take my work to the masses in the rural areas, and that I have not been able to involve them in my work. . . . I can only dream of a group of laborers playing themselves and destroying in the process all the familiar gestures and forms of our urban theater. As long as we do not realize that dream, we can only play with faint shadows of life and reality. It is a shame to be estranged from the people and the truth that they embody.[26]

The Bengali theater will continue to be "estranged from the people" so long as it continues to perform for a predominantly urban audience, so long as it remains satisified with the conventions of the proscenium theater, so long as it is reconciled to bourgeois actors from the city playing the suffering and oppression of the masses. A rapport with the people can only be achieved if the theater in Bengal is willing to confront its insularity and open itself to the immediate influence and participation of the people. Only then, perhaps, will Bijon Bhattacharya's dream of a people's theater be realized.

Afterword

We have examined the political theater in Bengal from its gradual emergence in the late nineteenth century to its development during the activist phase of the Indian People's Theater Association to its varied, often contradictory, manifestations in the contemporary Bengali theater. So much has happened to the theater in Bengal over the last thirty years that it is difficult to ignore the sheer momentum of its growth. Most practitioners of the Bengali theater, however, seem to have reached a state of ennui in their creative development around the mid-seventies. After years of experimentation in diverse forms and bold attacks on traditional taboos and norms, the Bengali theater seems to have settled down to a more predictable course of action.

Very few original Bengali plays have been written since 1975. The same old productions are repeated week after week somewhat listlessly. Prominent groups tend to present, at best, one new production a year. Many talented performers are diverting their attention away from the theater by concentrating on commercialized *jatra* and an occasional film. These activities are alluring because they are financially lucrative. It should be stressed, however, that no Bengali actor or director, to the best of my knowledge, can rely on the theater to earn his living. In fact, the economic instability of the Bengali theater may well be one of the primary reasons for its present lassitude and inertia.

This economic instability persists despite recent attempts by the Left Front government in West Bengal to provide financial assistance to various groups. In 1981–1982, twenty-two groups in Calcutta received grants of five thousand rupees each, and a year earlier, five groups received ten thousand rupees each and five others five thousand rupees each. The distribution of money has been a controversial issue since many of the members of the funding committee are also the directors of prominent groups which receive grants and prizes. Some stalwarts of the Group Theater movement believe that the increased availability of money will merely destroy the idealistic spirit of the theater in Bengal. Shekhar Chatterjee, for instance, has emphasized that the Bengali theater "has always survived on its own." But it should also be acknowledged that the economic crisis in West Bengal today is so acute that theater groups need some kind of financial security if they are to survive and experiment with new forms of theater.

Apart from economic problems, Bengali theater groups are reacting to their ideological differences in a rather petty and irresponsible way. The tensions between the supporters of the proscenium theater and the Third Theater groups, in particular, have escalated in the last few years. More perceptible than in the past history of the Bengali theater (which has always been turbulent), the feuds between the groups and the character assassinations of particular directors have not been constructive for the growth of the theater.

There was an attempt, however, on the part of established theater groups in Calcutta to establish their solidarity and commitment to professional theater. In 1980, groups like Nandikar, Chetana, and the Theater Workshop merged to form the Calcutta Repertory Theater, which produced an adaptation of Brecht's *Galileo*. Apart from thirteen performances of this production (which were sold out), the group has not staged a new production. Another organization with good intentions and a short life was the Group Theater Federation. Formed in 1979, it claimed to protect the rights of the smaller groups in Bengal and mounted a somewhat self-righteous campaign against the obscenity of the commercial theater. Unfortunately, the Federation seems to have exhausted its zeal, and the cabaret performances and smut of the commercial theater continue to titillate the predominantly middle-class audiences.

There are many problems in the Bengali theater today, but I am convinced that they will be confronted in the near future. The actors, directors, and intellectuals of Bengal care about the theater too much to allow it to stultify. They are acutely aware that the theater does not merely provide entertainment and raise the social and political consciousness of the people: it is essential to the very life of Calcutta. It never fails to amaze me how intensely the theater is loved in Bengal. After encountering the pervasive materialism and corporationlike bureaucracy of the American theater, I am positively invigorated when I think of Bengali groups like Satabdi and the Living Theater of Khardah responding to the theater *for the sake of theater* and not for fringe benefits of the theater like fame, publicity, affluence, and career opportunities in film and television. Since these benefits are not easily available in Bengal, most Bengali groups can afford to dedicate themselves to their work in the theater with few distractions.

The most insinuative form of distraction for Bengali theater practitioners is the commercial film in Hindi or Bengali. Utpal Dutt, in particular, has spent more time in film studios than at rehearsals in recent years. This probably explains why his recent productions lack the fire and meticulous coordination of his early productions. He simply does not have sufficient time to devote himself entirely to his plays. While I believe that Dutt should extend his ideas of the "revolutionary theater" to film (as he has done most convincingly in recent years), I also believe he should stop playing villains and buffoons in commercial Hindi films. These roles may be financially alluring but they are intellectually inane and numbing. If Dutt continues to work in Hindi films, his plays might begin to resemble them more closely than he would care to admit.

It is reassuring to learn, however, that Dutt is working on two ambitious film projects—an adaptation of Gorki's *Mother* and a historical film on the life of Lebedeff (the founder of the Bengali theater) to be directed jointly by Dutt and Victor Melnikov, a director from the Soviet Union. Dutt has also adapted two foreign plays—*Death of an Anarchist* by the renowned Italian satirist Dario Fo, and David Selbourne's *The Trial of Smt. Gandhi* (a documentary play on the excesses of the Emergency), which was produced by Dutt just before the last General Assembly election in March 1982.

Dutt also plans to revive a play by his acknowledged mentor in the nineteenth-century Bengali theater, Girish Chandra Ghosh. As we have seen in chapter 2, Dutt has modelled his "revolutionary theater" on the fervent, often rapturously patriotic, spectacle of Ghosh's historical plays. While acknowledging the emotional power of this model, I can only reiterate that it needs to be questioned with greater rigor by Dutt.

I would also like to see Badal Sircar and the actors of the Living Theater in Khardah broaden the scope of their theaters in the ways mentioned in the last two chapters. Though I do not prescribe Boal's model of the "forum theater" as their only possibility of development, I offer it as a direction and a source of inspiration that might be of some use to them. As I emphasized earlier, the model can be adapted to Indian conditions but it is not something that can be effortlessly assimilated. On the contrary, it will take a considerable amount of courage, thought, and self-sacrifice before Sircar and the actors of the Living Theater can create situations whereby underprivileged people can participate in open "forums" and speak freely of their grievances.

It is not possible to predict when the Bengali theater will transform itself into the "people's theater" that Augusto Boal practises and Bijon Bhattacharya envisioned. I can only hope that this transformation will take place soon. Life in Bengal has never been more impoverished and destitute. The suffering of the people has never been more perceptible. At no stage in the development of the political theater in Bengal has its allegiance to an oppressed people been more imperative.

Without the support of the theater, millions of people in Calcutta and the rural areas of Bengal who are denied the basic necessities of life will continue to accept their squalor believing that they are incapable of changing the conditions of their life. Without their active participation in a politically engaged theater, they will have to continue relying on the false promises of politicians and opportunistic bureaucrats. The theater, it is true, cannot substitute for concrete political action. But it is, perhaps, the most powerful and illuminating means of *preparing* people for this action. In the words of Augusto Boal, the theater may not be "revolutionary in itself," but it is, potentially, "a rehearsal of revolution."

Notes

CHAPTER 1
TOWARD A POLITICAL THEATER IN BENGAL

1. All references to the *Natyashastra* are from Manmohan Ghosh, trans., *Nāṭyaśāstra* (Calcutta: Asiatic Society of Bengal, 1950).

2. See Indu Shekhar, "Text and Date of *Nāṭyaśāstra*," in *Sanskrit Drama: Its Origin and Decline* (Leiden: E. J. Brill, 1960), pp. 42–44.

3. Shudraka, *Mricchakatika*, trans. J. A. B. van Buitenen, in *Two Plays of Ancient India* (New York: Columbia University Press, 1968), p. 180.

4. For an excellent introduction to the play, see van Buitenen, *Two Plays of Ancient India.*

5. Balwant Gargi, *Folk Theater of India* (Seattle and London: University of Washington Press, 1966); a comprehensive survey of the folk theater in India, its origins, conventions, and contemporary practices.

6. Sylvain Lévi, *Le Théâtre Índien*, vol. 2, trans. Narayan Mukherjee (Calcutta: Writers Workshop, 1978), p. 40.

7. Certain Indologists, notably Lassen and Klein, assert that the *jatra* originated even earlier in the *Gita Govinda*, an ancient poem celebrating the love of Krishna and Radha, written by the Bengali poet Jayadeva in the twelfth century. But there is little evidence to support their views that the poem was "a mystery play of the Hindus" enacted with songs and dances. It should also be stressed that the *Gita Govinda* was written in Sanskrit—a language that was not accessible to the people. Furthermore, as Sylvain Lévi reasonably objects, "It is a *kavya* (poem) and should not be forced into the framework of drama . . . it is still between the ritual hymn and drama." Most contemporary Indologists share this view and are more or less convinced that the *jatra* originated in the religious processions of Chaitanya's movement.

8. For a perceptive study of *jatra*, see Nisikanta Chattopadhyay, *The Yatras*

(London: Trubner & Co., 1882). Though the study concentrates exclusively on the *Krishna jatras* written by Krishnakamala Goswami, it is one of the first studies to examine the *jatra's* innate characteristics and structural principles with some authority. Despite Chattopadhyay's false conjectures and his tendency to make arbitrary connections—he relates, for instance, the three periods of Krishna's life (infancy, youth, manhood) to the three parts of a mystery play *(passio, sepultura, resurrectio)*—his book is full of insights and sharp observations. It is minuscule in size, but *The Yatras* is broad in perspective. It is an admirable introduction to a rich and complex area of research.

9. For an alternative reading of these facts, see P. Guha-Thakurta, *The Bengali Drama* (London: Kegan Paul, Trench, Trubner & Co., 1930), p. 65.

10. Quoted by Kironmoy Raha in *Bengali Theater* (New Delhi: National Book Trust, 1978), p. 10.

11. This enormous amount of money (more than sufficient to finance many theater groups functioning in Calcutta today for over a year) is quoted by R. J. Yajnik in *The Indian Theatre* (New York: E. P. Dutton & Co., 1934), p. 85.

12. Guha-Thakurta, *Bengali Drama*, p. 65.

13. Quoted by S. R. Mehrota in *The Emergence of the Indian National Congress* (New York: Barnes & Noble, 1971), p. 3.

14. See ibid., pp. 25–29, for more information about these societies.

15. Ibid., pp. 24–25.

16. Guha-Thakurta, *Bengali Drama*, p. 73.

17. Ibid., p. 74. This passage suggests an intricate connection between "orientalism" (as defined by Edward Said in his seminal work) and "occidentalism." Instead of condemning the "Asiatic air" of Byron and the "Orientalism" of Moore (which contributed to Western mythologies of the "exotic Orient"), Madhusadhan upheld these mystifications as poetic virtues, and thereby asserted his "occidentalism." Ironically, it was by passing through this phase that he was able to develop a clearer, more incisive, vision of what it meant to be an Indian living in a colonized society.

18. See Guha-Thakurta, *Bengali Drama*, pp. 75–78, for a detailed description of the play.

19. Quoted from *The Heart of Aryavarta* by the Earl of Ronaldshay in Guha-Thakurta, *Bengali Drama*, p. 84.

20. See S. Gopal, *British Policy in India 1858–1905* (Cambridge: Cambridge University Press, 1965), pp. 22–32, for a cogent analysis of the political background surrounding *Neel-Darpan*.

21. Quoted by Raha in *Bengali Theatre*, p. 19.

22. This idea is discussed at greater length in my analysis of *Ajeya Vietnam*, a production by Utpal Dutt (see chapter 2, pp. 80–81).

23. Quoted by Raha in *Bengali Theatre*, pp. 27–28.

24. Guha-Thakurta, *Bengali Drama*, p. 150.

25. *Bilati Jatra Theke Swadeshi Thiyetar*, ed. Subir Roychaudhuri (Calcutta: Jadavpur University Publication, 1972), p. 41.

26. Compared to the theater practitioners, the writers and social thinkers in

the Bengali literary circles were positively daring in their documentations of colonial oppression. Sankar Ghose calls attention to these documentations in *Socialism and Communism in India* (Calcutta: Allied Publishers, 1971), pp. 46–47.

Foremost among Bengali novelists, of course, was Bankim Chandra Chatterjee whose *Anandanath* later became the gospel of revolutionaries. In addition, this renowned novelist exposed the economic inequalities of the Raj in a series of articles on *samya* or equality. Earlier, Dwarkanath Gangapadhaya, a Brahmo social reformer who had lived in disguise among the coolies on plantations in Assam, wrote about the dehumanizing experiences of the workers in *Sanjibanee* and *The Bengalee*. It should be noted that two years after the Dramatic Performances Act was passed, Sasipada Banerjee instituted a journal dedicated to the labor movement in India. It was called *Bharat Sramjibee* (The Indian Worker). While theater practitioners memorialized the history of the Mughals and the Rajputs, the social workers, thinkers, and writers of Bengal were addressing the problems of the underprivileged workers in India.

27. Quoted by Lévi in *Le Théâtre Índien*, vol. 2, p. 106.

28. Girish Chandra Ghosh, *Collected Works*, Vol. 1, cited by Utpal Dutt in *Towards a Revolutionary Theater* (Calcutta: M. C. Sarkar & Sons, 1982), p. 140.

29. These figures are quoted by Percival Spear in *India: A Modern History* (Ann Arbor: The University of Michigan Press, 1972), p. 198.

30. Ibid., p. 199.

31. Quoted by Stuart Cary Welch in *Room for Wonder* (New York: The American Federation of Arts, 1978), p. 181.

32. Mehrota, *Indian National Congress*. See chapters 6 and 7 for a lucid analysis of the Indian National Congress.

33. Gopal, *British Policy in India*, p. 225.

34. Quoted by Guha-Thakurta in *Bengali Drama*, p. 155.

35. Ibid., p. 156.

36. Quoted by Raha in *Bengali Theatre*, p. 98. *Raghubir* is about Raghua, a tribal aborigine who is adopted by a Brahmin priest and given the name Raghubir. In a cataclysmic moment in the drama (described by Sombhu Mitra in his review), Raghubir abandons all the civilized virtues that he has learned from his foster parent and reverts to his savage state of being.

37. Raha, *Bengali Theatre*, p. 103.

38. Ibid., p. 104.

39. To indicate this increased militancy of the workers, it is significant to note that in 1936–1937 there were 271 unions controlled by the All-India Trade Union Congress and the All-India Kisan Sabha. In 1938–1939, there were 562 registered unions with 399,159 members. These figures are quoted by Ghose in *Socialism and Communism in India*, p. 63.

40. Excerpt from an amended manifesto adopted by the members at the Second All-India Progressive Writers' Conference held in Calcutta on December 24, 1938. Quoted by Sudhi Pradhan in *Marxist Cultural Movement in India: Chronicles and Documents (1936–47)* (Calcutta: National Book Agency, 1979), p. 21.

41. Quoted by Jawarhalal Nehru in *The Discovery of India* (New York: Doubleday & Co., 1959), p. 345.

42. My first and only reference to Tagore in this chapter requires some explanation. I have deliberately avoided speaking about him because I do not believe he can be associated with the professional theater in Bengal. Tagore's symbolic dramas have no precedents and, to my mind, no replicas in the history of the Bengali theater. They have to be studied in themselves. They cannot be categorized under any rubric nor can they be linked with any tendency, most emphatically not a political one. Though some of his plays have been interpreted in quasi-Marxist terms—his masterpiece *Raktakarabi* (Red Oleanders), for instance, has been interpreted as an indictment of colonial tyranny—I believe that Tagore's plays ultimately transcend any political interpretation. If one has to unearth historical and political meanings in Tagore's plays, one should remember that they are inextricably linked with metaphysical issues of the "soul." To trace the minutiae of historical detail embedded in the poetic texture of Tagore's plays lies beyond the scope of this book.

43. Quoted by Pradhan in *Marxist Cultural Movement*, pp. 107, 109.

44. Ibid., p. 137.

45. Ibid. These phrases are extracted from Hiren Mukherjee's inaugural speech at the first conference of the I.P.T.A.

46. Ibid., p. 141.

47. Ibid., p. 276.

48. Ibid., pp. 357–358.

49. Interview with Bijon Bhattacharya by Samik Bandyopadhyay, "Janshadharaner Ami" [I belong to the people] in first issue of *Proma* (Calcutta: Rup Lekha Press, 1978). It should be pointed out that though the interview was conducted in Bengali, Bijon Bhattacharya frequently used a number of English phrases and expressions that have not been altered in Dilip Kumar Chakravarty's translation.

50. Ibid., p. 36.

51. Ibid., p. 36.

52. See Amartya Sen, *Poverty and Famine: An Essay on Entitlement and Deprivation* (Cambridge: Oxford University Press, 1981). In this incisive study, Sen examines the intricate economic factors that cause the outbreak of famines in various parts of the world. Rejecting the common beliefs that famines are directly related to overpopulation and a scarcity of food, Sen substantiates with a most detailed statistical analysis that people starve when their "entitlement" is insufficient to buy the food necessary to keep them alive. Income distribution is yet another seemingly remote factor that causes famines.

53. I am grateful to Samik Bandyopadhyay for providing me with a copy of this unpublished document.

54. Quoted by Raha in *Bengali Theatre*, p. 131.

55. There is some irony in this symbol that Bhattacharya would surely have acknowledged were he alive today. For almost a decade, a tube railway has been "under construction" in a central area of Calcutta. It has proved to be a Kafka-

esque enterprise, so ridden with corruption and administrative blunders that the people of Calcutta have come to accept it as a bad joke. Not only are the soil conditions of West Bengal unsuited for the construction of an underground railway, the climatic conditions (particularly the humidity) and the incessant power cuts in Calcutta (lasting six to eight hours daily) indicate some of the problems that were not considered by the entrepreneurs of the tube railway scheme. Certainly it is far removed from the underground railway in *Haanshkalir Haans* envisioned by Bhattacharya as a symbol of "technological progress and change."

56. Quoted by Bandyopadhyay in "After Professionalism," *Drama Review* 15, no. 3 (Spring 1971):239.

57. Quoted by Pradhan in *Marxist Cultural Movement*, pp. 302–303.

58. I regret that I have not been able to discuss the immense contribution of Sombhu Mitra to the Bengali theater in this book. The reason for this seemingly irresponsible omission corresponds to that for not including Tagore in this survey. Like Tagore, Mitra's orientation as an artist is too ethereal, too poetic, ultimately too deeply personal, to be categorized as "political." It is no coincidence, therefore, that Mitra's greatest allegiance as an artist is to Tagore. He has devoted a substantial part of his career and life to unravelling the mysteries and consonances of Tagore's poetic dramas. And where others have failed ignominiously, he has triumphed.

In his article entitled "Building from Tagore" (published in the special Asian issue of the *Drama Review*) Mitra makes it very clear that the only way to achieve "a distinctive form of Indian theatrical expression" is through Tagore. Dismissing European models of realistic theater and criticizing contemporary *jatra* as "a poor imitation of the commercial theater in Calcutta," Mitra affirms that it is only by unveiling the poetic language of Tagore that the Bengali theater can discover its "origins." While he acknowledges that the contemporary theater needs to confront the turbulence of his age, Mitra still yearns for a "peace in rhythm," and an inner tranquillity. "Only Tagore," according to him "has been able to establish a connection with our Golden Age, in the midst of social and political conflict." This innately romantic yearning for a lost heritage is distinctly un-Marxist. It is no surprise, therefore, that Mitra's association with the I.P.T.A. was controversial and brief.

Since he formed his own company, Bohurupee, in 1948, Sombhu Mitra has staged a number of poetic dramas, notably Tagore's masterworks *Raktakarabi* (Red Oleanders) and *Raja* (King of the Dark Chamber). His performances in these productions are legendary. As a classical actor who relies primarily on his voice to convey the innermost feelings of his characters, Mitra has no peer in the contemporary Bengali theater. Whether he plays Oedipus or Stockmann or Tughluq, he surrenders to these roles with the intensity of a poet. His critics sometimes maintain that he tends to lose himself in his lyricism and that everything he utters on stage is uniformly mellifluous. While these are not qualities one associates with a proletarian actor, they are resplendent in themselves. If one had to write about Sombhu Mitra (or Sombhuda as he is affectionately called in Bengal), one would have to devote an entire book to him. One would have to find words to evoke the sublimity of his acting, a demand that lies outside the scope of this book.

CHAPTER 2
THE REVOLUTIONARY THEATER OF UTPAL DUTT

1. In his article "Little Theater O Ami" published in his journal *Epic Theater* (May 1977), Dutt narrates an incident when he was beaten by Kendall after a performance of *Romeo and Juliet* in Allahabad:

> I had Mercutio's part, I died in the middle of the play. Having finished my part, I went back to the hotel. Around midnight, Kendall entered my room with a pair of heavy boots in his hand and, before uttering a single word, he beat me mercilessly. Then I remembered that I was supposed to conduct the music in the last scene. As there were only fourteen of us in the group, we had to do practically everything ourselves. As I had neglected my duty for various personal reasons, Kendall became furious and constantly repeated the words: "Shame on you, you don't belong." You don't belong—you are not one of the theater. You are not a man of this profession. The Guru's reprimands hurt me more than the boots. That night I learned a lot. Kendall was an old type of British professional, who had learned by being beaten and who used to teach by beating. (P. 50)

2. A month earlier the CPI held its second congress in Calcutta, where it passed a resolution stating that "though the bourgeois leadership parades the story that independence has been won, the fact is that the freedom struggle has been betrayed and the national leadership has struck a treacherous deal behind the back of starving people, betraying every slogan of the democratic revolution" (quoted by Sankar Ghose in *Socialism and Communism in India* [Calcutta: Allied Publishers, 1971], p. 67). Ghose also states that in support of this resolution the CPI organized a number of strikes in the plantations, collieries, textile mills, and in the Indian railways and tramways. In March 1948, the CPI was banned and leading Communists were arrested under the Public Safety Act.

3. After the ban on the Communist party was lifted in 1950, the Bengal unit of the I.P.T.A. (which had been relatively disorganized since the aftermath of *Nabanna*) once again emerged as a powerful organization. Unfortunately, the schism between the "artists" and the "political" members of the I.P.T.A. continued to exist. Like Sombhu Mitra and Bijon Bhattacharya, Dutt could not tolerate the bureaucracy of the Party members.

4. Utpal Dutt, *Towards a Revolutionary Theater* (Calcutta: M. C. Sarkar & Sons, 1982), p. 32.

5. Ibid., p. 31.

6. Ibid., pp. 17–18.

7. Ibid., p. 71.

8. It should be pointed out that when Dutt produced *Macbeth* in a proscenium production in Calcutta, the effect was far removed from the early performances in villages. Blatantly operatic and lavish in scale, the production exemplified

some of the worst excesses of the nineteenth-century theater—melodramatic acting and posturing, a pretentious delivery of lines, and a fundamental lack of belief in the social and political resonance of the play. It was one of Dutt's most pointless productions.

9. Dutt, *Towards a Revolutionary Theater*, p. 140.

10. Ibid., p. 15.

11. All references to *Angar* are from the Bengali text of the play published by Jatiya Sahitya Parishad, Calcutta, translated by Dilip Kumar Chakravorty.

12. Quoted by Kironmoy Raha in *Bengali Theatre* (New Delhi National Book Trust, 1978), pp. 133–134.

13. Dutt elaborates on this idea in *Towards a Revolutionary Theater* (pp. 54–56) by hypothesizing about a worker shot down by the police. A bourgeois commentator would concentrate on the facts and note that "the worker had first thrown stones on the blacklegs and then dragged one of them from the company's truck and smashed his skull with an iron rod, whereupon the armed police, until then absolutely stationary, fired a single round, killing the worker." This report, according to Dutt, merely upholds "bourgeois truth." It does not include any perspective on the living conditions of the worker or the devious collaboration of the management with the armed police. Dutt believes that it is only by maintaining such a perspective that a commentator can uphold the "revolutionary truth" of the incident.

14. Quoted by Raha in *Bengali Theatre*, p. 134.

15. The Communist Party of India (CPI) split in two on April 11, 1964, when a faction of strong leaders within the parent party resolved to form a new party called the CPI(M)—the Communist Party of India (Marxist). The tensions between the factions surfaced when the Chinese attacked the Indian border on October 20, 1962. While prominent Communist leaders, notably Dange, assured Nehru of their support, the dissidents within the Party viewed this support as a form of "bourgeois nationalism" and a surrender of the Party's revolutionary ideals. Another controversial issue concerned the relationship of the CPI to the Communist Party of the Soviet Union (CPSU).

While the members of the newly formed CPI(M) asserted their political autonomy, the members of the CPI continued to follow the Soviet line of thought. Five years later, there was a split within the CPI(M) when the extreme leftist members of the Party advocated Maoism as the only true revolutionary mode of thought and action. This party, formed on May 1, 1969, was called the CPI(M-L)—the Communist Party of India (Marxist-Leninist).

For a succinct commentary on the ideological differences between these parties, see Bhabani Sen Gupta, *Communism in Indian Politics* (New York: Columbia University Press, 1972).

16. Bandyopadhyay, interview by A. J. Gunawardana, "Problems and Directions: Calcutta's New Theatre," *Drama Review* 15, no. 3 (Spring 1971):241–245.

17. Quoted by Dutt in "Little Theater O Ami."

18. All references to *Ajeya Vietnam* are from the English translation of the play by Dutt. The text is available at Grantha Bikash, Calcutta.

19. Roland Barthes, *Writing Degree Zero* (New York: Hill and Wang, 1978), pp. 67–73.

20. The mother cult is so deeply rooted in Bengali culture that even doctrinaire Marxists have used it to influence the minds of villagers. When Harekrishna Konar, the CPI(M) minister for land and land revenue, successfully implemented his policy of distributing land to the poor, he said: "We are witnessing reestablishment of [the] natural relationship between mother and her children." In the April 10, 1969, issue of *Paschimbanga*, he further elaborated on the mythical connection between land and the sacrosanct figure of the "mother."

> Under united front rule, the landless peasant and the agricultural worker have begun to get land of their own. . . . Land is the mother. The peasant is her first child. At Chaitanyapur and other villages, the *jotedars* (landlords) reddened the mother's bosom with her children's blood. And so the green fields are swelling with anger, the earth roars, there are stirrings of new life.

This passage and the reflection on the mother cult in West Bengal politics are included by Gupta in his admirable study on *Communism in Indian Politics*, p. 255.

21. It is possible that the black character in *Ajeya Vietnam* inspired Dutt to examine the predicament of the Black American in his play *Manusher Adhikarey* (The Rights of Man), based on the famous Scottsborough trial in 1931. In this production, Dutt played one of his favorite roles—Liebowitz, a pragmatic lawyer who defends his black client from the indiscriminate attacks of a white mob. The play, which is one of Dutt's most thoroughly investigated courtroom dramas, includes a prologue and epilogue about the Detroit uprising of the blacks in 1968.

Though Dutt's theater is intensely topical, it is significant that he has frequently used foreign subject matter such as the war in Vietnam and the Scottsborough trial to preach revolution to working-class audiences in Bengal. Apart from dramatizing the lives of revolutionaries in Bengal, Dutt has also written plays on Lenin, Mao, and Stalin. Overly rapturous in their adulation of these leaders and totally uncritical of their ideologies, these plays are effective only insofar as they humanize Lenin, Mao, and Stalin.

22. Dutt, *Towards a Revolutionary Theater*, p. 50.

23. Quoted by Gupta in *Communism in Indian Politics*, p. 228.

24. Ibid., p. 249.

25. Dutt, *Towards a Revolutionary Theater*, p. 74.

26. Dutt, interview by A. J. Gunawardana, "Theater as Weapon," *Drama Review*, 15, no. 3 (Spring 1971): 227.

27. Dutt, *Towards a Revolutionary Theater*, pp. 80–81.

28. Ibid., p. 80.

29. Dutt, interview by Gunawardana, "Theater as Weapon," p. 236.

30. All references to *Surya Shikar* are from the English translation of the play by Dutt published in *Enact*, a New Delhi theater journal. Page numbers from this translation accompany quoted passages from the play in the text.

31. It should also be emphasized that Dutt's use of *jatra* contradicts the some-

what fashionable trend among many theater practitioners (particularly in New Delhi) who have attempted to revive folk theatrical traditions. If Dutt turns to the folk theater, it is in order to use it for his own purposes, not to glorify its heritage.

One of the most ironic uses of the popular theatrical tradition in his oeuvre is the play *Ebar Raja Pala* (Enter the King). Specifically directed against the imposition of the Emergency by Indira Gandhi, the play questions the role of authority in a blatantly theatrical way. A group of travelling actors are startled to discover that their colleague who plays the king is actually a real king. When he ascends the throne, he promptly appoints his fellow actors as ministers. Together they improvise changes in the constitution which reduce the country to a state of chaos. Politics becomes a kind of amateur theatrical performance where the egos of the actors are more conspicuous than the honesty and commitment of their performances. At the end of the play, it is clear that these "politicians" are unable to distinguish between illusion and reality. They are as redundant as bad actors.

32. All quotations from *Tiner Talwar* are from the original Bengali text (Calcutta: Jatiya Sahitya Parishad). Sections quoted in this chapter, translated by Dilip Kumar Chakravorty, include page numbers from the Bengali text.

33. Dutt seems to have followed the advice of his young playwright-character by writing a play called *Titu Meer*. Unlike *Tiner Talwar*, however, it is not one of his most popular productions despite its panoramic action and elaborate scenography.

34. Dutt, interview by Vijay Tendulkar and Kumud Mehta, "In West Bengal: a political theater," *International Theatre Information*, Summer 1974.

35. All references to *Barricade* are from the original Bengali text (Calcutta: Jatiya Sahitya Parishad). Sections quoted in this chapter translated by Dilip Kumar Chakravorty.

36. Bertolt Brecht, "The Modern Theatre is the Epic Theatre," in John Willet, ed., *Brecht on Theatre* (New York: Hill and Wang, 1976), pp. 33–42.

37. Dutt, *Towards a Revolutionary Theater*, p. 94.

38. Ibid., p. 93.

39. All references to *Dushopner Nagari* are from the original Bengali text published in *Epic Theatre*. Sections quoted in this chapter translated by Dilip Kumar Chakravorty.

40. Dutt, *Towards a Revolutionary Theater*, p. 144.

41. Ibid., p. 147.

42. George Szanto, *Theatre and Propaganda* (Austin: University of Texas Press, 1978), p. 75.

CHAPTER 3
THE THIRD THEATER OF BADAL SIRCAR

1. Badal Sircar, *The Third Theater* (Calcutta: Sri Aurobindo Press, 1978), p. 76.

2. Utpal Dutt, *Towards a Revolutionary Theater*, (Calcutta: M. C. Sarkar & Sons, 1982), p. 99.

3. Sircar, interview with author, Calcutta, August 1979.

4. Ibid.

5. Bandyopadhyay, interview with author, Calcutta, August 9, 1979.

6. Dutt, interview with author, Calcutta, July 8, 1979.

7. Sircar, *Third Theater*, p. 77.

8. Badal Sircar, *Evam Indrajit* (Calcutta: Oxford University Press, 1977), p. 59. All quotations from the play are from this text.

9. Extracts from Samik Bandyopadhyay, "Badal Sircar: Middle-class Responsibilities," *Sangeet Natak* (a journal of the Sangeet Natak Akademi in India), no. 22 (October–December 1971).

10. Quoted by E. Alkazi in his director's notes published in the brochure for the Dishantar production of *Hiroshima*.

11. Quoted by Bandyopadhyay in "Badal Sircar," p. 8.

12. *Tringsha Satabdi* is discussed in greater detail on pages 163–169.

13. Badal Sircar, *There's No End*, trans. Kironmoy Raha (Delhi: Enact publication, November 1971), pp. 18–19.

14. Sircar, *Third Theater*, p. 28.

15. Ibid., p. 42.

16. Ibid., p. 41.

17. It is a pity that Sircar does not develop his ideas in *The Third Theater*, particularly on controversial issues such as the influence of the Living Theater. This reticence to speak about his theater has often made Sircar extremely vulnerable to attacks from various quarters. Utpal Dutt's vituperative condemnation of the Living Theater is well known among practitioners of the Bengali theater. In a polemical article entitled "Kabarkhana" [Cemetery] in *Epic Theater* (Dec. 1978–Jan. 1979, translation by Dilip Kumar Chakravorty), his fictional alter ego Japenda indulges in a preposterous diatribe against the Living Theater and the New Left. The following passage typifies Japenda's (Dutt's) polemical style:

> Indian spiritualism, yoga, Buddhist "samadhi" and meditation are all, I hear, the tools of the Living Theater. . . . They discover great truths in Hindu religion, keep their eyes drowsy by taking hashish, and engage in the most flagrant copulation. And this kind of living is regarded by them all as anti-establishment! Actually, they are merely the rotten intestinal parts of that corpse called the Establishment, the last shit of that corpse, the stains of its last vomiting. They call this the New Left. There can be no greater insult to the word "Left" than this. Don't forget that there are no laborers among this Left, not a single one. All are spoilt children of rich people and they are American intellectuals. (P. 30)

In the same article where Dutt/Japenda states that the Becks "find no difference between the lavatory and the theater, between the brothel and the stage," there are scarcely concealed references to the Third Theater, whose aping of the American avant-garde threatens to result in "sexual perversion, mass rape, public defecation, and urination on stage." While one cannot expect Sircar to respond to such "criticism," I believe that it would be very useful if he could articulate *his* criticism of the Living Theater and the American avant-garde theater with

greater clarity. By outlining the limitations of these groups, Sircar could emphasize that he has not been overly influenced by them.

18. Sircar, *Third Theater*, pp. 46–47.

19. Badal Sircar, *Spartacus* (Calcutta: Naba Granthakutir), pp. 54–55. Translation by Dilip Kumar Chakravorty.

20. Ibid., pp. 61–62.

21. Sircar, *Third Theater*, p. 71.

22. Ibid., p. 72.

23. This passage (included by Sircar in *Third Theater*, p. 72) does not capture
the ferocious energy and the disjointed narrative structure of Sircar's monologue
in *Prastab*. But since no text of the monologue is available, I have preferred to let
Sircar speak for himself about his central concerns as an artist. It is interesting to
observe some resonances of a text created by the Living Theater in the monologue of *Prastab*. The text, entitled *A Meditation on Money, with a Text on the
False Standard of Exchange that Enslaves the People*, was part of a series of
Seven Meditations on Political Sado-Masochism performed by the Living Theater in North Carolina in the spring of 1972 (shortly before Sircar met the group
in New York). Though the ideological thrust of *Seven Meditations* was far removed from anything advocated by Sircar in its equation of economic and sexual
repression and its masochistic evocation of martyrdom, there are some resonances of the *Meditation on Money* in *Prastab*. From Stefan Brecht's valuable critique of *Seven Meditations* ("Willing Martyrs," *Performance*, Fall 1973, pp. 29–
36), it appears that this particular Meditation was more rigorous and focused
than the other episodes in the production. The following excerpts from the *Meditation on Money* are similar to Sircar's terse, uncompromising statements on
money in *Prastab*.

> Under the money-system, all labor is wage-labor, therefore all labor is
> slave-labor. . . . Under the money-system, people die of starvation at the rate
> of one every four seconds, although we could produce. . . . Money is super-
> fluous. . . . Under the money-system, men have to sell their labor & time as
> though their lives & bodies were nothing but lifeless commodities. (Quoted
> by Brecht in "Willing Martyrs.")

24. The end of the Living Theatre production of *The Legacy of Cain* seems to
have influenced Sircar. In this production, a character impersonating Death
bound the wrists and gagged the mouths of all the actors in the playing area. This
was followed by what the Becks described as "the Rite of Liberation" where
members of the audience untied the actors and participated with them in a communal celebration. For more details of the production, see *The Legacy of Cain*
(in its earliest stage of development), in *Scripts* 1 (November 1971), published by
the New York Shakespeare Festival Public Theater.

25. All quotations are from Sircar, *Michil* (Calcutta: Naba Granthakutir,
1978), p. 5. Translation by Dilip Kumar Chakravorty.

26. Quoted by Bandyopadhyay in "Badal Sircar," p. 9.

27. Ibid.

28. The teachers in *Shukhpathe Bharater Itihas* seem to uphold the "banking" concept of education analyzed by Paulo Freire in his seminal study *Pedagogy of the Oppressed* ([New York: The Seabury Press, 1970], pp. 57–74). In this kind of education, the teachers do not communicate anything significant to their students. Instead, they "make deposits" of arbitrary facts and figures which the students "patiently receive, memorize, and repeat." Such an "act of depositing" operates on the principle that it is the teacher's task to "fill the students with the contents of his narration." And it is the student's duty to serve as a "receptacle" to be filled by this narration.

29. All quotations from various performances recorded by the author. A script of the play was published by Seagull Books, Calcutta, in 1983. In the preface, Sircar notes that there have been many changes in the production of *Bhoma* over the years. Certainly, my own observations of *Bhoma* (which I first saw in 1977) do not always correspond to the details in the printed script.

30. All references to Boal are from his *Theater of the Oppressed* (New York: Urizen Books, 1979), ch. 4.

31. The Nandikar production of *The Caucasian Chalk Circle* is discussed at length in chapter 4 of this book.

Chapter 4
Varieties of Political Theater in Bengal

1. Bohurupee is one such group that cannot be classified as "political." Founded by Sombhu Mitra after he left the Bengal I.P.T.A., the group established itself during the noncommercial Group Theater movement of the fifties with its extraordinarily lyrical production of Tagore's *Raktakarabi* (Red Oleanders) and somewhat romanticized interpretations of *Oedipus*, *The Enemy of the People*, *A Doll House*, among other classics. Today, without the direction of Sombhu Mitra and Tripti Mitra (Bohurupee's legendary actress), the group produces plays that are conspicuously contrived and removed from the pressures of life in Calcutta.

Other omissions in this chapter include the productions of Jochhan Dastidar and Ashit Basu. The former director has candidly admitted in an interview with Ella Datta for the *Business Standard* that he "goes through the mechanics of staging plays because it has become a habit." Ashit Basu, on the other hand, has become increasingly involved in commercial *jatra* productions. Once the protégé of Utpal Dutt, he created a stir with his dynamic production *Kolkatar Hamlet* (Calcutta's Hamlet), which addressed radical issues in a radical way. Unfortunately, Basu seems to have sold out to the commercial establishment of the Bengali theater.

The only omission in this chapter that I regret is a discussion of the open-air plays produced by Silhouette in Curzon Park. Performances of these improvised plays were banned during the Emergency Rule of Indira Gandhi. Unfortunately, they have not been adequately documented, and I did not personally see them. I should add that the documentation of most of the productions described in this chapter was recorded by me during performances I attended.

2. Nandikar, a prominent Bengali theater group in Calcutta, was first organized in 1960. It is noted for its adaptations of European classics, including *Six Characters in Search of an Author, Enrico IV, Roots, The Lesson, The Swansong,* and *The Cherry Orchard.* Ajitesh Bannerjee, a most accomplished and charismatic actor, directed most of the plays before he left Nandikar to form a group of his own. The productions of Nandikar in the late seventies include its adaptations of *Antigone* and *The Caucasian Chalk Circle.*

3. Bandyopadhyay, interview by Gunawardana, "Problems and Directions: Calcutta's New Theater," *Drama Review* 15, no. 3 (Spring 1971): 242.

4. Quoted by Samik Bandyopadhyay in "Bertolt Brecht," *Quarterly Journal of the National Centre for the Performing Arts* 8 no. 3 (September 1979): 41.

5. Bertolt Brecht, "Notes to *The Caucasian Chalk Circle,*" reprinted in vol. 7 of *Collected Plays of Brecht,* ed. Ralph Manheim and John Willet (New York: Vintage Books, 1975), p. 299.

6. Ibid., pp. 298–299.

7. In the section on "*Jatra:* The People's Theater" in chapter 2, I discussed Utpal Dutt's resistance to Brechtian techniques in relation to *jatra.* According to Dutt, "The Brechtian style interferes with the responses (of the Indian people) . . . who are accustomed to the dramatic atmosphere getting thicker and thicker, until it becomes almost unbearable." The principle of interrupting a play is fundamentally alien to the temperament of Bengali audiences. This is one of the reasons why Dutt does not produce Brecht. Unlike directors such as Rudraprasad Sengupta, he is aware of the considerable demands that Brecht makes on a director and an audience. Dutt is honest enough to acknowledge these demands even though he would never submit to them.

8. Utpal Dutt, "Kabarkhana," *Epic Theater* (Calcutta), December 1978–January 1979. Translated by Ella Datta and reprinted in her article "When Progressives Fight . . .," *Business Standard,* May 20, 1979.

9. Ibid.

10. Quoted by Bandyopadhyay in "Bertolt Brecht," p. 41.

11. Bertolt Brecht, "Does Use of the Model Restrict the Artist's Freedom?" in *Brecht on Theatre,* p. 224.

12. Dutt, "Kabarkhana." (Translation by Dilip Kumar Chakravorty), p. 26.

13. Some of the plays directed by Shekhar Chatterjee for the Theater Unit include adaptations of Durrenmatt's *The Visit,* Handke's *Offending the Audience,* Hocchuth's *The Midwife,* and Kroetz's *Das Nest.* All these productions were sponsored by the Max Müller Bhavan, an Indo-German cultural organization. They had shorter runs than most of the plays in the Bengali theater. One cannot expect the plays of Handke and Hocchuth, uncompromising and somewhat arcane as they are for most Western audiences, to be appreciated by the masses in Bengal. As much as I admire these plays, I cannot help feeling that they are cultural oddities when produced in Calcutta. Their dramaturgy utilizes nonrepresentational techniques and rhetorical modes of speech that are fundamentally alien to Bengali audiences. Their characters (insofar as a playwright like Handke uses characters) convey impulses and embody sensations that are specifi-

cally related to the cultural and psychic turmoil of postwar Germany. They cannot be understood by a Bengali audience whose cultural milieu is so different that it prevents them from grasping contemporary German attitudes toward guilt, individuality, responsibility, and sense of the past, among other problematic concepts and issues. When Shekhar Chatterjee attempts to find Bengali equivalents for these concepts and issues, he either simplifies them or else indicates how essentially remote contemporary German life is from Calcutta, its daily problems, its precarious survival, its squalor and destitution, its innate resilience.

14. Dharani Ghosh, "Towards a Rich Theatre," *The Statesman*, July 25, 1982.

15. Ella Datta, "Group Theatre Wars," *Business Standard*, Sunday, April 11, 1982.

16. Ella Datta, "Where Have All the Good Plays Gone?" *Business Standard*, Sunday, April 4, 1982.

17. Ranan Banerji, "*Marich Sangbad* by Chetana," *India Now*, November 1980, p. 8.

18. This quotation, which describes the emotional state of Jagganath so accurately, is extracted from Lawrence Chisolm, "Lu Hsün and Revolution in Modern China," *Yale French Studies* 39: 238.

19. All references to *The True Story of Ah-Q* are from Gladys Yang's celebrated translation published in her edition of Lu Hsün's writings entitled *Silent China* (London: Oxford University Press, 1973).

20. Urmimala Lahiri, "Calcutta: the commercial chaos," *Sunday Standard Magazine*, November 30, 1980.

21. Bhattacharya, transcript of a recording by Samik Bandyopadhyay, August 1977. I am grateful to Mr. Bandyopadhyay for providing me with a copy of the transcript.

22. As we have seen in chapter 2, Dutt is the undisputed master of the *pathnatika* in the Bengali theater. Most recently, he created a play called *Petrol Bomb* for the election campaign of the Left Front government. Performed seventy-seven times in twenty days, the play focused on a violent incident in which the *goondas* of the Congress(I) party reputedly bombed a crowded state bus, and thereby murdered three aged women and wounded several of the passengers. The impact of the play was phenomenal. Commenting on one of the performances staged during a "cultural show" organized by the Communist party, Samik Bandyopadhyay asserts that Dutt scored over all the other political groups in the show who tried to be "arty" and "aesthetic" in their agitprop plays. By using a "rugged verbal style, with no frills whatsoever," Dutt preached his message with force and clarity. The other groups lacked his experience and knowledge of the *pathnatika* as a medium of propaganda.

23. Probir Guha, interview by Chhanda Dutt, *Hindusthan Standard*, June 7, 1980. Guha's understanding of a "physical theater" is clearly inspired by Grotowski's seminal reflections on acting in *Towards a Poor Theater*. It is significant to note that Grotowski conducted workshops for the Living Theater early in 1980. He later invited Probir Guha and two actors in the group to participate in an international workshop based in Poland. Guha also had a unique opportunity to work with Eugenio Barba. Reflecting on this intercultural exchange, Samik

Bandyopadhyay emphasizes quite accurately that "this was undoubtedly the most important international connection that the Indian theater has had in recent years" (*Hindusthan Standard*, May 15, 1981).

24. Samik Bandyopadhyay provides a pithy summary of *Aami Tumi Aamra* in an article on the Third Theater (*Business Standard*, August 10, 1980). According to Bandyopadhyay, the play dramatizes the predicament of

> a frustrated, disgruntled man from the Earth who finds himself in a non-Earth, ruled by Egotism, Ambition, Sloth, Rage. The man pleads and cringes at first for his freedom. He soon encounters a spirit man, a man killed by the demons of the non-Earth but still with the power of magic in his words. The spirit man calls upon the new victim to revolt, to challenge the non-Earth with his faith in love, in flowers, and in human relationships. . . . The man tears down one of the rock walls that protect the non-Earth from the waves of human passion—a new wind enters the non-Earth and shakes it up to its core.

25. For more information on Aranyak, see "Liberated Theatre," a booklet published by Najma Anwar for the Second Festival of the Indigenous People's Theatre Association at Peterborough, Canada, July 30–August 9, 1982.

26. Bhattacharya, transcript; recorded by Samik Bandyopadhyay in August 1977.

Index

HAWAI Production Notes

This book was designed by Roger Eggers. Composition and paging were done on the Quadex Composing System and typesetting on the Compugraphic Unisetter by the design and production staff of University of Hawaii Press.

The text and display typeface is Compugraphic Caledonia.

Offset presswork and binding were done by Vail-Ballou Press, Inc. Text paper is Writers RR Offset, basis 50.